Short Walks in Shangri-La

Peter Francis Browne

SUMMERSDALE

Summersdale Publishers Ltd
46 West Street
Chichester
West Sussex
PO19 1RP
UK

www.summersdale.com

Printed and bound in Great Britain.

ISBN: 184024 194 2

Cover photograph© Alec Le Sueur, 2002. Reproduced with kind permission.

With thanks to Cambridge University Press for permission to quote from *Nepal Himalaya* by H. W. Tilman, 1952; Faber for permission to quote from *Collected Poems* by Louis MacNeice, 1988; Penguin for permission to quote from *Under Milk Wood* by Dylan Thomas, 1977; A. P. Watt Ltd on behalf of Michael B. Yeats for permission to quote from 'Epitaph' and 'When You Are Old' from *Selected Poetry* by W. B. Yeats, Macmillan, 1963; Nikki Anderson at Lonely Planet Publications for permission to quote from *Trekking in the Nepal Himalaya*, seventh edition, Lonely Planet, 1985.

Although every effort has been made to trace the present copyright holders, we apologise in advance for any unintentional omission or neglect and will be pleased to insert appropriate acknowledgement to companies or individuals in any subsequent edition of this publication.

About the Author
Peter Francis Browne is an award-winning documentary maker, film producer, director and playwright. He lives in Devon with his wife.

Other books by Peter Francis Browne
Fiction
Land's End
Sassenach

Travel
Rambling on the Road to Rome

In memory of Angela, loving sister and a great friend

Before

'Have you climbed the Eiffel Tower yet?'

'I'm only halfway up.'

'How long'll you be?'

'Another half hour.'

'That's too long. The chops're nearly done.'

'I can't rush it.'

'It's your choice. Unless you want them burnt?' Mimi, my wife, sounded fraught.

'Then turn the bloody gas down,' I replied.

'Anyone'd think you were attempting Everest. You're only going for a sodding walk in Nipple.'

'Nipple's not walking, it's trekking.'

'What's the difference?'

'Altitude.'

'So?'

'So I might die of pulmonary oedema.'

'What's that?'

'I'm not sure but it's in the guidebooks along with pneumonia and frostbite.'

'Why do you always have to dramatise?'

'Because I have imagination.'

'Imagine burnt chops.'

The kitchen window, ajar, inhaled a balmy March evening in Devon, eerie with tawny owls. But what if my neighbour heard? Would he see his positive equity slump because of the loonies living next door?

'OK, I'll finish after I've eaten.'

I was going to the Himalaya. My boots, the finest Italian leather with rubber soles – none of that lightweight synthetic crap – required breaking in, and my leg muscles, 54 years old, were in need of retreads.

I had read that walking up and down hills for weeks was a prerequisite of Himalayan travel but I lived in a cul-de-sac despite being on the edge of Dartmoor. No rehearsal there; my theatre closed by foot-and-mouth disease. Not a public path open. So I had hatched a plan. I calculated the height between my hall and landing. Ten feet. The Eiffel Tower is 984 feet high. Thus a hundred ascents of the stairs would be the equivalent of climbing and descending 1,000 feet: just like a scene from *The Lavender Hill Mob* but without the vertigo – to which I am prone.

Up, and a vista of the farmed-salmon pink of the WC rising like a weak autumn sun above the treads. Down, and an exquisite woodcut of a hot-air balloon hovering above St Ives, chiselled by my eldest son. Up, down. Up, down. Sweat dripping from my unfit forehead. And always the danger of a fall from the untacked fifth tread.

Not like Everest? Nonsense. It was a real adventure. After all, more people die on stairs than they do in the Western Cwm.

The first Nepalis I encountered were sprawled in a transit lounge in Dubai, where I waited for my connecting flight. They were flying back to their families after a season of guest-working in the Gulf for minimal wages – although most had the accoutrements of Western civilisation avalanching onto the concourse: oblong ice-falls of microwaves, TVs and ghetto-blasters, all to be bluffed into the aircraft as hand luggage.

I worried about the extra weight. Would the airline make allowances? When the Captain called 'Rotate' at the crucial moment prior to take-off, would the plane actually leave the runway or plough into the Gulf? But when the flight was called, and the Nepalis stood up, my fears evaporated. They were all very short with not a beer belly amongst them. One Nepali, even with a 24-inch TV nonchalantly clutched against his hip as if it were a lunchbox, must weigh less than the average American. And surely the Seattle-based aeronautical engineers must have been aiming for the US market – despite giving their planes wings that seemed far too small, presumably on the scientific basis that, theoretically, a bumblebee is incapable of flight?

Oh! That wonderful moment when the plane trundles and lurches towards the runway, its oil-stained engines shuddering as it negotiates the omnipresent low-tech potholes, its Heath Robinson flaps – far too flimsy – being tested. They work. Hurrah! We can fly. And then, from static to roar. Only those with turbocharged cars can experience that thrown-back-into-the-seat thrill of pure acceleration.

The terminal building that must, logically, be halfway along the runway, scudding past. But still on the ground, like an attempt on the land-speed record. Get the bloody thing *up*. And then, that little slurp of fluid in the semicircular canals that tells you you're airborne.

I was nose to the porthole as we bisected the Makran and Talar-I-Band deserts of Iran and Pakistan: desolate beaches, ripe for development, declining into the bikiniless green of the Gulf of Oman and the Arabian Sea. An antediluvian map of a landscape. Black, white and yellow aridity, like Dartmoor granite viewed through a magnifying glass; mica, feldspar and quartz. Dry wadis snaking down from barren mountains towards the sea, but no hint of vegetation anywhere. But there were roads, of a kind, leading to villages whose camouflaged houses cast just-discernible shadows. Even in this emptiness people survived, somehow. Fathers and mothers, no different to you and I, bringing up their children in a sunbaked desolation where the stamina of a single goat means the difference between milk and no milk. Life and death. That simple.

India was hidden by clouds, and with nothing to watch apart from a film espousing the superiority of Dubai golf courses, I succumbed to sleep until my ears told me that we were approaching Kathmandu.

I had selected a seat on the right in order to see Everest but it was late in the afternoon, and the Himalaya were veiled in grey. But as we broke through the mist I saw the foothills: khaki ridges, amphitheatred by rice paddies, dry in the pre-monsoon, and everywhere precipitous footpaths linking communities where delivery vans were still a fantasy as everything arrived by foot.

It was what I expected but, as with all travellers, the reality coalesced with preconceived images gleaned from *National Geographic*. But this was *real*. I was here, despite a gnawing feeling that I had cheated.

Quote your credit card number and, twelve hours later, you can be where you have always wanted to be.

In 1967, aged 20, I had tried to reach Kathmandu overland, hitching and taking cheap trains, but it didn't happen. There was a war. In Istanbul, Russian warships were entering the Aegean via the Bosporus. By the time I had reached Erzincan in eastern Turkey, I was told that the six-day war between Israel and its Arab neighbours precluded travel through Iran. The world was about to explode in a nuclear catastrophe. Actually Iran wasn't directly involved and I could have made it to Nepal had it not been for the incompetent advice of a jobsworth at the British Embassy in Ankara.

No doubt, having risen in the ranks, he now gets by on an extravagant pension, growing rare orchids in his Shropshire farmhouse, beneficiary of a lifetime's disinformation.

But, despite him, I was here now. I was in Nepal.

– 2 –

Coming out of Kathmandu Airport is a kick in the kidneys. You are there to see the Himalaya. All you have read about it being a Third World country has been forgotten. You simply want to sleep, see a temple or two, and trek off into the hills. But it's not like that.

Into the 35-degree heat and into a swarm of barefoot beggars and sharp-eyed touts held back by whistle-blowing police strutting and posturing like demented referees. Tourists are gold, and I realised that the mob was after me: a Westerner whose weekly income would keep a Nepali family in rice for a year.

'Safe taxi, sir?'

'Nice hotel, sir?'

I had booked a room by phone, at random, for my first night. Someone would meet me, I had been assured. Cardboard, felt-tipped with names, jigged up and down like placards in a political demonstration. Maybe I should get a taxi to the city centre and wing it from there? And then I saw a sheet of paper with my name, misspelt, amongst the mayhem. I dragged my rucksack across the no man's land towards my contact whose name was Hari.

I shook hands; my first faux pas, for this Western demonstration of being swordless is an import and no part of Nepali culture.

'Mr Broom?'

'Yes.'

'Come with me please, sir.'

Someone grabbed my rucksack and held it aloft like a trophy as we barged through the throng. I tried to get it back.

'It's all right,' said Hari. 'Is safe.'

Several Nepali in rags accompanied us to a cab scarred with rusty wounds. In my naivety I assumed the entourage were porters employed by the hotel, but after I was pushed into the vehicle I realised that they were simply impoverished. Grubby hands, palms up, snaked in, Kali-like, through the open windows.

The man who had purloined my rucksack was demanding money. 'Rupees, sir?'

'I don't have any rupees. I haven't changed any money yet.'

'American money – for my coin collection.'

I delved into my pockets, but could only find a two-pence piece. I gave it to him. 'That's all I have.' He snatched it and then we were off, in a puff of exhaust, into Kathmandu.

I stuck my head out of the window, trying to savour my first impression of the capital renowned, outside Nepal, as being south of the one-eyed yellow idol.

The sun was setting as we careered through chaotic city streets towards Thamel, the district where people like me invariably end up.

We were driving on the left, theoretically, but people and skeletal sacred cows – the slaughter of either incurred a penalty of years in prison – had to be avoided at all costs, even if it meant death by head-on collision. At roundabouts there was no logic, no right of way, but a bedlam of hooting, shouting and hitting of brakes, and at each lurch I was reminded of seat belts that worked. Holding one in a damp hand just isn't the same.

Hari wanted to know all about me. 'Your first visit to Kathmandu, sir?'

'Yes, but please, I'd just like to look at it right now.'

'You are coming from England?'

'Yes.' Hari knew where I came from but he was so charming that I had to go through the motions.

'You like Kathmandu?'

'So far.'

The entire city seemed an alien settlement on a noxious planet, its lower atmosphere composed entirely of carbon monoxide belching from the exhausts of motorised rickshaws, vans and motorbikes all running on lead-rich fuel. Already I could feel oxygen and chemicals vying for attention in my lungs, but the pollution was pretty.

The sun saturated the smog with backlit orange light, casting bright spectres of pedestrians against pink-tinged walls like shadow puppets.

Then we drove tortuously through Thamel, seemingly a sort of innocent Soho, until we turned into a dusty road and my hotel, which was far from the dump I had envisaged: red bougainvillea concealing cement which proclaimed a tourist boom.

'Come,' said Hari, shouldering all my luggage, his teenage arm muscles appearing even more meagre than mine.

There was a gatehouse of sorts, a cross between a pillbox and a cottage, from which emerged a tall, thin Indian-looking man, all in white, who joined his hands like a priest offering an amen.

'Namaste,' he said, bowing in welcome; the first of countless namastes – the unfailing Sanskrit salutation that means 'greeting to the god in you'.

The hotel was a family affair run by a Buddha-eyed, flat-faced, high-cheekboned Tibetan couple who were dressed from neck to ankles in yellow and black patterns like bees.

The wife offered me a room that was nice enough.

'How much?'

'Ten dollars.'

My guts were rumbling and I found myself asking, 'Anything en suite?' This was daft. I was meant to be roughing it.

She led me up carpeted stairs and into a huge double

room with an adjoining sit-down lavatory, bath and shower, and *two* loo rolls. She ran the tap. 'Always hot water.'

'How much?'

'Fifteen dollars.'

I should have haggled but said, 'I'll take it.'

She switched on the ceiling fan, and its rotors ruffled my hair.

There was a window-box, pink with busy-lizzies, and I glimpsed a large brown rat scurrying between the petals. Not roughing it, but it wasn't a Hilton.

A thud of drums, accompanied by chanting, suddenly erupted close by but I didn't regard it as an intrusion; rather a fanfare welcoming me to a country I had visited in my imagination since adolescence. All those adventures described by Tilman, Herzog, Shipton, Morris and many more, camouflaged as textbooks in the school library as I pretended fascination with the Corn Laws and *The Knight of Burning Pestle*.

'You want to eat?'

'No thank you.'

She smiled and inclined her head. 'Sleep?'

The bed offered crisp white sheets, more tempting than a lover's flesh, her face an exquisite blank pillow. But how could I possibly sleep? It was one of those moments all travellers must experience: that sudden up-welling of happiness, where you want to shout, 'I am here! I'm bloody here!'

'I'd like a beer!'

'Here or on the terrace?'

'The terrace, please.'

'Tuborg or San Miguel?'

Endemic Catholic guilt kicked in. I had been expecting a monk's cell of a room, and a fetid hole in the floor for a toilet, but I was in the lap of luxury. Continental beer was a step too far.

'I'd like something Nepali.'

'Tuborg or San Miguel?'

'Tuborg.'

'You want to shower first?'

I didn't take the hint, if it was one. It was true that I hadn't washed since leaving Devon and I was vaguely aware of odours resonant of Cornish pasties, rich in onion, wafting from my armpits, but there is only so much a roll-on can do.

She led me down to a door opening on to a roof garden where I sat alone in the gloaming surrounded by flowers. I could smell jasmine. The earthenware pots around me sprouted familiar blooms: sweet williams, marigolds, nasturtiums and geraniums, all glowing out of focus as all flowers seem to do in the last light.

An open space on the far side of the road was umbrellaed by tall trees with flaking boles like eucalyptuses. Crows croaked, invisible in the foliage, and towards the west I saw the silhouettes of egrets, their legs trailing as if palsied, heading home to roost.

Hari arrived with a bottle sequinned with ice crystals and poured my beer into a glass he cleaned with his fingers.

'Sir, you are going to the mountains?'

'Yes.'

'I have a friend. Tomorrow, nine o'clock, he will come to see you. No problem.'

I wasn't entirely sure what he meant but I didn't give it another thought.

Hari remained, hovering by the table, and I cracked the embarrassing silence between us blandly.

'Does your family come from Kathmandu?'

'No, sir, I am from Trisuli.' With pride.

'It's a good job?'

'Yes, sir. A thousand rupees a month.' Less than ten pounds.

'You work all year?'

'No, sir. Only in the tourist season.' About four months altogether, spring and autumn.

'And when you are not here, what do you do?'

'I go home.'

'And work?'

'No, sir. No work, no jobs.' He smiled. I wondered why.

While I was staying at the hotel, whatever the time, night or day, Hari was never absent and always busy. On duty twenty hours in twenty-four.

I supped Tuborg, imagining the bellies of 747s, pregnant with bottles, on special missions from Scandinavia.

It was only much later I learned that it was brewed just down the road.

Time to see Kathmandu. At least a bit of it.

The track was like a maze and dimly lit by street lights. Bats patrolled between bulbs, and crickets thrummed from a patch of wasteground. I stepped on a run-over rat, flat as a photograph, and had to sidle between three skulking feral mongrels, all mange and ribs, who sniffed my legs as I passed. But for once dogs did not concern me, even in this city where rabies is endemic, for I had endured the jabs.

Then out into streets that should have surprised me, and did. Mini-marts, trekking agencies, an Internet café, and shops selling cheap kukris, carpets, crudely carved Hindu gods, and T-shirts emblazoned with tigers, snow leopards, and statements such as 'I've rafted the Kali Gandaki' and 'I've been to Everest'. Not *climbed* Everest. But you can. Anyone. For $40,000. Before leaving England I read a feature in an outdoors magazine advertising an ascent which included a pre-expedition training weekend in North Wales. Day 3: Free for last-minute shopping in Kathmandu. Days 19–57: Climb Everest. Day 64: Last-minute shopping in Kathmandu or relaxing by the pool. Nowadays nowhere is beyond the well-heeled tourist: not even space.

A man tapped my shoulder. 'You want stuff?'

'Stuff?'

He inhaled smoke from an imaginary spliff, exhaled with a rolling of eyes, and grinned.

'Not today, thank you.' He might have been an agent provocateur.

Tourists creaked by in bicycle rickshaws, like minor Raj officials. Something pincered my arm. It was a woman's bony fingers. A ring through her septum, a newborn baby shawled in her free hand.

'Money, sir? Milk for my baby.'

Her wrinkled skin and gummy mouth made me suspect that she was the grandmother, but how can one tell in a country which, even in the Third World, has the distinction of being one of the few where women die, on average, younger than men? I had no change and could do nothing for her.

'I'm sorry, but I can't help.'

Later, I changed money and went in search of food.

The distinction between traveller and tourist has gone forever. Even explorers are devalued. What is left to explore? No one has hopped to the North Pole blindfolded, but someone will eventually. In my hubristic youth, when I despised tourists – aka holidaymakers – I would have sought out an insanitary joint serving authentic food on principle, but I didn't want the squits on my first night, so I selected a salubrious rooftop restaurant. A moustached bouncer, turbaned and uniformed, saluted me before I climbed wrought-iron spiral stairs leading to starched tablecloths glittering with cruets.

A bow-tied waiter pounced and ushered me to a table designed for four, overlooking the street.

This was going to cost me a bomb, but I didn't care. It was my first night. The menu arrived. I was shocked. It listed everything a hungry man could desire: Western and Asian cuisine, but the price! Nothing over £2 and ALL SALADS SOAKED IN IODINE SOLUTION FOR 40 MINUTES. Something cooked, but what? It had to be *daal bhaat*, the staple diet of Nepal. My waiter's face dropped. It was the equivalent of ordering ham, eggs and chips with ketchup at Le Manoir aux Quat'Saisons.

Chaos ruled below as a policeman, screaming through his whistle, prevented taxis damaging a man crawling across the junction on hands and knees. The cripple moved painfully slowly and methodically, like a praying mantis on a branch, his spindly limbs like bones painted brown.

My meal arrived on a stainless steel dish shaped like an over-designed hubcap for a mid-range family car, each asymmetrical indentation overflowing with food: white rice, lentil soup, chutney, spiced potatoes, chilli peppers, and chicken chunks in goo or ghee or something. It tasted delicious, but the chillies sandpapered my throat, causing me to cough.

'Water, sir?'

All around me, innocents were drinking water but I knew that a blue cellophane wrapper around the bottle cap did not guarantee purity. Bottling plants in Nepal aren't as regulated as they are in Leamington Spa. Cholera and giardiasis were only a sip away.

'Tuborg, please.'

I was learning fast.

* * * * *

Kathmandu closes at ten. Tired and tipsy, I walked back to my hotel through almost empty, shuttered streets. On the deserted track leading to my hotel I was accosted by a man who jumped out of the shadows, barring my way.

'Father, my father. Help me.'

'What's the matter?'

'Father, my father. My son is sick. He needs operation. I have no money.'

My first thought was that this was a scam, but as he continued to rant I began to believe him. His desperation was genuine. Fearing a poor rate of exchange at a streetside booth I had changed only a few pounds, and I handed the man the change in my pocket. Not much.

'Father, my father. This is not enough. He will die.'

I didn't care whether it was true or not, and – foolishly perhaps – I said, 'Come back tomorrow. I will give you more.'

'Thank you, father. My father.'

If he had been a mugger he could have produced a knife and taken everything I had there and then. But he seemed a good man: a man who had rejected pride in favour of his family. In the West, such men are rare.

Back in my room this anonymous victim obsessed me. What right did I have to be here? It was true that my foreign currency could help a bit; a grain of sand on the beach of inward investment, but my primary purpose was selfish: the wish-fulfilment of my boyhood dreams and, ironically, a compulsion to take time out from being a father for a while.

Those of you who are not parents will not understand. Those who are might. Witnessing the birth of your baby is the best and worst event in life. Death comes a close second. I have talked to few fathers who failed to burst into tears when they first saw a purple head squeezing through the ripped, bleeding, gunky, shaved anatomy that had been the object of their desire.

When my boys were growing up I was blessed by long periods of unemployment. My wife and I carried them, backpacked, over mountains and moors and beside roaring rapids. And when my first son left home, I fell apart. It occurred gradually. There were favourite places, haunted by his small living ghost, which I could no longer bear to visit. I even wrote the first line of a poem: 'I must find other paths to take.' It was that thing I had read about: a breakdown, but I had responsibilities and dared not knuckle under.

I've seen men like me at weekends, striding over Dartmoor, disconsolate, alone. Divorcees mainly, I suspect. And, like quiet King Lears, I know that they are inwardly howling for their Cordelias. You try to console yourself with memories, but suddenly *whole years* are extinguished, perhaps as an amnesiac self-protection mechanism.

My GP was jolly and glib. 'It's called "Empty Nest Syndrome",' he explained, glued gratefully to a diagnosis and its concomitant solution. 'I can arrange cognitive therapy if you like.'

'No thanks.'

'Then I'll give you some pills. They'll help in the long run.'

How could they? A chemical solution to an insoluble inevitability. But I took the prescription to my village chemist who would now view me professionally rather than as a mere consumer of shampoo and dental floss.

I never swallowed a single green-and-white capsule. I got by. And then, two years later, my second son left home, and there was a reprise.

But again I got by. What else can you do?

Coping with a crisis, with self-immolation ruled out, was one of the main reasons I was in Nepal.

Aged 55 and having been US president, Teddy Roosevelt joined an expedition exploring an Amazonian river. After three months of privation and death-defying brio, he emerged from the mud. The Brazilian government renamed the river after him. And why had he done it? It was, he said, 'My last chance to be a boy again.'

That is what I wanted too. To see the world afresh, with a child's eyes, although, deep down, I knew that this was impossible. Simply not to repeat the past would be enough, despite knowing that I had, without doubt, passed the halfway point. After all, who lives to be 108?

In Nepal it was time to exalt. *Be a boy again.*

– 4 –

A woman inside a sari swept the courtyard beyond the hotel. The sun, awake before me, turned her long shadow into a right-angle across the cement and up the wall, her witch's broom causing clouds of gold dust.

There is a shrine there, a few oval boulders from a river saturated in red like boiled eggs dyed for Easter. Sacred stones. Why not? When I was eight I collected special pebbles and built altars to them in caves clawed from an earth bank in my garden, lit by pink and purple birthday cake candles. It was a secret ritual but perfectly normal, or so it seemed to me, although I doubt that my preparatory school chums, all from bookless petty bourgeois homes, would have understood. I did not make it a topic of conversation but pretended an interest in test match scores instead. It was safer that way.

Clunking metal security blinds were being rolled into cylinders above all the small businesses in Thamel as I wandered, wondering what to do, for I had no plan; no circumscribed itinerary planned at the kitchen table. But you can't afford to be too preoccupied in Kathmandu for you run a watery gauntlet, risking a soaking from bucketfuls chucked by shopkeepers in a futile attempt to prevent midday wind covering their wares with patinas of grime.

An old man carrying a menagerie of parakeets crammed into mean little wire cages got his feet splashed and he shouted abuse at the thrower who I wanted to applaud. The birds' feathers, green as fresh grass, were squashed against the mesh and their long blue tails protruded like soft spikes. Fifty pairs of round yellow eyes looked panic-stricken. And although I am guilty of anthropomorphism, I think I can safely say that they were not happy even if – this being Nepal – they were dumbly accepting their *karma*.

All around there was the sound of a dawn chorus different from Devon: men hawking, spitting and snotting into hands that then shook the mucus into the street with deft wrist and finger movements, like yo-yo adepts.

Most of the Nepalis I encountered in Kathmandu coughed a lot; respiratory problems caused not only by emissions of illegally adulterated fuel but from tuberculosis.

It was not rare to see globules of yellow sputum in the gutters flecked red with haemoglobin.

Back at the hotel Hari was lighting joss sticks while outside my room Buddhists were indulging in a walking meditation, shuffling mindfully in slow motion, round and round like inmates in an exercise yard. No drums, no chanting, but a blissful – for me – silence.

The raked solar panel on the roof, still cool, provided a tepid shower and I remembered, just in time, not to clean my teeth with tap-water. And so began the almost religious ritual of purification. Fill a water bottle, drop in an iodine tablet, and shake into a cocktail. Wait twenty minutes, then add a neutralising pill to eliminate the foul taste. Wait another five minutes and, hey presto!, you can drink. The only drawback is guessing when you are going to be thirsty thirty minutes beforehand.

The hotel was now a Buddhist enclave. Monks, wrapped in material the colour of dried blood, came and went carrying briefcases like delegates at a convention which, perhaps, they were.

The only truly fat people I saw in Nepal were monks, but it's not so surprising. Like all religious middlemen they have got it made. Cast a spell or two and the poor will grease chubby hands with whatever they cannot afford to part with. Spread a little instant wisdom to rich, earnest Westerners on a fortnight's crash course in enlightenment and bingo, you're in nirvana.

I ate breakfast on the terrace, already baking by nine, but eschewed the shade of a bamboo clump in favour of dazzle. Rooted in the shade, toying with yogurt, were two antipodean women to whom I had said hello without getting a response. They had both glanced at me disapprovingly when I ordered beer with my scrambled eggs, and as I crunched toast I tried to eavesdrop. It was almost as difficult as trying to overhear a confession in a Catholic church, but I gleaned enough to realise that thirty-something A was running a self-fulfilment course of some kind, and that fifty-something B was a client undergoing a personal tutorial.

The only time I heard complete sentences was when A raised her voice and said, 'Of course you should leave him.'

'But I'd feel such a shit.'

'It's men who're the shits!'

Imagine going all the way to Kathmandu to listen to such platitudinous sexist remarks. And paying for it.

A shadow fell across my plate. 'Mr Broom, sir?'

'Almost.'

'I am Mr Pradhan.'

Mr Pradhan wore a dapper made-to-measure black suit, white shirt and tie. His shoes were ebony.

'May I sit?'

'Of course.' Who was he?

He put his attaché case on the table and began his spiel. 'Where do you want to go?'

'I'm not sure.'

'Mountains or jungle?'

'Mountains. Excuse me, but who are you?'

'Didn't Hari tell you? I am from the trekking agency.'

'Oh.'

'You have many choices.'

'I know that.'

'You want to travel in a group?'

'Certainly not.' Imagine being stuck with a dozen random strangers for weeks on end and discovering, on day two, that they were all Seventh-Day Adventists.

There are advantages in travelling school-party style, for there are fascinating places in Nepal like Mustang, where only groups are permitted, sleeping in tents. But picture snuggling down beside a severe case of halitosis or flatulence in a hermetically sealed nylon bubble.

Mr Pradhan smiled a charming smile. 'I can tell that you are an individual who wants to travel alone.'

'Not entirely.'

'I can supply a guide.'

'I only need a porter.'

'I can supply a guide and porter.'

'I can't afford both.'

'Same man.'

I had read that guides consider themselves superior to mere carriers, and that finding one prepared to combine both functions could be difficult. Apparently not so, and I was delighted. I had envisaged days of trekking from office to office in search of a paid companion.

Mr Pradhan could sense my relief. 'Now all we have to decide is where.'

I didn't hesitate. 'Annapurna.' It would do for a start.

It is true that there are less frequented wilderness areas but I had no desire to walk in a landscape devoid of people. Glaciers and tarns are all very well, but they don't speak.

I could tell that Mr Pradhan was appraising me like a doctor in a surgery.

'It's very hard. Over seventeen and a half thousand feet.'

'I'll be OK.'

Would I? I was older than many of my acquaintances who, having paid into pension plans since the age of eighteen, were already taking early retirement.

'Are you sure?'

I stubbed out my cigarette. 'I'll give it a go.'

'I can offer you an all-in package. Guide, transport, all accommodation, meals, including morning tea, for only – ' And here he quoted a price that would have bought me a fortnight's self-catering in Tenerife. It seemed too good to be true and I accepted, although I was to learn, later, that having a guide and paying your own way is considerably cheaper. I think it was the offer of morning tea, supplied by my own personal Sherpa, that tipped the balance.

Mr Pradhan handed me his business card. 'Come to my office at six.'

'When can I leave?'

'Tomorrow.'

The temples would have to wait.

* * * * *

It is wise to register at the British Embassy, not simply to let them know you are there, but to give them your insurance details in case you break your neck or suffer acute mountain sickness and need to be helicoptered out. In an emergency it's life or death. You can be weeks away from medical attention and without confirmation that your bills are going to be paid, you can be abandoned to survive or perish, as the Nepali are.

I walked to the embassy and passed the Royal Palace, its architecture grandiose Tesco, surrounded by a tall fence of steel pikes designed to keep the population, Maoists included, out. The main gate was guarded by soldiers in Ruritanian uniforms, augmented by modern weaponry, keeping the mob at bay. But the threat was from within: King Birendra, Queen Aiswarya and their family still alive then, but not for much longer.

Opposite this opulence there was a suppurating

testimony to the country's corruption. A woman in rags was lying on the pavement, her arms outstretched but not quite touching her baby who lay alongside her with bubbly nostrils; a grim visual equivalent of Michelangelo's fresco of the creation. They were dying. But what can you do? You can't dial 999. No one will come. No one stops to help, even if they could. After all, this madonna and child might, literally, be untouchable in a religion that classifies its adherents according to caste. Not to worry. The baby is a victim of original sin. The baby might be reborn higher up the scale, so let her die. She might even make it to the top of the league: become a Brahman.

And just across the street, the king and his cohorts, those spiders clinging to the web of corruption stifling the country, were doubtless eating imported smoked salmon for breakfast, washed down with Buck's Fizz.

That dreadful palace. How, in 2001, could the concept of a kingdom still survive? Because cultures are out of phase.

In his brave book, *Bleeding Mountains of Nepal*, Aditya M. Shrestha lifts the lid on the festering corruption literally killing the Nepali people. Let's take two examples at random. He quotes the Office of the Auditor General of Nepal, a statutory body that examines the propriety of the use of public funds:

> *1. Rupees 293,000 was diverted from the programme on family planning and maternity and childcare to repair and maintain the vehicles of the health minister.*
> *2. Rupees 2,400,000 was spent for the maintenance of the minister's vehicles from the leprosy-control programme.*

Let's not beat about the bush. Government ministers in Nepal have been murdering their compatriots for the price of an off-shore account.

Soon after I had filled in the requisite forms at the embassy I realised that I had lost my passport. Bad *karma* for a world traveller. I ran back, passing the dying mother and child. The Gurkha recognised me and let me in.

There it was on the floor, the maroon document which proved I was who I was; a combination of cardboard and paper that a billion world citizens would give their eye-teeth for.

* * * * *

I climbed to a rooftop restaurant up stairs as disconcerting as those in an Escher print. Each floor was a textbook example from *The DIY Guide to Jerry-building*; load-bearing walls of single-brick thickness pointed with crumbling sand, and rusting spirals of iron, like dead flowers, sprouting from cubed vases of reinforced concrete. No building regulations here.

The last major earthquake to shake Kathmandu was in 1934. But when the next one hits there will be a catastrophe. The restaurants and apartments will crumble like packs of heavy cards.

I sat opposite a North American couple bickering over their bill.

SHE: *But I didn't order chutney.*

HE: *You ate it, didn't you?*

SHE: *But I didn't order it.*

HE: *Here. Let me see.*

(HE snatches notebook from HER in which SHE is accounting for every cent spent.)

HE: *OK. So you didn't order it.*

SHE: *Jeez! I'm tired of being ripped off.*

I looked at the menu. She had been ripped off four pence.

I had climbed the leaning tower in order to see the Himalaya but the smog at midday had gained altitude in the heat, rising like mercury in a thermometer. Maybe it was a patch of snow I saw through the haze but I couldn't be sure.

I had bought two items from an excellent bookshop opposite where, in the second-hand section, they had everything from rattling good family sagas by Catherine Cookson to unreadable, pseudo-philosophical tomes about Nepal such as *The Chorten In Your Brain* and *Prayer Flags Know No Nations*. Stuff like that.

Once bitten, twice shy. On my first visit to Greece I had bought a worthy book, Henry Miller's *The Colossus of Maroussi*, which I assumed would give me an insight into the culture of the people who George W. Bush calls the Grecians; but it was not one of Henry's best. None of the moist sexiness of his *Tropics*, but a memoir as dry as an unharvested Aegean fig. Since then I have made it a rule only to finish books that encourage me to turn the page rather than books I ought to read.

My *Birds of Nepal* was condomed in cellophane like a porn magazine, so I unfolded my map of the Annapurna region instead and spread it on the table. Published by Himalaya Kartographisches Institut, it sported worrying additions to which I was not attuned. Arrows pointed to specific paths. *Danger of theft* read one. *Group trekking suggested* read another. And, enigmatically, *Fields of marijuana*. A warning or an inducement?

Ordnance Survey doesn't go in for this sort of thing. If they did there would be symbols: a giggly man for marijuana fields and a head split open by a kukri for probable mugging sites.

* * * * *

At six I presented myself to Mr Pradhan in an office suffused by incense. A teenager was sitting in a corner.

We did our business, which mainly meant me signing countless travellers' cheques, and then Mr Pradhan introduced me to my guide, the boy in the corner.

He stood and said, 'Namaste,' looking me straight in the eye. For the second time I knew I was being appraised. 'My name is Iman.' His silky black hair was carefully parted above perspicacious brown eyes.

'My name is Peter.'

'We will have a special time, sir.'

'Please don't call me sir.'

'Peter then.'

I liked him immediately but worried that he might be too slight to carry my load, which included an excessive number of heavy underpants and socks.

Iman took over straight away. 'We leave tomorrow. Be here at six. The bus for Besisahar leaves at seven. You have boots, sleeping bag?'

'Yes.'

'Then no problems. You are healthy?'

'I think so.' Best, at this stage, not to mention the dandruff.

'Good, because we climb very high.'

'You've been to Annapurna before?'

He smiled, showing perfect white teeth. 'I was there last week.'

'And Thorung La was clear?'

'No problem.'

Thorung La, the pass separating the valleys of the rivers Jhargeng Khola in the east and Kali Gandaki in the west, is the key to completing a circuit of the Annapurna Himal, but its ascent is dependent upon the caprice of the weather gods. In theory it was open from mid-April but this was mid-March.

But Iman's optimism enthused me. There would be no problem. Or so I thought then. However, it is nearer to 18,000 feet than 17,000 feet, and it didn't care a jot that I was coming.

31

I went for dinner at the same restaurant I had visited the previous evening, working on the assumption that, having been spared amoebic dysentery during the past twenty-four hours, it was a safe bet.

As I picked at my *sekuna*, spiced chicken – I think – I watched two young Englishmen devouring buffalo steaks; buffaloes, genetically not sacred cows, being acceptable fodder. One was having to slice the meat for his friend whose left leg was encased in plaster from heel to thigh, his right arm, likewise swathed from wrist to funnybone, limp in a sling.

Robert and Tarquin – the latter the Semi-Invisible Man – were ex-public schoolboys, both aged nineteen, on a gap year working for a charity renovating a school.

'I fell through the fucking rotten floor,' Tarquin told me. 'But that's the best thing that's happened to me in six months. Now I can go home.'

I asked if they'd gained anything from helping an underprivileged people.

'Yeah,' said Robert. 'Learnt what it is to be fucking bored. Out in the fucking sticks with only fucking *daal bhaat* to eat day after day.'

So that was why they were drooling over the bloody steaks, like hyenas at an abandoned kill. Only much later, deprived of meat, was I to understand this craving for flesh. While Nepal is heaven for vegans, it is purgatory for omnivores like me.

While Robert assisted Tarquin down the stairs they were passed by a Nepali man in bizarre garb: a pleated plastic Sherlock Holmes coat and a red woolly hat. He sat down at the nearest table, produced sheaves of magazines from his briefcase, and tried to sell his wares, tolerated by the management who obviously knew him. No one was buying, but when he was about to leave I called him over.

He was on the editorial staff of *The Quarterly Development*

Review, an English-language publication that draws attention to the plight of most Nepalis, although I suspected its credentials; its opening pages being given over to portraits of His Majesty the King Birendra and his wife, under whose photograph there was a simpering message: *We express our hearty felicitations to Her Majesty Queen Aiswarya Rajya Laxmi Devi Shah on Her Majesty's Auspicious Golden Jubilee Birthday.* How objective could it be?

But at least the country's problems were being aired in articles written by a motley crew of contributors ranging from politicians to academics. No solutions though. Simply setting it out. The role of women for example: *Child marriage, rape, bonded labour, trafficking and selling into prostitution are everyday realities and very few steps have been taken to lessen crime against women.* Why not? *Reports show that even the parents are involved in the trade of their daughters. In some cases, a young man marries a girl, leaves the village for a job in a faraway city (usually in India) and then sells his wife to a brothel.*

Rock music erupted from across the street. A live band. The Rolling Stones, Pink Floyd, Bob Marley. And it was very, very good. Almost indistinguishable from the originals. A green banner stretched across the street advertising St Patrick's Night at Paddy Foley's Bar, and with the sing-along lyrics of 'Satisfaction (I Can't Get No)' and 'Money' echoing in my head, and the promise of ice-cold Guinness, I was drawn, fogey-like into my past.

Nepali entrepreneurs in slick suits guarded the doors, but they let me into a time warp of a joint, heaving with international youth bopping to the very music I would have heard had I made it here back in '67. Even the superficial manifestations were the same: Jesus hair, bell-bottomed jeans for the men, hipsters and Francoise Hardy hairstyles for the women, and I knew the lyrics better than any of them – but there the ambience ended. There were no glasses for a start, and with bottled beer nippled to my mouth, I tried to chat as I would have done in the sixties. But they didn't want to know. They weren't impolite, but I was an Oldie who shared neither their recent experiences in Bali, Thailand and Vietnam, nor their craving for a no-strings-attached one-night stand, which is the unspoken/spoken *raison d'être* of such raves.

When I was their age I constantly heard the elderly on radio programmes saying that when they were past 40 their self-image was still that of a teenager. Bullshit, I thought, but now I can confirm that it is true. Be warned, drunken revellers at Patrick Foley's Bar. When you return, nostalgically, in 2025, you will want to sidle out, as I did, while the tribute band pays homage to the late, great Rolling Stones.

I was happier alone in Kathmandu's streets, ambling wherever the mood took me.

You get used to being alone when you are growing old. It's not just that friends have ended up betraying you. Some still survive. It's a fact that meeting new ones is influenced by past disappointments: so-called friends failing to call you when the chips are down, when you're no longer useful to their careers (for most of our friends stem from our chosen profession). And then, when you are on the up again, they can't wait to buy you a drink.

Yeats' epitaph, in Drumcliff churchyard under Ben Bulben, is:

Cast a cold eye
On life, on death,
Horseman pass by!

I hated this when, as an undergraduate, Yeats was a hero. It seemed so antipathetic to a man whose passion for life and language somehow seemed to echo mine. But I was in love with romance. Then even a poem such as 'When You Are Old' was beyond my understanding, except in imagination. I could only imagine Yeats imagining Maud Gonne growing old in his imagination.

When you are old and grey and full of sleep,
And nodding by the fire, take down this book
And slowly read, and dream of the soft look
Your eyes had once, and their shadows deep …

My wife is grey now, and my experience of people has taught me to cast a cold eye, but not stemming from an innate cynicism. On the contrary, I want to believe that people are inherently good. It's just that, amongst most of those I have met recently, I see a lack of compassion – love even – and that irrevocably separates them from my aspirations. They are like androids whose egocentricity and quiet cruelty separate them from a human race to which I still feel privileged to belong.

* * * * *

I walked through the silent streets, passing ambiguous massage parlours and businesses advertising so-called therapies for gullible Westerners such as tarot and crystal healing. Plaintive music in a side street lured me into a restaurant where a quintet was strumming, bowing, tapping, key-boarding on the bellows and singing. I have no idea how authentic they were in cultural terms, but their sound was pleasing. And the words meant nothing. They could have been *'The moon in June'* or *'Praise be to the Red Flag of the Revolutionaries attempting to overthrow the regime that makes our ability to eat dependent on tourists' tips'*.

The *sarangi* player, expertly fiddling on an instrument similar to those I had been offered by street vendors, was in a world of his own; his arpeggios worthy of Kennedy. I tipped them and left.

I had money ready for the man with the sick son but he did not appear from the shadows; only the scabrous dogs which any animal rights activist worth his salt would have chosen to help in preference to a dying child.

5

Iman ushered me into a taxi at six the following morning and we drove through the slums of Kathmandu, already an ants' nest of activity before sunrise. We drove over a river which, in this dry season, was a sewer of turd-brown water in which women were washing clothes while their children paddled and splashed. Poor people littered the streets, each with something to sell that no one needed. Why would the poor buy orange plastic parrots from other poor people? A man with no legs, his buttocks encased in cut car-tyres, propelled himself between belching vans with his hands, like a crab. Everyone looked thin and exhausted at the start of a bright new day.

The bus station was a chaos of rusting charabancs, circa 1959, parked in a confusion that even Iman could not fathom. Eventually we found our vehicle but it was not destined to leave on time. There are two kinds of buses in Nepal: public and tourist. Taking a public bus saves the trekking agency money. I examined the tyres of the public bus. They were as bald as Grand Prix slicks; no treads at all. A cockroach's antennae would puncture them.

A wild man confronted me and, without ceremony, smeared my forehead with a thumb red and sticky with some potent ketchup. Iman intervened, greasing the man's palm with a pittance.

He was my first sadhu, follower of Shiva, some of whom are said to tie stones to their penises in an effort to prevent erections. There is a philosophical aspect to this which some might consider logical: the eschewing of worldly preoccupations. Having raised families, and seen their offspring on their way, they revert to the spiritual side of their lives that has been interrupted by the day-to-day penance of earning a living. They opt out, like septuagenarian hippies, in a last-ditch attempt to discover a meaning to breathing. They wander alone, divorced from all that went before, abrogating parenthood like cuckoos flying south in an arrogant dismissal of responsibility. I've done my bit. Let them cope. And what happens to sadhus' wives? Presumably they get by, somehow, proud of their husbands' integrity.

Iman buckled my rucksack to the roof rack which would stop it falling onto the road but offered no protection against theft from the men making the bus a double-decker.

Although local, the bus boasted a business class: a whole compartment, glassed-off from the plebeians, where favoured passengers sat adjacent to the driver in his cockpit.

A man trying to sell single strips of chewing gum leapt off as we jostled into the traffic leaving Kathmandu. Poverty was all around: blue sparklers of oxyacetylene in garages mending state-of-the-ark vehicles; meagre fruit and vegetable stalls. Dust. Dogs fucking. People simply wandering, aimlessly, or squatting with nowhere to go. Heat and hooting. And occasional children emerging from stinking alleyways, spick and span in blue blazers, grey shorts, white socks and shiny shoes: boys who would pass muster at any snotty English public school. Upper caste kids. Girls too, pleated skirts and plaited hair, while around them men defecated in ditches.

Then past a temple. An enormous Buddha, the colour of custard. But why? Why this cult-of-personality sculpture as crass as pre-glasnost Lenins in Soviet parks? I had always envisaged Buddhism as being intellectually beyond the equivalent of a blue-robed Lourdes virgin or a Hindu elephant god, but there he was, as pot-bellied as a darts player, enticing the faithful.

Buddhism not a religion in the way we Westerners understand it? Pull the other one. It has all the trappings of Catholicism. Buddhists can't simply adhere to the philosophy. They have to have all the tools of the trade. Portable altars (not even Christians go in for that) and special candles to light, like Christians. And they chant – God, do they chant – for hours on end, like monks at compline, as if their mantras can affect anything but their own inflated sense of non-importance.

'It's prayer' they say. But when I object to the paradox of influential prayer versus free will, I am told that I am being *too logical*. How can you be too logical, not to question hocus-pocus?

It comes down to faith. Doesn't it always? I made a series of religious programmes once, but refused to allow Christian propaganda. The cameraman asked me what I believed, and I said that I was an atheistic Christian.

'What?'

We were in a pub in Plymouth's Barbican. The floor was made of slate and I said, 'This floor is made of slate, right?'

'Yes. So?'

'So if I say "God says it's slate", does it make it any the less – or more – slate?'

'No.'

'And if I say "Love thy neighbour as thyself", is the imperative dependent on it being dictated by God? Or is it merely an inspired phrase of revolutionary moral philosophy? In other words, why should Christian ethics be dependent on all the other claptrap? Resurrection, ascension into heaven?'

'Because Christ claimed it.'

'No he didn't. Journalists did. The Apostles.'

* * * * *

As we left the outskirts of Kathmandu, the air became

breathable and the muzzles on cyclists and rickshaw drivers less noticeable. In the centre many mouths had been covered by white prophylactics looking like single bra cups, worn in an effort to filter out lead and other pollutants adding to an already unacceptable mortality rate.

As soon as we were on the open road, I realised that our driver had a death wish, or rather a reincarnation wish, to be reborn as a chauffeur to a government official.

I wanted to appreciate the landscape but for several hours my attention was riveted to every decision the driver made. He had turned tailgating into an art; so much so that I had the impression of being towed behind the vehicles in front. And then he would overtake, choosing blind bends in preference to straight sections of the road, his gaudy postcard of Shiva, destroyer and creator, stuck above the dashboard our only insurance.

As a child, I was sceptical that the St Christopher medal in my father's car had statistical significance. Before each journey, even to the shops, we had to recite, 'Dear Saint Christopher, please protect us from the perils of the road.' If it worked, then surely insurance companies would lower premiums for devout Catholics?

I tried to rationalise. Our driver was over forty. He must have been doing this job for years and was still alive. The chance of us dying simultaneously was remote, but then we reached a pass, no worse than you might encounter in the Alps; the usual hairpin bends and vertiginous drops which, taken sensibly, were no hazard. But not for our Shiva-believer. Each corner was a challenge to be tackled at maximum machismo speed. Just getting from A to B had become a compulsory fairground ride.

Then there were people in the road, peering over the edge, and we had to stop briefly. From my window seat, on the vertigo side, I had a clear view down. There, 300 feet below, was an upside-down bus, its plunge attested by snapped trunks that cut a swathe through the forest like a ski-run. There it lay, cushioned in green foliage. No smoke, no fire, no sign of life. Most had to be dead. And the injured must have been trapped in a topsy-turvy world, devoid of any hope of rescue. No paramedics five minutes away trained to abseil into the abyss. Just another Third World accident. I doubted that it would even make a headline in the local newspaper. After all, these things happen. It is *karma*.

Far from sobering up our driver, the accident drove him to even more reckless overtaking and last-second braking. Perhaps our delay would result in a pay-penalty? Or perhaps, as I suspected, he was just plain stupid.

We entered the valley of the Trisuli River, flowing slow and uncut-emerald green between khaki bluffs and sandbanks with occasional rapids just exciting enough to raise a squeal from Western rafters. It has surprises that the Wye and Colorado don't offer. I met an English girl who, after three days cruising the river, decided to plunge into the freezing water in lieu of a bath. Swept downstream, she clambered onto rocks and found herself sitting beside a barbecued corpse. It is a Hindu custom to incinerate their dead beside water and, when the river levels drop in the dry season, Davy Jones' locker is left as bare as an estuary at low tide.

We stopped for tea, and a couple I had not noticed in the back of the bus came blinking into the sunlight, although they chose to stay by the door sipping bottled water rather than join Iman and me. They were both in their late twenties: she svelte with cropped black hair; he chunky, ginger and shy-looking. I thought they might be Irish. A profusion of flies was licking the sugar but the peaty tea, the first cup of many gallons I was destined to drink, cleansed the dust from my palate like a mouthwash.

The bus driver hooted and glared out through the

windscreen like a Hannibal Lecter in a glass cage. Iman tried to pay for the tea, but the proprietor couldn't cope with his 100-rupee note so we had to wait for other customers – not from our bus – to pay in coins to provide the change.

The bus driver was becoming frantic, thumping the horn with his fist, and when I heard him putting the engine into gear I stood steadfastly in front of the bus in a mock-heroic gesture. Tiananmen Square it wasn't, but the driver's wild eyes and intimidating revving unnerved me.

I wasn't worried about missing the bus. There would be others; but all my worldly goods were strapped to the roof. I used sign language, pointing to my watch. I smiled. The man was mad. He put the bus into reverse and I had to follow it to prevent him pulling out. The phrase 'over my dead body' came to mind but I doubted that the driver would commit murder to remain on schedule. Or would he?

Iman, grinning, joined me, and we leapt onto the bus, already heading west.

I had hoped for a glimpse of the Ganesh Himal, or Manaslu to the north, but the foothills intervened. Even if there had been a flat plain between us and the great peaks we would probably have seen nothing. At this time of year, by mid-morning, the tallest mountains have the habit of wrapping themselves in white surplices, neck to toe, with a bonnet of clouds to cap their highest ridges.

I asked Iman where he lived.

'In Kathmandu, with my wife.'

'Does she work?'

'Oh yes, for a travel agent.'

'Do you have a house?'

His head moved equivocally from side to side. 'Not a house exactly, more like an apartment.' Before leaving Nepal I visited Iman's 'apartment' but I will tell you about that later.

'You're very young to be married.'

Iman giggled. 'Not so young. I'll be twenty-two in July.'

'Children?'

'Soon, I hope.'

'Were you born in Kathmandu?'

'Oh no. I come from a little village not far from here called Salyan Kot. My father is a farmer and I am the oldest son. I have a brother, Kalyan and sister called Maina.'

'So you'll inherit the farm when your father dies?'

'Oh yes. It is a very beautiful place, four thousand feet up in the mountains. One day you will come and visit me there, perhaps.'

'Are you a Hindu?'

'Yes and no.'

'You're a member of a caste?'

'My caste is Magar. My full name is Iman Singh Rana Magar.' Here, confusion reigned and it was never properly resolved, for, as I understand it, the Magars are a highly influential people whose culture was absorbed several centuries ago by the arrival of Hindus from the south.

'My ancestors originally came from Mongolia and there was much of Buddhism in our lives.' More confusion. There was nothing in Iman's physiognomy to suggest forebears having journeyed from the north; none of the features that predominated as we skirted the Tibetan border later in our travels. He would not have stood out as a foreigner in Delhi or Madras.

'Were you happy living on the farm?'

'Oh yes.' From his broad grin I could tell that his memories glowed with fond nostalgia. 'But it was hard sometimes. I was very lucky. I went to school. Six days a week I would get up at four o'clock in the morning to prepare my homework. Then I'd wash and drink some tea and help my parents on the farm until eight o'clock and then had to walk for an hour down the mountain to my classes. It took an hour and a half to walk back and then I had to help with the animals and the crops for five hours. I would go to sleep at eleven o'clock.'

'What animals and crops did you have?'

'We had goats, pigs, buffaloes, chickens. And we grew rice and many vegetables. We still do.'

'You go back?'

'Oh yes. I am a guide for only a few months each year. The rest of the time I'm a farmer.'

'And you're a guide because …?'

'Because my family needs the money. And because I enjoy it. I like the mountains and meeting strange people.'

'Most people who live in the mountains can't understand why strange people like me want to visit them.'

'That's true, but I've always loved the mountains. When I was a boy I would spend all my time, when I could, walking alone up to ten thousand feet with a picnic. Sitting in the jungle. And twice I saw tigers, but luckily I saw them first. Otherwise I wouldn't be here with you now, Peter.' He laughed.

'Tigers? You mean leopards?'

'No, tigers.'

Iman must have meant leopards, for tigers lived only in the lowland jungles of Nepal. It was only a glitch in translation, for throughout our travels every oak or bamboo forest was labelled jungle by Iman.

'How did you become a guide?'

'I knew someone.' Always the best route for a career. 'I started off as a porter, carrying heavy loads, but I got a lot of experience.'

'Have you climbed any big mountains?'

'No, only little ones. Up to twenty-two thousand feet.'

Twenty-two thousand feet little? I knew I was in safe hands.

We stopped for lunch in Mugling, an oven of a town, down-at-heel and fronted by insalubrious greasy spoons, many, so it's rumoured, serving not only execrable food but also live flesh to the kind of truckers whose wives don't understand them.

There was no menu, and *daal bhaat*, the spam of Nepal, arrived within a minute. No cutlery, so I followed Iman's lead, eating the rice and bony chicken bits with my right hand. You *never* use the left, which is reserved for the other end of the alimentary canal.

I imagined a slick celebrity chef making a *Flavours of Nepal* series, nauseatingly enthusing about authentic traditional ethnic dishes and how they could be improved with just a smidgeon of basil and some sundried tomatoes. Of course, the camera would stay strictly on close-ups, avoiding the bacteria factory of the kitchen and the poor little girl squatting in a pool of diarrhoea on the restaurant steps. It might put off the viewers.

The 'Irish' couple were muttering in a corner while their porters sat apart, cramming rice balls into their cheeks as fast as competitors in a pie-eating contest. The woman spoke to them, and I was surprised to hear a French brogue.

She turned to me. 'I think you're lucky.'

'Why?'

'Because your guide talks to you. These two aren't too bright. Where did you find him?' I introduced Iman and invited them to join us.

Marie and Philippe were Parisians. Marie bought clothes for a posh frock shop, and Philippe worked for an international news agency. Their trip was spur of the moment, triggered by a rainswept urban winter and a palpable dissatisfaction with their jobs.

There are prides of lions and charms of goldfinches, but the collective noun to describe Marie, Philippe and their ilk, would be a sigh.

'Are you going to Annapurna?' Marie asked.

'No, but around it.'

'Us too. But we haven't much time.' She glanced at her watch.

'How long?' asked Iman.

'Two weeks.'

Iman showed concern. 'That is not enough.'

'We don't go all the way,' explained Philippe, as if talking of heavy petting. 'We're flying out of Jomosom.'

Iman proceeded to lecture them in a quiet, authoritative tone. He explained that the weather could be unpredictable and that skimping on acclimatisation days would be irresponsible, but Marie shrugged off his advice with a '*que sera, sera*'.

Throughout our conversation they had been looking at me oddly, not in my eyes, but above them.

'Are you all right, Peter?' Marie asked.

'Why do you ask?'

'Your face.'

As far as I knew, there was nothing wrong with my face that cosmetic surgery couldn't put right.

'You're bleeding.'

There was a cracked mirror on the wall supplied by a cola company, and as I rose into frame between swigging blondes, circa 1959, I was met by a victim of a vicious assault or a sudden bizarre stigmata, a nail having been driven into my forehead.

The laws of physics proved that, optically, it had to be me. The same shirt. The same hair. But I was covered in blood. Tributaries flowed down my cheeks from a lethal wound. I rubbed the spot frantically and discovered unbroken skin. And then it dawned on me: it was the red mark of the sadhu, which, mingled with sweat, had stained me cochineal. Iman had been too discreet to mention it.

6

The Prithvi Highway splits beyond Mugling. Those looking for horned rhinos and crocodiles in the Chitwan National Park turn left, while those in search of red pandas and yetis turn right.

In the Marsyangdi River Valley we crossed a dam built a decade ago to provide hydroelectricity to businesses and the tiny proportion of Nepalis who have access to power. It's true that electricity helps to prevent the wholesale destruction of forests for fuel – but only in those regions where there are cables linking generators to customers, and this is largely restricted to the Kathmandu Valley. But at least it's one of the aid projects, largely financed by the World Bank, that has not been accused of corruption and the siphoning of dollars into officials' pockets.

I dozed as far as Dumre, the next bifurcation, and when I opened my eyes I saw a woman with a shallow reed basket, wide as a coracle, picking out individual black rice granules from a million, and discarding them.

The town was a linear rubbish dump, coloured plastic predominating, along with bottles and rusting tin cans. But why should the population care? Civic pride must come low on the list of priorities when the feeding of your family takes precedence over everything.

Documentary makers love images of decay. They are so *visual*, and they serve a conservative view. All those slum-dwellers in Glasgow and Tower Hamlets. Those Other Ones. The ones who, thank God, we don't ever have to meet except via the telly. Those scroungers, devouring our taxes with handouts. How can they live in such squalor? The answer is simple: because they have no choice.

Through a water splash and up a meandering road into hills, away from the dirt. Into a corner of the world entirely divorced from previous experience; the very reason for travel. Sheer novelty. Nothing with which to compare it. Freshness, like a new love. New lips. New taste.

We sped through villages and by well-managed farms as neat as patchwork, their ochre fields almost bare of crops between seasons, their barns parasolled by thatch resembling Robinson Crusoe hats. Terraced rice paddies in arcs like crude pottery, dry now, but planted with millet and vegetables. Sheep and goats in the shade of strange trees for which I had no names, some crowned with crimson blossoms. One species, with shark-fin buttresses supporting them, intrigued me, and Iman told me that they were banyans, the same under which Buddha is alleged to have attained enlightenment.

Banana trees, their trunks straight as Greek pillars, had Corinthian tops feathered with drooping, pointed, green leaves a yard long. And papayas with clusters of fruit, like little melons, ready for plundering.

In each village were young girls and their mothers, bare-shouldered, but modest in red and orange saris, bending forward to wash waist-length silky black hair under spouts of cold mountain water that joggled pendulous gold earrings.

Kites, distinguishable from eagles by their forked tails, spiralled in thermals above bluffs of rock turned wobbly by the heat. And in the roadside bushes, brief glimpses of small birds with bright plumage, flitting from cover to cover.

As the sun began to sink and the shadows grew long, every colour was transmogrified; the entire landscape becoming vibrant with subtropical pigmentation that I had only experienced second-hand via the paintings of Gaugin which, until now, I had suspected of exaggeration. Not so. That is how it is.

We were now only 2,000 feet above sea level, and close

to the end of the road which meant more than 15,500 feet of vertical ascent to come.

That is one of the great attractions of Nepal. Within ten days' walking, not only will you climb through several climatic belts with their varied flora, fauna and geomorphology, but also through cultural zones reflecting religion, architecture and a myriad of other differences.

Besisahar, chief town of the Lamjung Region, is the end of the road. No more bald rubber tyres, but Vibram soles from now on. It is a bazaar, a straight street half a mile long fronted by every conceivable business from bank to *bhatti*, largely run by retired Gurkha soldiers, whose UK wages are way above the Nepali national average. But they earned them; not only by leaving their families for years on end, but often with their blood. From the Indian Mutiny to the Falklands War they have been sent into the front line, dying and winning medals out of all proportion to their numbers. And how do the British reward these brave men when they are past their usefulness? Retire them on a pittance of a pension, considerably lower than their British counterparts.

You can imagine a sub-committee in the Ministry of Defence concluding that these mercenaries should be grateful for whatever they get. After all, none is an officer – they are not allowed to be – and the price of rice in Nepal is considerably less than at Safeway.

'Where are we staying, Iman?' I was used to choosing my own accommodation, and was worried that my comfort might be compromised by deals struck between the trekking company and the lodge owners.

'Very nice place.'

It *was* very nice; at the far end of town with a balcony overlooking the street. Marie and Philippe were lost in the crowd, guided elsewhere by their taciturn porters.

I sat on the balcony drinking beer, listening to a hacking

cough that emerged from a Dutch girl who was obviously very ill, her male companion most concerned that the trek might be off.

Between splatters she explained that she had only been in Nepal a fortnight, and I wondered if she could have contracted TB so soon. After all, it only takes a gob in a bowl of rice if you've not been vaccinated.

'Tomorrow, if it's not better, we return to Kathmandu,' her gallant companion explained, 'which would make the whole trip a fucking waste of time.'

A heavily laden German couple stopped outside the lodge. Even in the street they were using fashionable telescopic walking poles, guaranteed to decompress knee gristle in the over-fifties. They reminded me that I needed a stick, and I went in search of one.

I visited shops that looked as though they might sell such things, but no one could help. I was about to give up when I was advised to try a furniture shop. Why not? Stick shops didn't sell them. The great bear of a man who owned the emporium understood immediately, and led me to a stack of pink mattresses.

'No,' I said. 'I need a stick.'

The bear lifted the mattresses with one hand and divulged two bamboo walking sticks, hidden like family heirlooms. The first was straight and dull; the second perfect. It was shaped like a crosier, but how it had been bent was a mystery. It must have been fashioned while still green and left to dry, but there were burn marks on the curve which implied later engineering. It was a one-off, and I saw nothing remotely like it in the whole of Nepal. Higher in the hills it produced looks of amazement, and people simply wanted to gape at it as if it were Merlin's wand.

It was light and strong, and after some haggling I agreed a price. Less than a pound. And no better pound was ever spent, for later it was to save my life.

Supper was a formal affair in a dining room wallpapered with roses. It reminded me of fifties' B&Bs in Swanage where, as a boy, I had spent my summer holiday provided by my father who I loved beyond reason. When he died, when I was 13, I gave up God; and it's largely his death which, I think, accounts for my obsessive love of my sons. A way of making up for my father's leaving too early. He didn't want to go. It was a blood clot in his wonderful musician's brain, but I wished it could have been my mother instead, who I loved less then. Now she has gone too, killed by a blood clot on the brain, so I can write this without offence.

What does this have to do with going to Nepal? Everything. If you want a guidebook, buy one.

I lay on my bed, the fan swishing like a slow propeller above my head, and turned on the short-wave radio that my youngest son, Padrig, had bought me for the journey. He knows me to be an insomniac, forever glued to the BBC World Service, but with several bands to choose from I could only find one clear channel; The Sons of Christ, or some such fundamentalist US international Christian propaganda. It combined bigotry with linguistic education. Some southern Baptist was saying, *very* slowly, 'If John says my wife, Claudette, was looking at Jim, at the barbecue, with lustful thoughts in her mind, what does this mean?' Pause. 'It means that John, at the barbecue, intuited that his wife, Claudette, was looking at Jim with lustful thoughts in her mind.'

I envisaged villagers across Nepal thinking, 'OK. I've improved my vocabulary, but what the hell is he trying to tell me?'

– 7 –

The hacking Dutch woman woke me before dawn, and I walked out onto the balcony under a canopy of stars so dazzling and unprecedented that they resembled a special effect from a Spielberg movie; which must mean that Spielberg had got it right. I am thinking of *Close Encounters*.

I sat in a plastic chair, waiting for dawn. It arrived slowly, the stars disappearing sporadically. There was a cloud, a pink one, an edge of an ember, to the north. As the sun rose over China, the cloud became snow; the rim of a great mountain, Lamjung Himal, nearly 23,000 feet tall, my first Himalayan peak. I wanted to tell someone about it, but the entire town was asleep, and no one at the lodge was awake. The purity of it. Nothing to besmirch its simplicity and grandeur. It was the antithesis of all I had left behind; the world of television in which I had been obliged to earn a living working for commissioning editors who had no insight into the *wonder* of life.

I needed a crap, but a German and his wife were trimming their moustaches with nail scissors at the washbasin outside the khazi. No choice. It had to be done. All those Western inhibitions gone with the wind. But the hole! It turned pleasure into a mere function. It's true that squatting on your haunches eases evacuation, but where's the fun? You're so concerned with balance and, in this case, going quietly, that all the usual perks go by the board. You can't read, for a start, because the knees start to tremble after a minute, and there's always the fear that your book might plummet into the pit. And all the while the Germans conversing beyond a wooden door with *cracks*. Fart, and how can you face them over breakfast?

Iman and I set off slowly. We were passed by the Germans going at a pace any triathlete would be proud of, their clever sticks turning them into scuttling quadrupeds.

Iman frowned. 'Why so fast?' he asked them.

'Because we have to get there,' said the male enigmatically.

We caught up with Marie and Philippe on the edge of town, just as we began to descend a stone staircase leading into a gorge.

I counted aloud. 'One, two, three.'

Iman glanced at me but said nothing.

Halfway down I began again, '103, 104, 105 ...'

Marie asked, 'What are you doing, Peter?'

'Counting the steps. I want to know how many paces to go around Annapurna.'

'Are you serious?'

'No, it's a joke.'

Marie didn't laugh, but Iman did.

We were all going too fast and so I slowed down, wondering if Iman was testing me. We had a long way to go, maybe two hundred miles or more. But I was going to do it at my own pace. Marie and Philippe pulled ahead as we crossed the Powa Khola on a precarious plank bridge. It was time to set the agenda.

'Have you heard of the Alps, Iman?'

'No.'

'They're mountains in Europe. Not as high as here but I've walked there many times and I've learned one thing.'

'What?'

'Go at your own speed. I used to rush, stopping every ten minutes for a rest. But then I watched professional guides. They plodded along slower than me, but they always reached the huts before me. I'm here to enjoy myself, not take part in a race, so I'll do it my way.'

I recounted the fable of the tortoise and the hare, and Iman understood.

The walking was easy, following a crude road destined, eventually, to reach a hydroelectric project still on the drawing board. The Marsyangdi River, aquamarine, squeezed between black boulders beyond thatched farms.

A platoon of fully armed infantry ran towards us, the squaddies' heads slippery with sweat, AK-47s pointing at us. They were wearing camouflage – greens and browns – suitable for a jungle. Here, amongst the sun-bleached rocks, it was as effective as flamingo pink. They were the first and last army personnel we were to see for a long time, the security of the high valleys having been given over to poorly armed police who, then, were – for political reasons – the only antidote to the Maoist guerrillas who control 70 per cent of the country.

Why? Because the people, especially those in the rural regions, are not receiving proper medical help and education: particularly the women. And when the government fails, where else can you turn? Not democracy but a dying child doesn't have a vote.

Policemen are regularly massacred and only now has the Nepali government decided to use the army as frontline troops. The catalyst was the blowing up of 34 policemen in a truck in the western region.

We caught up with a wrinkled old man, possibly in his forties, who Iman knew. He carried a huge sack full of grain, supported by a leather strap around his forehead, and I assumed that he was a peasant returning to his village. But no, he worked for the government; a well-educated PR man advising farmers on irrigation, fertilisation and disease-free seeds.

'Don't the farmers object to you telling them to change their ways?' I asked.

'Oh yes. They have been doing the same thing for hundreds of years – but then I explain that they'll make more money and then they listen.'

Butterflies fluttered amongst spring flowers blooming by the roadside; purple vetch and yellow daisies. Pale butterflies, like cabbage-whites and occasional exotic species resembling ebony swallow-tails with vermilion streaks across their wings. And birds, an eagle above, and in a bush a black-lored tit with a triangular inky cap fringed with yellow, identified through the lightweight binoculars my American brother had given me for the trip.

Often we had to step aside, pressing rucksacks into rocks, to let mule trains through, led by the most experienced beasts whose heads were capped with red embroidery like circus ponies. On this eastern edge of Annapurna everything is carried by mules, not only what the people have always needed – salt and rice – but the things that interlopers like me demand: beer, cigarettes, and soup. But I felt no guilt, for people like me provide jobs, and we have no right to say that this culture should be preserved in poverty-stricken aspic.

In the eighteenth century, before Thomas Cook encouraged the English to visit the Alps, many far-flung mountain communities in France and Switzerland epitomised ignorance and ill-health. Look at photographs taken in the Himalaya 75 years ago and you will see people hideously swollen by goitre. No longer, at least where Westerners tread. In the Alps, two hundred years ago, there were the same deformations.

Now, in Nepal – or at least some of it – there are schools, doctors, hospitals, and modern communication. And it has all happened within 50 years. As a direct consequence less people die which must be beneficial. And if, in a few years, the villagers watch Juventus playing Barcelona via a satellite TV instead of coughing their guts out in an electric-free hovel heated by yak dung, then it's all to the good. It may not be civilisation as we would wish it, but it is civilisation as we know it, and we have no right to withhold it.

Snow-covered peaks to the north came no nearer as

we walked towards them. Spindrift plumed from their tops and I could see the blue tumbling of glaciers four vertical miles above us. But it was the near at hand that took my attention.

'Stop,' I said suddenly.

A lizard, speckled black and yellow like German mustard, lay flat against a boulder, its tongue sniffing the air.

'The lizard is a very lazy animal,' Iman told me. 'There is a story about him. Would you like to hear?'

'Please.'

'Every morning he wakes up in his cold hole and says, "Today I will collect some firewood to heat my hole." But he climbs out onto the rock and it is so hot that he just lies there and eats a fly or two and he forgets the firewood. And then, when the sun goes down, he goes back into his hole. He says, "Tomorrow I really must collect some firewood." But again he crawls out in the morning and the sun is so nice he just lies there eating flies. And slowly the winter comes and he has no firewood, and then he dies because he is too cold.'

I waited for the denouement, but that was it, and Iman looked at me quizzically. And then I got it. The bathos. And I began to laugh hysterically, with Iman joining in. Tears of joy streamed down my cheeks, not because the story was *that* funny, but because I was suddenly aware of not being in gloomy Devon, only a few days in the past, under a canopy of smudgy grey clouds blowing in from the Atlantic, drizzling the landscape of my life.

We crossed the Khudi Khola on a rickety bamboo bridge and skirted a village via a short-cut known only to Iman, through a school whose playground was a forest of tall deciduous trees beside a sparkling stream.

The children, all in snow-white shirts and blue blazers, were sitting in classrooms reciting by rote, or huddled at their desks writing in exercise books. I was impressed, mainly because I assumed that education like this was a right. Not so. Later I was to learn that education is largely for wealthy merchants and landowners and the poor who are prepared to sacrifice everything for their children's sake.

It must have been 90° Fahrenheit in the shade, but there was no shade, and my tongue had turned to leather.

'Tea,' I told Iman. 'I must have tea.'

And there, in the middle of this desert, was a tea house blessed with a bamboo canopy under which I slunk, while Iman propped my pack on the stone shelf outside. The husband and wife running it were brimming with laughter and I exalted in being there for no reason other than *being* there.

A Swiss couple was approaching – Swiss, I knew, because of little flags embroidered on every item of their high-tech trekking gear. It's only the Canadians and Swiss who do this; maple leaves and colour negatives of the Red Cross, and I wonder why. What do the Canadians and Swiss have in common apart from a sense of isolation?

Wanting to drum up business for the lovely proprietors, I leapt out in front of Heidi and Willam Tell and suggested that they stop for a cuppa. But they were very proper, very Swiss, with Calvinistic faces, and they walked past, embarrassed, content with caffeine-free water.

The only other customer was a porter who, again, Iman seemed to know. I sat back in the shade. Two stick insects emerged from the dust. It was the Germans who must have stopped for a break in Khude. Click, click, click they came, their clever poles pricking the dust. They passed by, and the porter called out. They ignored him. The porter stood and shouted after them. They deigned to turn but there was no flicker of recognition on their serious-walker faces.

'It is me,' said the porter.

The man paused and walked back, recognising his rucksack on the shelf.

'Ah, so it is you.'

It was his porter, with whom he and his partner had travelled from Kathmandu, but whom they had failed to recognise. An easy mistake to make: after all, these foreigners all look alike.

At Bhulbule I faced my first rope bridge which, being close to the road head, was made of steel. I had worried about these back in England, wondering if the rushing water below coupled with no visible support apart from engineering, would cause vertigo. But there was no choice. I set off across a 200-metre span. These bridges are firm at first, close to the anchor point, but then they begin to bounce, and when you look down through the gaps it is as if you are walking on air. Logic tells you that they are safe, but some primitive feeling informs your guts that the gaps are an unnecessary economy. Why not fill the holes?

I had asked Iman to wait until I had got across so that I could photograph him, but when I reached solid ground I was accosted by the village idiot who wanted to touch me all over. As I checked the f-number, and focused on Iman, I was aware of wandering hands. But I took the pictures and when Iman arrived he shooed the man away. I asked Iman what happened to people who were mentally ill.

'Their families look after them.'

'But if they're seriously ill?'

Iman shrugged, and I wondered how schizophrenics and manic-depressives would cope, for there are no psychiatric hospitals in the hills. I suppose they get madder.

We stopped for lunch and I sipped onion soup the colour and taste of dishwater. Iman dug his fingers into *daal bhaat* and I couldn't understand why I didn't want to eat, but throughout our travels I was never truly hungry, despite having carte blanche and burning more calories than I had ever done in my life. Perhaps it was the altitude, but in two months I was to lose two stone.

Before leaving the village we had to check in at a police point where our permit was franked; then out into the country with glimpses of high mountains disappearing into the inevitable morning haze.

We passed Heidi and William Tell shouting at their porter. He was so short he looked like a child being scolded by angry parents. Apparently he was going too slowly, and the Swiss wanted their luggage waiting for them when they reached their lodge. The fact that the carapace covering the porter's back from neck to knees weighed many times more than Superman and Wonderwoman's knapsacks appeared irrelevant. He was their servant and had to be put in his place.

I could not imagine anyone arguing with Iman, and I asked him if he ever found clients difficult.

'Oh yes. It's nearly always couples. They're not used to being together for long periods and so they fight. And because they don't want to be seen fighting with each other they get angry with their guide.'

'Are some nationalities more difficult than others?'

'The Australians and English are very good, Irish too, and Scandinavians. The Americans are sometimes difficult. They expect things to be modern like in America, but the most rude are the Germans and the Israelis. Some guides I know refuse to travel with Israelis even if it means losing money.'

'Why?'

'Because they treat you like –' he pointed to the ground, '– mud. But not everyone. They are all people, some better, some worse than others.' He laughed. 'There was one Italian, part of a camping group I was leading. He hated everyone and slept in a tent on his own. He would wake up before everyone else and go off alone and we'd only see him in the evening at the next site. He didn't speak to anyone for two weeks, and it was very bad for me because I was responsible and didn't know where he was all day. And it was a wild place. No lodges. He could have died easily. And my reputation would have become zero.'

'But you have regular clients who ask for you?'

'Oh yes. They are the best. They are my friends.'

To the west, beyond the river, there were high forests but we walked through a barren landscape, passing occasional farms and crossing tributaries on stepping stones.

What you see most on a walk is your boots, hour after hour. To twist an ankle would be foolish, and so you concentrate on each step, although after a time an autopilot kicks in, working out the next ten strides. But you don't walk and look at the same time. If you want to absorb the images around you, you must stop. And so it was that afternoon. Brief pictures. A waterfall splashing into a black pool. Stooks of hay smelling sickly sweet. Tall trees bursting with exotic red flowers. A dizzy climb, down which an avalanche of mules threatened to trample us. Stinging nettles that I pretended to touch, causing Iman to shout a warning. And Iman patient as I took photo after photo of everything new to me.

The first days are always the photo days. Later you become blasé, or perhaps more discriminating, and the travelling more personal; no longer fitting your perceptions into slides.

It was mid-afternoon when we stopped in the village of Ngadi, a single street paved with great flagstones steaming with soft mule turds. Iman dumped my rucksack between the tables of a lodge and said, 'This is it. We are here.'

'So soon?'

'You want to go further?'

'No.'

'It is our first day. You have done well, Peter.'

He might have been a nurse complimenting me on traversing a hospital ward after major orthopaedic surgery, but his remarks were genuine. Although the day had not been too taxing he was relieved that my old limbs had coped. Indeed I felt wonderful; tired but not exhausted after our six-hour tramp, and very glad that I had climbed the Eiffel Tower so methodically before setting out.

The lodge owner, a droll man with Tibetan ancestors, welcomed us and offered to show me my room, but, like John Mills in *Ice Cold in Alex*, I had been envisaging an end-of-day beer, so ordered one for myself and another for Iman.

We sat and watched the ebb and flow of people in the street: an old woman with Brazil nut striations in her face, carried in a basket on the back of a dutiful grandson, a gold ring through her nose like a bull's; young women, barefoot, their saris and scarves clashing greens, pinks and greys, patterned with dragons and other mythical creatures. The best seat at a fashion show; the street the catwalk, with beauty shining from these unintentional models who professional clothes-horses would give their capped eye-teeth to look like.

My room, reached up an almost vertical staircase, was a crude cabin; its walls sawn coffin lids, its ceiling cardboard. The only available light was a stub of candle on the windowsill; not even a saucer to stick it in, but a splodge of white wax, like a dead jellyfish on a beach, on which to perch it. It was the same everywhere and I was amazed that half the lodges in Nepal hadn't been burnt to the ground by drunken trekkers fumbling in the dark.

They might have been had even a small proportion of trekkers actually let their hair down. Most, although far younger than me, resembled – psychologically – maiden aunts who might indulge in a small sherry at Christmas. Hardly anyone I met in the Himalaya wanted to get pissed and stay up until the small hours, becoming silly or funny or boring. Trekkers are the careful people: those afraid of disclosing the darker side of their minds – although I suspect that most are inexorably dull, with no vices to reveal; young fogies and old Boy Scouts and Girl Guides who trekked, it appeared, for the *exercise*. That and a puritanical nature-worship recalling, in my mind, those thirties' home movies of Nazi *wunderkinds* leaping, naked, into icy Bavarian alpine tarns for the good of their perverted souls. Not there to enjoy, but to endure.

Politics pervades everything. There's no getting away from it even if you want to. Take Heinrich Harrer. Harrer was one of my boyhood heroes: a member of the team who first conquered the Eiger's North Face. Seen recently in a documentary, he was revealed to have been a member of Hitler Youth, his motives for the climb held in question. Still alive, just, but his reputation tarnished. Doubtless a brave man and a consummate mountaineer, but now irrevocably diminished in my eyes.

Four Germans sat at the table beside us. I introduced myself, but although they all spoke perfect English they were only interested in themselves, and treated our host as if he were something that had missed a branch on the Darwinian tree.

One was a doctor, one a lawyer. The others were something in appalling middle-management. All were educated but divorced from the world. They indulged in this male bonding every year. Their beards and moustaches were a hymn to topiary; each chin and bit below the nose a bonsai bush which only rigorous daily gardening with nail scissors could have achieved.

After failing to engage in conversation with the

Germans, and with beer banishing political correctness, I pushed Iman to explain why the guides so disliked Israelis.

'Because they are soldiers. Men and women. They all have to serve in the army and then, when they are set free, they all want to leave Israel as fast as they can. Leave the prison of their country. Travel. Anywhere, including here. And they do not know how to behave. For the first time in their lives they do not have to follow orders. They can give them instead, and they do.'

Iman's explanation made sense. In a beleaguered nation, with conscription blighting the transition from childhood to independence, there isn't the space for natural rebellion against parents and authority. No rite of passage which is our right in most Western countries. Instead, Israelis break free in their twenties; old virgins trying to get laid, socially. And schizophrenic, politically. A Middle Eastern country that looks West. Only West. They even participate in the Eurovision Song Contest, whereas their neighbour, Lebanon, doesn't receive an invitation. One nation, they keep insisting, but have you ever heard Terry Wogan commentating on a Palestinian song?

Marie and Philippe joined us and we ate from a menu given the seal of approval by the local council, printed and sealed in plastic, its joint aims to give lodges parity and lessen the chances of food poisoning. Eggs, rice, vegetables, all safe, all bland, all seasoned to Western taste like supermarket curry.

They seemed an unlikely couple: Marie, relaxed and loose limbed, with inquisitive blue eyes, Philippe stiff and straight under his parted ginger English-public-school haircut. We sat under oil-lamps, talking inconsequentially, until Philippe suggested bed. It was 7.30 p.m. Iman left too, and I sat alone in this extraordinary place drinking beer, wanting to talk – to anyone – but the entire town had gone to sleep with the only sound the surge of the

Marsyangdi River. No distant traffic for I was, at last, where not even a motor-cross champion could follow.

The courtyard outside my room was lit by a ceiling of stars as bright as a palais de danse with only the music of the spheres for accompaniment. I stood there, aglow with contentment, bordering on the elusive happiness we all crave. And its cause? Who knows? Probably as simple as sheer novelty, which is easy. Go to your nearest travel agent, book a flight, and there you are, in Shangri-La, for the cost of a washing machine.

I lit my candle, snuggled into my sleeping bag, and heard a siren voice.

'Is that you, Peter?' It was Marie, separated only by the wooden partition.

'Yes.'

'Goodnight, Peter. Sleep well.'

How kind to be so cruel. Philippe said nothing. He was already fast asleep.

8

A cockerel outside the window woke me, and I rubbed a porthole in the windowpane to watch it. There it stood on a bale of pink hay, its iridescence tinged orange by the rising sun, singing 'Cock-a-doodle-doo', as they all do worldwide, although the French transliterate it, perversely, as 'Cocorico'. Why? It's not even close.

Eggs! I must have eggs for breakfast, but not before a wash. Smelling bad isn't compulsory in Nepal despite a dearth of hot showers. BO – body odour – was *the* thing *not* to have in the early sixties when, as an adolescent conditioned by unprecedented TV commercials, it meant becoming a pariah. I remember camping in winter under Tryfan in Snowdonia with my friend Chris, both aged 14. We were about to ascend this rockiest of Welsh peaks but not before, in sub-zero temperatures, I found a pool, broke the ice, stripped off, and washed my creases. Such is the power of advertising.

I opened the door and there was Iman in the courtyard, already brushing teeth that Pepsodent would have died for. He smiled, foam frothing on his lips. And in all our days together I never woke to anything other than a smile; not the professional grin of a lackey, but the greeting of a new day with genuine optimism, as if there were no alternative.

Nepali fried eggs look much like ours, with yellow surrounded by white, but subjectively they taste so much better, their gooey yokes made from high-altitude worms.

Our host tried to sell me a black stone, already split in two, which he opened like a magician to reveal a fossilised ammonite which had been carried across Thorung La from the Kali Gandaki Gorge. I declined, hoping to find my own if I ever crossed the pass, although it was sobering to be reminded that this entire upland landscape in the middle of Asia was a seabed more than 100 million years ago.

Marie and Philippe sauntered into the dawn and began cleaning their teeth at the village pump. Like a barefoot doctor I admonished them for their foolishness.

'We're only cleaning our teeth,' said Marie. 'We don't swallow the water.'

'Do you want to be ill?'

'You English. You are so predictable. So like servants.'

* * * * *

Iman and I left a Ngadi already congested by the traffic of mule trains and headed north towards Jagat, our next night stop. On the outskirts of the village we met a photograph of grinning children running up from the river, the youngest only a toddler. The eldest boy held up a trophy: a branch of grey fish impaled on bamboo, their pierced gills red like the insides of figs. The fish were no fatter than Dartmoor trout, but they were obviously plentiful and I asked Iman why they hadn't been on the menu.

'Very bony. Taste bad.'

Few fish taste bad, and I didn't believe him. Perhaps they are forbidden for economic reasons, because of pollution. Sick tourists are unhappy tourists, and Nepal relies on word of mouth to encourage visitors. And although the river was a fairytale green below us, I knew that in this still-Hindu region it was both a liquid cemetery and an untreated sewer for all the people populating and visiting the valley.

I was about to ford a stream when I realised that I had left my bamboo walking stick in my room. Iman immediately offered to retrieve it. Before I could object he had set off at a jog. Left on my own I sprawled on a flat boulder beside the stream, white peaks on the horizon, and closed my eyes.

Boots scrunching on rocks roused me and there was

Marie, with Philippe, staring at me. Marie spoke first.

'We met Iman running back to fetch your stick.'

'Running?'

'Yes. Running.'

'I didn't ask him to run.'

'He wants to please you, so of course he'll run.'

In my celibate imagination I imagined that she was flirting. They moved on together, as if handcuffed.

A brown dipper plunged into the stream below me and, having walked underwater, emerged onto a rock, its bib white like snow. Just like home. The same genus, the same gurgling stream, the same sounds, the same person perceiving it all. But there, all around, the Himalaya. Taller than my Devon tors. Not the same at all.

Iman returned with my crook and we followed the river to where a tributary, the Ngadi Khola, rushes down from the eastern hills, which necessitated crossing suspension bridges that no longer held any fear for me. Instead of dashing to get across as quickly as possible, I lingered at the elastic centres, watching the rapids far below without a qualm.

Then up through rice terraces towards Bahundra, a hilltop village, passing farmsteads that I couldn't help but feel were designed with me in mind. By this I mean that they seemed perfectly stage-designed: the stooks of sweet-smelling hay, black oxen, women in crimson saris sitting on wooden steps leading to thatched houses, men ploughing the fields below. All linked by a perfect stone staircase.

You are there, but it is not *you*; at least not the you you recognise from months or years of stultification. It is as if you are seeing it second-hand, via a film. But the steps, rising thousands of feet, have been there for centuries, reminding you that you are not in a theme park. These farmers are *real*. Their grandfathers had never seen a

Westerner. And they are uninterested, perhaps. You are merely passing by. They have crops to tend and harvest. Families to bring up in primitive – by our standards – conditions.

And everywhere the perfect photographs that you cannot demean yourself to take, despite the voyeur in you. You transpose yourself and see yourself from *their* point of view. Them with cameras snapping at you as you pass, intrigued by your clever rucksacks and pale skin. You'd be insulted. And so you try to entrap these images in your brain, but for a purpose that is as obscure as your befuddled reason for being there in the first place.

We caught up with Marie and Philippe, huffing and puffing, and overtook them. I felt flamboyantly fit, each step as easy as a treadmill, or so I thought until my muscles filled with lactic acid and I had to stop.

Marie passed me. 'Run out of breath, old man?'

Again I intuited flirting. But not just with me. It was with all men. She enjoyed the game for its own sake, just for fun – which is both generous and erotic and an art lost by too many women whose true independence has been crushed by hard line activists whose misandry has conditioned the semi-educated into lonely emulation. Oh how the strictures of the theorists proscribes the wonder and excitement of simply being alive; open to random events. The Curia of conformity gnashing their teeth at humanity.

We reached Bahundanda, last Brahman village of the valley, just as Marie and Philippe were leaving.

'So you finally made it?' she said before turning her back on me.

Iman ordered tea while I peeled off stinking socks to stick Elastoplasts on raw corners of my feet. But no blisters, and there were to be none, ever, so well made were my Italian boots.

Having climbed 2,000 feet we had to descend 2,000 feet. That's the frustration of Himalayan travel. Impenetrable gorges dictated the route, but with two litres of black tea inside me I almost skipped down the steep path with incomparable views of Lamjung Himal to the north-west, its snow so bright it seemed to be lit from within.

Hector Breeze is one of my favourite cartoonists. One illustration shows two sketchily drawn characters on a mountain peak, with one saying, 'Did you know that you can see five postcards from here?' From my vantage point I counted at least eight.

At the small settlement of Ghermu Phant I glimpsed Marie and Philippe lolling against a wall trying to talk to their porters, and I told Iman to run. The trail was flat and we sped past at high speed.

'Sorry,' I called out. 'We can't stop. We're behind schedule.' We continued running, without looking back, until we were out of sight, with the porters' laughter echoing in our ears.

Drenched with sweat, I stopped and Iman asked why I had done something so foolish.

'For amusement. My way of saying that although they're young enough to be my children I'm not a decrepit old man.'

It was time for food and I wondered why Iman hadn't stopped at one of the *bhattis* in the village, but his local knowledge proved golden for he led me to a house on a green alp bathed in sun, overlooking a gorge into which a magnificent waterfall fell thousands of feet. Anywhere else in the world this spectacular photograph would have been given a name, the Bridal Veil or some such, but here it was just a part of the scenery.

We ate vegetable curry spiced with chillies, and drank beer whose price had already accelerated to fifty pence a pint. Across the valley the sky became slate, and a perfect rainbow arced over the cascade.

* * * * *

Thunder echoed like timpani and heavy raindrops splashed on our plates. Quickly we put on anoraks and over-trousers but we were still only 4,000 feet above the Bay of Bengal, and rain doesn't preclude heat; the sweat engendered under such a soft carapace at least equal to an unprotected drenching.

Down a steep, slippery path that had become a gravy trail of viscous brown mud, and into our first real forest: oaks and rhododendrons whose splattered leaves rose and fell in the wind at random, like wagtails' wings.

We passed a gaggle of porters crouching under an inadequate overhang of rock, their heads tented by polythene as they tried to cook rice on a fire more smoke than flame.

The river, already discoloured by dislodged topsoil into a frothy cappuccino, roared under the suspension bridge leading to Syanje. Flash! Flash! Crash! went the lightning as if Iman and I were celebrities ambushed by paparazzi at a premiere. And as I crossed the windswept bridge I took care not to touch the metal handrail, balancing instead like a bird on a wire, trusting my Vibram soles to insulate me. Flash! The entire gorge a *son et lumière,* devoid of script, and scary.

Syanje, squeezed under cliffs, had all the charm of a claustrophobic Welsh mining village and so we pressed on, upwards, between clumps of rattling bamboo. Here I had my first crisis of confidence. Each step up – there were none down – caused pain. I began to sing, quietly, an obsessive lyric like a mantra which I hoped would overcome my physical hurt: 'I talk to my knees but they don't listen to me.' Over and over again. But perhaps the answer lay at my feet, literally. Little weeds grew all along the trail. I had never seen the serrated leaves in the flesh before, but I recognised them instantly: marijuana, the dandelion of the Himalaya. They were so profuse that, had they grown thus in England there would be a proprietary brand called Hashkill to control them. (That said, they do grow in Britain. Look in Collins' *The Wild Flowers of Britain and Northern Europe*, and, hidden under 'Hemp', you will find '*Cannabis sativa*, a tall strong-smelling annual' which is 'casual (sic) on wasteground, also illegally sown as a source of marijuana'.)

I wondered if I might munch the leaves, as Bolivians chew coca, but was inhibited for two reasons. One, I simply didn't know if undried leaves might be injurious, and two – and most important – I didn't want to offend Iman; for in all my time in Nepal I never witnessed any of the indigenous people smoking it. Even if it were done in the privacy of their own homes I am sure I would have recognised its pervasive and particular smell. Only Hindu holy men (there are no holy women) are allowed to partake, and only as a way of communicating with the gods, with a giggle.

I simply could not go on, and I told Iman, who frowned.

'Soon we will stop and you can rest. Sleep.'

'How soon?'

'Soon.'

Iman set off and I followed solemnly until I found an excuse to halt. There, beside the trail, in the middle of nowhere, was a mill. The clouds parted briefly and a shaft of sunlight lit the interior of a bamboo-thatched hut in which the miller sat, her gold earrings glinting beneath an Oxford-blue scarf knotted at her nape. A red blouse and long skirt, like sackcloth, encased her as she fed grain into a crude timber hopper, tapering to a stone doughnut of a wheel powered by an audible but invisible stream under the hut.

I felt guilty even while asking Iman to ask her if she minded having her photograph taken. Iman appeared reticent, but spoke to the woman. 'She says OK.' And so I took my photos, but felt diminished at each click of the shutter. Then the sun went out, and I put my camera away.

When H. W. Tilman travelled here, fifty years ago, the cliffs of the Marsyangdi Khola were just passable hereabouts.

> To overcome these the builders of the road had exercised boldness and ingenuity, stringing wooden galleries across the face. Such structures, known as parri are common in the Gilgrit region where they are usually stout enough; in the Marsyandri (sic) they were pretty frail.

I was to meet such log galleries later, but on a much smaller scale. Meanwhile technology, handed down by Alfred Nobel, had solved the problem of guaranteed access to the Manang District.

Dynamite had blasted a C-shaped path into the precipitous crags and although objectively safe, it is, subjectively, a horror for those prone to vertigo. The rock curves above, claustrophobically, while the edge ends in an abyss of nightmare proportions; the river, in spate, providing a soundtrack to a sequence that made my knees wobble. Do you have children? And have they ever gone close to a steep drop? And have you almost frozen in terror, chemicals in your brain affecting your ability to put one foot in front of the other, even to save them? If the answer is yes, then you will have some idea of my cowardice. If no, you will just have to imagine it. And for those who have walked this path and think I seem a wimp, all I can say is that you are privileged to be blessed with a lack of imagination. I don't mean that at all. What I really mean is that you are cursed.

I read H. W. Tilman's *Nepal Himalaya* uncritically when I was a teenager. It was a spiffing adventure, but now I realise that Tilman was no Biggles. Yes, he climbed mountains; made inroads into a country hitherto forbidden to lovable English eccentrics. But look at the *words* he wrote. When referring to Angtharkay, one of his Sherpas, he says, 'In fact I suspected that he had not long come down from his tree'. Then, when giving his expedition scientific credence by collecting beetles, he kills them in what he describes as, 'my battery of Belsen chambers, small test-tubes impregnated with amyl acetate'. This from a man who had distinguished himself fighting the Nazis?

Jagat is a Buddhist village whose thatched houses are built between boulders as big as the eggs of impossible birds. The steepness precludes more than one street and it is paved with a mosaic of metre-wide slabs. Sparks fireworked from a forge in the half-light of dusk; the blacksmith glistening with sweat, naked to the waist, hammering iron while his boy assistant squeezed bellows made of stitched animal hide.

Marie and Philippe, sulking under a leaking plastic awning, were already eating, as the French do, in compensation; passionately caring about the thrills that the various sections of their tongues imparted.

The rooms were as crude as rows of garden sheds stacked one above the other. I glanced at my view: a lavatory lashed by rain. But my room was dry as a tomb, I had a candle for warmth, and I no longer had to crunch my knees which, in my mind's eye had become as levers needing oil illustrated in a GCSE physics text book. Darwin had to be wrong. If the theory of evolution were true we would be born with lubrication valves just above our patellae.

A Nepali man wearing a well-ironed blue shirt joined our desultory group under the plastic awning, his cuffs studded with gold that perfectly matched two capped teeth. Even under a duvet jacket I was shivering, but the man seemed oblivious to the cold. A smiling Tibetan woman put *daal bhaat* in front of us, poked the awning with her arm, and waterfalls briefly fell all around us. It was like being in a cave under a cascade in a Raoul Walsh Western; the Sioux too stupid to look for us there.

And then the Nepali man did something unwonted. He ate with a fork. We exchanged names, but of the two I only remember mine. He was a merchant and hotelier from Kathmandu making a tour of inspection of his business interests. Confident and well educated, he spoke perfect English, but his suavity seemed at odds with a village which, to all intents, was living in the Middle Ages.

I rubbed my knees.

'You're sore?'

'A bit.'

'Not like your English roads, eh?'

A brief memory of being stuck in traffic on the A38, commuting to the TV studio. England? Tarmac? Already another life.

'At least here it doesn't matter if you're rich or poor,' I said. 'Everyone has to walk.'

'Unless you have a horse.'

'You have a horse?'

'Of course.' He spoke as if it were axiomatic.

In the Himalaya travelling by horse is the equivalent of having a chauffeur. It denotes status, and the fact that this slick operator was travelling on horseback fed my prejudice; for, already, I did not like him.

No doubt there are businessmen who achieve success ethically, but they are few and far between. In my experience most are egotistical users of people: they swallow them when their flavour is valuable, then vomit them out into the gutter when their usefulness is past.

'Where are you going?' he asked ingenuously, for there was no deviation from the route I was on.

'Thorung La.'

He clicked his expensive teeth. 'I doubt it. This rain here is snow higher up.'

'Thanks for your pessimism.'

'Be careful tomorrow. A woman was killed on the trail by stonefall yesterday.'

'A trekker?'

'No. Just a Nepali. No one important.'

Sensing my previous antagonism he smiled his gold smile, knowing indubitably that he was, ethically, in the right. And I felt ashamed.

I excused myself and walked down the empty stream of a street until I reached an open door. Inside there was a flickering light and I saw a woman's face, oscillating between shadow and glow as she sat at a table, sewing. She looked up and smiled.

'Sir? You would like a drink?'

'Have you a beer?'

She called into a back room and a man rushed out to fetch a bottle for me. She ushered me in, and I sat opposite her. Embarrassed silence. And then I noticed a little boy of five sitting at another table, biro gripped in his hand as he wrote in an exercise book lit by the smoky flame of an oil lamp. The mother spoke a few words of English and so the following dialogue is not what we spoke, verbatim, but how I remember it.

'Your son?'

'Yes, but I have a daughter too.'

'Where is she?'

'At school. In Bhulbule.'

'That's a long way.'

'She stays there during the week and walks back to see us when she can, but in the monsoon she has to stay there. The trail is too dangerous. Mudslides and rockfalls.'

'How old is she?'

'Fifteen.'

'You must miss her.'

'Of course. She is my daughter. I am her mother. When we are apart we become half of what we are.'

'Is the school free?'

She laughed. 'No. It's a state school but I pay 1,500 rupees a month.' Fifteen pounds. A fortune.

'How can you afford it?'

'With difficulty.'

The back room was lit by flames sparkling from an oven where the silhouette of a second man cast distorted shadows on the wall. A man cooking. Women's work. But then I remembered that I had left the last of the Brahmans with their despicable attitude towards women and was now amongst Buddhists whose attitudes are, by Nepali standards, far more liberal. The fact that this gentle woman's daughter was being given an education at all bore testimony to this.

Only half of the Nepali male population is literate. A quarter of females. Domestic violence within Hindu marriages is rife, stemming from the fact that women are considered almost less than nothing. Daughters are just more mouths to feed. That is why hundreds of thousands – literally – of Nepali girls are sold into prostitution. Indian pimps ply the hills for trade, pick the prettiest, offer £150, and buy the children, who are often prepubescent. They are then sent to India where they spend their childhoods being fucked by wealthy Indians. And when these poor mites have passed their sell-by date, they sometimes try to return to the bosom of their families. Many have AIDS and are rejected as unclean by the very parents who sold them into slavery in the first place. And why are these girls so abused? Because of religious tradition.

Just before writing this, I watched the news. Brave 'loyalists' in Northern Ireland had just entered Catholic schools in Belfast, brandishing baseball bats and terrorising the children. Why? On behalf of their

Protestant god, presumably. Why Good Queen Liz hasn't disavowed their perverted fealty is beyond my comprehension. What are they being loyal *to*?

Oh you profane users of religion, Catholics and Protestants. Oh you Hindus, despoiling your children. Oh you zealots, shooting Palestinian sons and daughters. Oh you Islamic fundamentalists murdering Israeli babies. Oh you Sikhs, killing in Kashmir. Oh little boy, scratching with your biro in that poverty-stricken house in Jagat, use your bright mind to rid the world of superstition, even if it means throwing your shibboleths into the rubbish heap they deserve.

Many travel writers fall on their knees to show deference to religious beliefs. I cannot. I realise that people are involuntarily trapped in their culture, but respect has to be earned. Otherwise you are 'respecting' a *fait accompli* and I can't kowtow to condescension. When we read about Greek gods we call it mythology. We *know* that there was never a woman called Medusa who had snakes growing from her hair. But when it comes to Moses receiving the Ten Commandments on tablets of stone, or Buddha being the ninth incarnation of Vishnu, we are supposed to take it seriously. Nonsense. Entire cultural edifices built on the sandy foundations of sheer nonsense. Superstition ruling the world.

There was a poster of Tower Bridge on the wall of this Jagat house where the little boy scribbled. Under it was the explication *London Bridge* which I pointed out to the mother. A detail, perhaps, but the truth. And without that, where are we? Nowhere.

9

Before dawn. Up and out before everyone, I walked along the trail to the edge of the village, steamy white mist rising from the valley, Turneresque, the sun still two hours away beyond chaotic mountains.

Sitting on a boulder I listened to distant birds, expecting – as if by right – rare species to flit amongst the bamboo spikes and oaks, but all I saw was a sparrow. I was hoping to see mammals; monkeys maybe, or even a Himalayan black bear sauntering back from a night's foraging. Too low for a snow leopard, but the one creature I truly wanted to watch was my favourite animal in the world: the red panda, even though I did not know if it was to be found here.

I had only seen one, half-asleep, yawning and blinking charmingly at the top of a tree in Paignton Zoo, its raccoon-like tail wrapped around it. No bigger than a koala, it is the ultimate cuddly toy. If there were a Hamleys in Kathmandu it would be a bestseller.

Perhaps I was too close to the trail and its smell of people, so I clambered up into the brush, pulling myself up on saplings as my feet slithered in the mud. Crouching in silence, I waited. And waited. Not even a yeti.

Through my binoculars I scanned the valleys opposite. It was there, I decided, that any sensible animal would choose to live. Corries, protected by unscalable turrets, disappeared and reappeared in the fog, and I doubted if human beings had ever entered them. So close but entirely unattainable, and this – being Buddhist territory – made me doubt that even hunters would risk life and limb in search of ancestors to kill.

If yetis exist, this is where they would live; not on the high peaks where there is little to eat. I imagined them looking back at me through abominable telescopes made of quartz crystals, having just left their troglodytic dwellings, glowing spliffs held between hairy fingers.

'What can you see, man?'

'One of them human creatures.'

'Chill out, man, they don't really exist. You've been smoking too much fresh grass.'

If yetis do exist I hope that they are never found. Eric Shipton photographed inexplicable tracks during the 1951 Everest reconnaissance, and the grittiest, bluffest climber, Don Whillans, claims to have watched one in 1970. Even the doyen of mountaineers, Reinhold Messner, said that he had seen one in Tibet in 1986. So maybe?

A bird landed on a branch level with my eyes. It perched for a second or two, then leapt off and flew in a circle, like a balsa boomerang, before returning to its twig. Through my binoculars I saw that its plumage was iridescent blue-black, glistening as if it had just bathed in oil. But its most remarkable feature was its curlicued tail feathers, curving outwards into a stringless lyre; doubtless the key to its acrobatic forages in search of flying insects. I looked it up in my book (we all need to call everything something) and discovered that it was a drongo, although whether it was a black drongo or an ashy drongo will never be known – one being 28 centimetres in length, the other 29 centimetres.

Iman, looking anxious, was waiting for me back at the lodge.

'Where have you been, Peter?'

'Looking for pandas.'

'There aren't any here.'

'Why not?'

'They live in Helambu and Langtang.'

'Where's that?'

'In the mountains north of Kathmandu.'

'Then we'll go there next.'

Iman laughed. 'OK, if you say so.'

'I have to see a red panda before I go back. If you don't find me one they'll be no tip.'

Iman frowned. 'Really?'

'No, Iman. A joke.'

No wonder he didn't find it funny. Tips are a serious preoccupation with guides. They depend on them for survival because the trekking agencies pay them peanuts. Iman never brought the subject up, but I have heard of trekkers who have paid their guides nothing, or perhaps twenty US dollars, after relying on them for their lives for months. The price of a few beers withheld through ignorance or sheer meanness.

I could not believe that the scrawny chickens strutting in the streets could produce the feast of saffron-yoked eggs I ate for breakfast. And with eggs in mind I told Iman I had seen a drongo.

'What?'

I showed him the illustration in my *Birds of Nepal*, and he flicked through the pages, amazed by the plethora of species to be found in his own country. But that didn't surprise me. Ask the average Englishman to name thirty species to be found in his garden, and after blackbird, blue tit, thrush and robin, he will usually hit the ornithological wall.

Iman closed the book and chuckled when he saw the cover, illustrated by an absurdly pompous-looking bird, a pheasant with a green plume spurting from its head like a freeze-frame of a splash.

'I know this one. I often see it.'

'What's it called?'

'I don't know its English name.'

I looked it up. It was the Himalayan monal.

'Ah,' said Iman. 'A monal. It's Nepal's national bird.'

There and then I decided to bequeath my book and binoculars to Iman before I left.

As a prophylactic against dhobi itch I entered an icy shower in a Stygian lavatory, and feeling as invigorated as an unbuggered Gordonstoun royal, I was ready for the trail.

As we left, I said *au revoir* to Marie and Philippe who were supping porridge in silence. Their room had been directly above mine, and no love had been made. I would have heard.

The shadows on the mountains above us to the west fell imperceptibly until we were suddenly aware of our spectres wandering on the rocks beside us as the sun squeezed between the eastern cliffs to come and go, like hyphens, between rocky bastions.

We walked down towards the Marsyangdi whose water had reverted to jade during a dry night, then up through trees to Chamje and down again to a suspension bridge, on the far side of which was a vast field of marijuana.

My camera case craved to be opened and I wandered into the wild crop, crushing enough botany to keep a yardie in *bijouterie* for a year. I picked a leaf, crushed it, and held it to my nose. That old, familiar, pungent smell. I lit a cigarette.

On we went, up and down, sometimes on narrow paths across landslips where a false step would have been fatal. But the clay was dry and I enjoyed conquering my fear, even though the river churned below. If I slipped, I slipped, and there was nothing I could do about it. In my diary I had written a note to my wife and children. 'If you get this when I am dead, then be glad that I died in a place I have always wanted to visit and where I am supremely happy.' Melodramatic, I know, but heartfelt.

A long, knee-crunching climb in a furnace of heat brought us to a ridge, and there, spread out before us, beyond the curve of a suddenly slow, meandering river, was an intermontane plateau, perfectly framed by a recently constructed gateway welcoming us to the district of Manang.

After the penned-in valley with its potentially dangerous paths, this vista was benedictory; safe paths, fields, and a village, far away, offering food and tranquillity. The Tal Valley was once a lake. 'Tal' means 'lake'. Presumably the valley was dammed by the gigantic boulders prevalent hereabouts, but I do not know whether a flood or an earthquake had shoved the rocks downstream.

Iman and I strolled down and sat on the riverbank where I watched grey wagtails – which are yellow – flitting between long rocks resembling salmon struggling upstream.

The architecture was suddenly different; flat roofs held down against the wind by heavy stones. And real horizontal fields, black as coal, in which farmers and their wives ploughed, following oxen so dark that only their horns and eyes differentiated them from the soil in which barley and potatoes were to be grown.

Potatoes! I ordered a plate and ate them all smothered in salt that I knew was bad for my blood pressure but essential for my muscles. Only a cube of butter, melted on the blotched, steamy skins could have improved it. Iman was perplexed.

'Is that all you want?'

'Yes.'

'But you can have anything on the menu.'

Perhaps it is my Irish ancestry? If I can have spuds, I am content. Clever dishes concocted into leaning towers, surrounded by drizzled sauces and coulis, like nosebleeds, leave me cold; the playthings of a modern society who 'have' everything but actually have nothing apart from money and an infantile obsession with their tastebuds.

Eating and masturbation have much in common. A

sensual pleasure that cannot be properly shared, even in company. There should be a restaurant called Onan: single eating booths curtained off and discreetly lit, with walls peppered with seductive photos of *salad Roscoff with lobster and basil mayonnaise* or *breast of Trelough duck with puy lentils, lardons and Sauternes sauce*, intimately photographed from unusual angles.

But tinned spaghetti on toast or seared salmon with watercress and spring onion crème fraîche all end up as indistinguishable turds.

Marie and Philippe drifted in.

'Potatoes?' Marie observed accurately. 'How dull.'

'They're wonderful.'

She wrinkled her nose like a character played by Stéphane Audran in a Luis Buñuel film and perused the menu with disdain. I visualised her in a restaurant in the Quartier Latin, pooh-poohing a hundred cordon bleu recipes. Why was she here?

'Perhaps I can recommend something that's not on the menu?' I said, tapping my nose.

'What?'

'Ox tongue marinated in balsamic vinegar pan-fried with heart valves.'

'Very funny.'

'I forgot the freshly chopped coriander.'

'Even funnier.' But Philippe understood and laughed. I feared that another celibate night threatened.

With an eagle spiralling in the updraughts between cliffs, Iman and I left Tal via a trail hewn in the rock, but I was beginning to enjoy the exposure and walked on the outside edge, gazing down like an old hand, enjoying the sheer drop only inches beyond my boots. Treat these paths like urban pavements and you are safe. After all, how often do you fall off a kerb into the road?

Clouds choked the valley and rain fell, or rather it was

pushed; its velocity beyond belief. Soaked to the skin, we crossed and recrossed the river until the trail took us under a *kani*, a symbolic Buddhist archway defining the entrance and exit of a community. Soaked through and exhausted, I craved the equivalent of a Travel Lodge but Iman led me past a new hotel, The Eco, whose alpine-style rooms blazed with generator-produced electricity, and up the dark, dismal street to a lodge whose interior reeked of damp. My room, a wooden box, had a window – no glass – and overlooked yet another lavatory. I began to rebel.

Shivering, I joined Iman in the kitchen where a Tibetan woman offered me tea laced with *ghee*, clarified butter, that made me want to throw up.

'You want to eat?' Iman asked.

'It's only five o'clock.'

'So what do you want to do?'

'Meet people, but there's no one here to meet. We are the only ones bloody staying here. How much does this place cost?'

'Fifty rupees.'

'And The Eco Hotel?'

'A hundred.'

Fifty pence difference. Suddenly I knew I was being ripped off, not by Iman, but by the trekking agency. Deals had been made. Iman got free lodging if he supplied a client and it was *de rigueur* to eat in your own lodge. I was paying way over the odds.

'I'm going out,' I said, like a petulant husband in a rocky marriage, heading for the pub.

Iman, crestfallen, said nothing, and I stormed out into the night, stumbling down the black street in search of light to write my journal.

I sat in The Eco Hotel's restaurant and ordered a quarter bottle of approximate scotch.

Four men sat in a corner. One had his socks off and his fetid feet, toes wrapped in old plasters, provided a still-life beside the condiments on a table. Another, his hair dreadlocked, was smoking a joint, thereby compromising the hotelier. The third played a bamboo pipe, badly, filling the room with cacophony. And the last simply sat, eyeing me with what he imagined was an inscrutable stare. They were Israeli.

The whisky, as coarse as emery, smoothed my mood and I began to write, but then Dreadlock marched past me and shouted into the kitchen: 'We want food.'

A voice from the kitchen: 'Soon, sir.'

Dreadlock returned to his pack. I wrote some more, but Dreadlock wasn't happy. He strutted past again.

'We want to eat!'

'Soon, sir,' said the voice.

'How soon?'

'Ten minutes. Fifteen.'

'What's that supposed to mean precisely? Ten minutes or fifteen?'

'When the stove is hot enough to cook on, sir.'

'So will it be ten or fifteen minutes?'

I stood, aware that my hands were visibly shaking in anger, and addressed the gang. 'How dare you treat these people as if they were nothing but servants?'

Suddenly these arrogant young men turned to mush. I could tell that none of them had *ever* been spoken to like this. They were lost for words and stared at me dumbly, as though, with my white face, I was a treacherous ally.

'Why can't you be kind?' I asked. 'Why can't you learn from travelling the world that everyone deserves respect? What gives you the right to feel you're superior? Behave like fucking Nazis?'

I'd gone far enough, and made my exit into the rain, but halfway back to my lodge I realised that I had not paid for my whisky. I had to go back. There they sat, huddled in a corner behind rain-streaked glass, muttering amongst themselves, but they shut up when I re-entered, no doubt expecting an additional diatribe. But I had said enough already.

Iman was waiting for me at the open door of the lodge, like a father anxious about an aberrant teenage son.

'Where have you been?'

I gave the standard reply: 'Out.'

'You want to eat in the dining room or the kitchen?'

The dining room was dark, empty and uninviting. Three generations inhabited the hot cave of the kitchen. The grandmother, her face as wrinkled as an old mussel shell, was hunched over the stove feeding pine spillikins horizontally into the flames while the mother fussed about her pots. The daughter, aged sixteen but already looking twenty-six, sat by an oil lamp learning English from a book.

'We eat now?' Iman asked.

'Yes.' And I suddenly felt mean, for I knew that a guide never eats before his client. Hungry, Iman had waited for me, and I was belittled.

'You want more whisky?'

'More?'

Iman smiled. He could smell it on my breath.

'Yes, please.'

'It's Nepali whisky. They make it themselves.'

Glasses and a jug appeared and the mother poured what looked like water.

We lifted our glasses and Iman said, 'Cheers!'

A clink, and my first taste of Nepali moonshine – although anyone can brew it legally, each home with its own distillery. Made from rice, or whatever grain is available, it had little in common with whisky as we know it. Its generic name is *raksi* and its taste varies, I was to learn, from place to place. Here it resembled a diluted concoction of scotch and vodka, smelling vaguely of methylated spirits.

Copious *daal bhaat* arrived, and Iman wolfed it down, dipping rice balls as big as tennis balls into the lentil soup, while I contented myself with marbles. I wasn't a quarter-way through when Iman's second helping arrived. Iman and the concerned mother spoke conspiratorially.

'She wants to know if you don't like the food.'

'Tell her it's very good but I eat like a sparrow.'

Iman translated, and the whole family burst out laughing as though I had just told the world's most hilarious joke. Relief, I suppose. Culinary pride had been assuaged, but I felt obliged to leave not a single grain of rice on my plate.

After supper, Iman helped the daughter – who had taken a shine to him – with her English. He read from the book, asking questions, while the girl behaved coquettishly, resting her chin on her chest, and looking up to reveal the whites of her eyes, as Princess Di once did.

'*Who* is that man?' Iman asked. '*Where* is that cat? *How* do you do?'

As a fluent speaker, I thought I should do my bit to help, but whenever I asked the daughter questions she replied, 'I don't know.'

'What is your name?'

'I don't know.'

'How old is your grandmother?'

This she answered, but in Nepali. Iman translated. 'Fifty-seven.'

Christ! The woman who looked as if she might have been *my* grandmother was only three years older than me.

I asked Iman about the girl's prospects. 'She's obviously very clever. Could she ever become a doctor or a lawyer?'

'Oh yes.'

'So if she passes her exams she can go to medical or law school?'

'Yes, if she can afford it.'

'But how could this family possibly afford it?'

'They can't.'

And no doubt while this Cinderella fought to understand the intricacies of the world's *lingua franca*, her sovereign, surrounded by his Prince Charmings, sat in his palace, dining in splendour.

After all, it is the tradition.

* * * * *

Having apologised to Iman, I took to my bed with half a day of night ahead of me.

I managed to pick up the BBC World Service and heard a report from an English journalist who had accompanied a four-year-old Palestinian child suffering from cancer in a taxi, along with the parents, in their frantic effort to reach the hospital providing chemotherapy. For the fourth day in a row, Israeli soldiers at a road block had turned them back. Like all soldiers, they were only following orders.

I woke in the night needing to crap, and donning my waterproofs and headlamp, stumbled out into the rain and up the garden path to the pit.

My lamp picked out two reflectors, like tiny diamonds, a centimetre apart. They were the eyes of a spider lurking on the wall directly above the point where I was destined to squat. Its body and legs took up less space than a chimp's palm-print, and I had not read of venomous spiders in the Himalaya. I just got on with it. After all, I was in Buddhist territory, and to squash a spider would be unacceptable. If it had been a bad spider it might have been reborn as a fly.

Iman woke me before dawn and we ate porridge sprinkled with grated apple, although I declined the goat's milk, for it can make you ill. The carved shutters rattled and rain, corkscrewing like little twisters, had transformed the rocky street into rapids. I sipped black tea slowly, wanting to go nowhere, but I could sense Iman's impatience. My gentle taskmaster wanted to be off and so, draped in theoretical waterproofs, I followed him into a gloom that would have sent sufferers of seasonal affective disorder reaching for their panic buttons.

The family waved us goodbye, including the daughter destined never to practise medicine. Mind you, I bet she'll be able to rustle up a mean porridge.

Shortly after leaving Dharapani we passed through Bagarchap where, in 1995, a landslide decimated the village, killing Nepalis and trekkers indiscriminately. In the West we equate landslides with minor mudslips, and the occasional highly publicised avalanche in the Alps. Here the scale is different. Entire mountainsides can fall. You can see it when the trail takes a new path on the opposite side of the river to the original trail that has been obliterated by landslips of unimaginable proportions. Some, half a mile wide, and too recent to have attracted even the growth of weeds, scar the green valley with colossal shards and splinters of rent rock that expose the bleak bone of our planet. Igneous, metamorphic or sedimentary. It doesn't matter. Just rock. Dead as a fossil and appallingly lifeless.

And then, suddenly, I was having to cope with real fear.

The trail crosses mudslips but, unlike the previous day, the grey clay was wet and glutinous, the 'path' sometimes only a boot's width wide, shelving outwards like slippery slate, with a roof below falling towards a chaotic river.

Imagine walking such a sliver, slippery as a fish, on the roof of Durham Cathedral. It would be mad. You simply wouldn't do it. But here, because your mind is reassured by the term 'path' you continue. My legs trembled and halfway across the first mudslide, where I needed to jump down into a boot-tread, I voiced my fears.

'I don't like this, Iman.'

'It'll be all right, Peter. Just concentrate.'

I thanked a god for my bamboo crook. I thrust it into the mud and wedged my boot behind it again and again. But it was like crossing a steep ice-field without a rope or belay, trusting to luck.

These horrid traverses had taken their toll physically and psychologically, and when we reached Timang Besi, I insisted on a rest.

Despite the tea house being fuggy with stove smoke, my breath was condensing in the cold, and I clutched my hands around a cup for warmth.

A 22-year-old middle-aged American, bespectacled and half bald, was sitting in a corner, guarding silvery metal luggage of a kind favoured by camera crews; all rectilinear and clever clasps. Wayne was a scientist from a Wyoming university researching the Marsyangdi River, and he was already missing Buffalo.

'What do you actually do?'

'I'm a hydrologist. I measure the river.'

'Why?'

'For my Ph.D.'

'No, I mean why?'

The question seemed to perplex him. 'There's an arrangement with my university and the government of Nepal.'

'So what do you actually do?'

'Go down to the river with this equipment' – he tapped his metal cases – 'and measure the flow.'

'Is the government planning a dam or something?'

'I don't know.'

'Then why are you doing it?'

'Because I was asked.'

'All on your own?'

'I've got porters.'

He gesticulated towards the kitchen where two shivering men, shamefully underclad in clothes not granted by a US university, were steaming beside the stove.

'Do they understand what you are doing?'

'Why should they? They're only porters. And between you and me I'm having trouble with them.'

'Why?'

'They don't understand what I'm doing and it's tough work getting down to the river and asking them to wade out with the equipment. They complain of the cold.'

'Why not take a day or two off? Wait until it warms up?'

'Oh, I couldn't do that.'

'Why not?'

'I've got a schedule.'

'See what you're doing set against the entire history of science. If you and your porters have a break, would it really interfere with the progress of human knowledge?'

'If Newton had stayed in bed instead of sitting in an orchard he would never've seen the apple fall.'

'Did he really do that?'

'Now you ask, I'm not entirely sure.'

Rain rattled the windows with even more ferocity, and thunder bounced along the canyon. It was like being in a car with broken wipers, and I was perfectly content to sit out the storm in this lay-by that provided warmth, of a kind, and hot liquid.

Iman began pacing up and down like a caged leopard, so I said, 'OK, let's go.' But we didn't leave until I had pilfered my rucksack for every bit of protective clothing I possessed.

It was hard to see anything with raindrops pummelling our corneas, but I suddenly felt inexplicably fit, and I took the lead until we reached a concrete bridge, once spanning a chasm, now ripped from its metal moorings by the sheer force of water.

Iman pointed down, and we climbed into a steep gully reminiscent of a Cornish zawn, crossed the raging torrent on a tree trunk and clambered up again to meet another of those blasted-into-the-cliff paths with even further-to-fall cliffs beyond the lip than I had previously encountered. But I was almost beyond caring as the rain turned to sleet.

More mudslides, the paths now no more than thin ribbons of mud over which a grey waterfall poured, sometimes fifty metres wide. And the river below filled the air with a horrible noise, the rapids now an incontinence of orange urine, while below the surface boulders continuously scraped against the bed. If you have ever had the misfortune to hear horses' teeth being rasped with a metal file you will be able to imagine the sound. Blondin, tiptoeing across Niagara Falls on a tightrope, must have had little more adrenalin pumping through his heart than I had.

Then we met an avalanche chute where the path had simply been swept away. These chutes are the shape of Neolithic axe-heads, the cutting edges embedded in the river. Higher up the blade, where it is narrowest, is where the path – where there is one – follows a quick but precarious passage. We scrambled down through undergrowth until we were just above the river. Then we gingerly threaded our way through the charnel house of a dismembered mountain whose gigantic bones littered the ashen slope above us, just waiting for that final millimetre of water to send them crashing down.

It was a recent fall. Not a blade of grass grew in the mud, and I tried to move as fast as I could across these 500 metres of what proper mountaineers call 'objective danger' – meaning there's not a hell of a lot you can do about it. But weariness dictated my pace, and I distracted myself by trying to work out the relationship between speed and probability of disaster. Was it better to run – not that I had the energy – thereby getting across quicker? Or take my time? If I shot across I might be struck by a boulder on the far edge, whereas by going slowly I might avoid it and survive.

I heard clattering rocks echoing high above but we crossed in safety and climbed through underbrush back onto the trail. At least there were no leeches. They were dormant, waiting for the monsoon, but how they could tell the difference was beyond me.

Guidebooks glibly tell you that trekking in the rainy season has advantages. 'You're less likely to meet other people on the trails.' Oh yes? And what's the advantage of that, apart from appealing to misanthropes?

We had met no one the entire morning, moving up or down, and I had an inkling as to the reason. The clouds evaporated, and only a few hundred feet above us, the valley was white with wet snow, the branches of the pines on the bluffs opposite drooping under its weight.

Our altitude was only 7,000 feet and Thorung La rose more than 10,000 feet above us. My spirits sank: all this way to be thwarted by a late winter. And what if we had to cross mudslides higher up? They would be impassable if covered by snow.

As we approached Danagyu we saw desultory couples and individuals, their eyes downcast, heading back.

Iman and I sat in silence in a lodge where we had stopped for lunch, neither of us daring to voice our fears. A Dutch family came in, grey snow capping rucksacks which they punished by throwing into a corner. The father, whose elephantine ears protruded from a cropped head, sat opposite his mousy wife while the son, perhaps 17, pretended to take photos of the salt cellar with a state-of-the-art digital camera that had been bought for him with more dramatic pictures in mind for the family album.

The husband had a carefully trimmed moustache, and I guessed that he was in the military. I had to ask.

'Where have you come from?'

'Manang.'

'Over Thorung La?'

'No. It's impossible. We spent five days in Manang waiting for the snow to stop but we've run out of time.'

'It's bad?'

'Very bad.'

Their dream, possibly planned for years, had been ruined by snow crystals, and my heart went out to them. Perhaps the couple had planned to share some last great experience with their son before he left home for ever, but it was not to be. In a few days they would fly out of Kathmandu and back to their niceish home in Tilburg or Eindhoven where they would resume the routine that had propelled them here in the first place.

Marie and Philippe burst in. 'What a shitty day!' Marie said when she saw me. 'What a shitty path! We thought we would end up fucking dead!'

I turned to Iman. 'What do we do?'

'It's your decision, Peter.'

'We go on.'

He smiled. 'Who knows? We might be lucky because there's Tibetan bread on the menu.'

How I love such non sequiturs. They are poetry. 'Is it good with eggs?'

'Oh yes.'

And so I sublimated my fear, ordering four fried eggs

which appeared beside a soft round cake, like a Yorkshire pudding, that tasted both sweet and savoury.

We had two beers each, and feeling full of food and alcohol and optimism, set off into sunlight dappled beneath a canopy of pines smelling of retsina, Iman leading me along paths that only he knew, sometimes across mudslides already dry and safe compared with the morning's horrors.

We walked down to the river, suddenly green again, under the cackle of jays lumbering amongst the branches of firs and oaks. Rhododendrons, in bud, were close to blossoming, and I could only imagine how the forest would have been stippled with pink in a normal spring.

Yellow flowers with white crowns perched on fleshy stems sprinkled the woods beside the path; like English stonecrops but bigger and flashier. Dippers splashed into the river and I glimpsed gold-feathered finches flitting amongst the pines, their bills like octopuses' jaws. The mountains above were tiled with snow and black rock like Tuscan cathedrals, but the giants of the Himalaya were still hidden. Children's laughter filled the air and around a corner we saw them playing by the river, half-naked in the heat.

We shed our sopping top clothes and ambled slowly through the forest, steaming, ironed by the sun, stopping every now and then for no particular reason. By late afternoon we had reached the outskirts of Chame. There, on a knoll beside the river, was an extraordinary sight. Two enormous people, their backs to us, were talking to a man with a Sony Betacam, a professional camera I knew well, slung from a leather shoulder strap. He was adopting a pose, not because he was being watched, but because it is second nature to video and film cameramen worldwide. Their cameras are akin to guns – of course, they shoot – and they are always the macho members of any crew.

Holding a sound-mixer or a clipboard simply doesn't herald the same kudos. And that powerful zoom lens! It's the business. You see them at airports, hurrying to news assignments, looking neither left nor right because *they are on a mission*.

I assumed he was Japanese, and he was obviously artistic for he had grown his hair over his shoulders and wore tinted spectacles. He even had a goatee. Seen from behind, his companions resembled sumo wrestlers. Their hair was swept back in the sumo style, kept in place by grips, and their arses were the biggest I had ever seen, squeezed into skin-tight pink and lime-green trousers that exaggerated every adipose bulge of their buttocks, which overhung thighs as rimmed with folds as Michelin Man's.

Inquisitive, I shouted a greeting. 'What are you making?'

'A documentary.'

The wrestlers turned. They were wearing make-up; scalding red lipstick and false eyelashes like millipedes' legs. Green eyeshadow extended up into their temples Cleopatra-style, and blusher on their blubbery cheeks only heightened their bizarre appearance. I would have taken them for transsexuals had it not been for the enormous breasts, truly as big as balloons, that struggled to rise from their gaudy T-shirts. Even a struck-off Moroccan cosmetic surgeon could not have inserted so much silicon and lived with himself. Iman turned away, and I could hear his stifled giggles.

I had to ask. 'What sort of documentary?'

'Oh, you know. About Nepal.'

I didn't know, and my ignorance was compounded by two men, Tweedledum and Tweedledee, their breasts almost as erotic (but only to those who believe size is all) as their companions'.

They had been having a quiet pee in the forest, and one was still zipping his fly, although his micturition must have been accomplished by touch rather than sight, for his belly was nine months pregnant and even his toes must have been invisible except when he was lying down.

We moved on into Chame, followed by the strange quintet who began to sing and dance, clapping their pastry hands and bellowing with laughter. What an odd crew, I thought. Surely the four fat ones couldn't all end up on the credits as executive producers; and for those of you who don't understand the Emperor's New Clothes parlance of the media, such a credit means that they do sod all.

Chame is the district headquarters of the Manang District, and is a proper town. There is a hospital and local government offices, but it is a bit of a mess.

Iman led me to a lodge where people were actually staying, evidenced by wet clothes hanging from the balcony, failing to dry in the cold evening sunlight.

I walked to the top of town and watched local lads playing volleyball barefoot on a patch of dirt. Dust, backlit by the last rays of day, formed brief orange puffs, while above them, to the east, I saw an extraordinary cloud edged with pink, resembling a high plateau of snow, curling like a breaking wave.

'Manaslu.'

I turned, and there was my guardian angel, Iman.

'What?'

'There. Manaslu.'

The cloud was a mountain, the first 26,000-foot peak I had seen, and the way to the summit seemed so simple, a bit of a plod. That is what is so hard to appreciate in the Himalaya: the sheer scale of the things. In the Alps there is usually some point of reference: a mountain hut or a *téléférique*. Even on Mont Blanc or the Matterhorn you can usually pick out climbing parties in day-glo, rescue-me pink through binoculars that put the faces and ridges into proportion. In Nepal there is nothing between you and them except air, and you cannot comprehend the height. The angle from your eyes to a summit may be no more than five degrees, but that is akin to viewing Leith Hill from Crawley, and this crude goniometry somehow diminishes them. Only when you know a mountain is over five miles high does it impress you, for in my travels I saw many peaks, considerably lower, which made a more immediate impact.

But a plod it is not. Manaslu is known as the 'Japanese Mountain' because of several attempts by Japanese expeditions to climb it, resulting in success in 1956. Many have climbed it since, but for every three who have made the summit, one has died. Not odds to impress your local insurance broker, so best not to try unless your name is Reinhold Messner who managed it in 1972. Then you can say, 'Piece of cake. I've done it before. And of course I've done Everest too, and ...'

The sumos back at the lodge were beginning to eat. A table had been laid out like a banquet, and course after course was being shovelled into bodies that seriously challenged the craftsmanship of the carpenters who had made the chairs. I had to know what was going on, so I approached the cameraman.

'You are from Japan?'

'South Korea. Simple mistake. You all look the same to us too.' He laughed and took a gulp of beer.

'So what are you doing, exactly?'

'A slimming programme.'

Tweedledum was squashing a ball of rice into a mouth already congested with potatoes, while Tweedledee's chin glistened with yellow noodle fat. The sumo-ettes were scrapping over a curry bowl, good-naturedly, like sibling sows at a trough.

'I see,' I said, in the English way.

'Tonight's the last night,' the cameraman explained. 'From now on, they *starve*.'

'I see.' I didn't.

'Tomorrow we weigh them in order to find out how much they'll lose by the time they reach Jomosom.'

'You're going over Thorung La with them?'

'That's the plan.'

'You must be mad.'

He guffawed. 'Good television, yes?'

No, I thought. Very bad television; the television whose mainspring is humiliation and exploitation. But in today's climate, good television. Cleverly advertised, it would probably beat all comers in the Seoul afternoon ratings war. And cheap, not only in concept, but also to produce.

'Come,' said Iman, 'I've got someone you'd like to meet.'

Paul was sitting in the kitchen, eating rice with his fingers, and I sat beside him at a crackling stove. He hailed from Wolverhampton. Inspired by celebrity chefs – on TV of course – he had decided to begin at the bottom of the ladder as a commis. But the rungs leading to the apotheosis of *Ready, Steady, Cook* are greased with lard and he became an adviser for a non-governmental organisation in a polytechnic in Pokhara instead, teaching the Nepali to cook. Understretched by a lax regime, he had volunteered to spend concurrent time in the hills for another NGO, proselytising culinary hygiene.

'You wouldn't believe the way they handle their food,' he explained. 'Wipe their arses and then leave their fingerprints all over the plates. No wonder there's so much diarrhoea. And worse. I've arranged a meeting tomorrow night, but I doubt they'll listen. They don't seem to believe in germs.'

'At least you'll be doing some good for the locals.'

'Locals've got nothing to do with it. I'm talking to the

lodge owners. Tourists with the shits aren't good for the economy. It only takes one poor sod with giardiasis to go scuttling back to Cincinnati and there's a dozen potential tourists booking into Disneyland instead.'

'What about the others? Those living in the sticks?'

'Hopefully it'll filter up, eventually.'

It was time to mention the M-word.

'Have you had any contact with the Maoists?'

'Oh yes. In the west. I was in one place where they invaded the school and forbade the kids and teachers to sing the national anthem.'

'But they didn't interfere with you?'

'Why should they? Health's high on their agenda, and anything that helps, helps.'

Before leaving England I had been told about a charity worker who had been advised to take the organisation's cash supply from the local bank the day before an armed robbery. The Maoists got money to finance their collective banking system, and the charity continued its work unhampered.

Now the Nepali government has changed its policy. Following the massacres of even more policemen by insurgents, the army has finally been co-opted into fighting the dissidents who claim to represent the impoverished. And no one else can make this claim, despite the Maoists' terror tactics. Once again it's a battle between the corrupt and the revolutionaries. Haven't they read Aristotle?

'So it's all in the west?' I asked. 'Not here?'

'Don't you believe it.'

'We're in a Maoist area here?'

'Not like it is in the west. They don't control the economy here. They don't run the local councils, banks and schools, but they're here all right. The revolution doesn't stop just because Westerners like us are buoying up local businesses. They're wherever there're poor people. And there're poor people here, believe me.'

In 1994 the Communist Party of Nepal, United Marxist/Leninist, was the first democratically elected Communist government east of the Urals, but it was a minority government, and was terminated by the Supreme Court in 1995 on a technicality. Since 1996, the Nepal Communist Party (Maoist), once a recognised and legitimate organisation, has been at war with what it considers a venal government; its aim to inspire a peasant-based revolution in the manner of that achieved in China.

In purely geographical terms, over 60 per cent of Nepal is now controlled by the Maoists, and there is no rapprochement between them and the government; an impasse that has resulted in atrocities on both sides.

The cities are still free of Maoist control but the countryside, comprising most of this small nation, is largely under their thumb. The government treats those fighting 'the People's War' as terrorists, and the Maoists see the government as terrorisers, denying basic human rights to the rural and urban population. It is a *real* civil war, little publicised in the world's media, that seems destined to continue for many years. And its outcome? No one knows.

I returned to the dining room, where the fat Koreans were still eating: apple pies and fruit, each diner like the glutton played by Terry Jones in *Monty Python's The Meaning of Life*. I wished that, like him, they would all explode.

I sat in a side room, along with the Koreans' porters, and experienced my first *kotatsu*, a simple but ingenious method of keeping warm. A charcoal brazier is placed under the table and the maxi-length tablecloth is draped over your legs, trapping the hot air, warming blood vessels in the legs which then spread heat into your upper body with the inevitability predicted by William Harvey.

Its only disadvantage is footstink, but imagining a bowl of shredded Parmesan on the table neutralises any inclination to throw up.

The sumo-ettes squeezed in and, emboldened by vats of alcohol, decided to flirt with their porters who, being servants, didn't complain. Instead of sitting beside their wiry objects of desire, the slimmers sat *on* them, fat fingers like curling tongs fondling their hair.

The porters, who had been at the *raksi*, seemed happy to be crushed but there is always a problem having a lascivious woman sitting on your lap. You know what I mean. You're coming back from the pub and the car's full, so the woman you fancy a bit sits astride you. You're concerned that she's not wearing a seat-belt, but that's the least of your worries. But if the leering porters were prone to stiffies I doubt if their teasers would have been able to tell through their posterior flab.

As I left for the sanctuary of my cell, two porters stumbled in from the dark, bent double, and dumped their impossible loads on the floor: cases of Tuborg together with two boxed laser-jet printers for a PC, and I wondered if they understood what had been breaking their backs.

11

I don't know about you, but I have always considered going for a Number Two a private affair. Someone waiting just outside the door is always inhibiting, and next dawn I found a tripod pressed against the privy and I could see the cameraman through the porthole. Had he switched his microphone on?

In the final documentary there would be exquisite shots of the sun's rays turning the Annapurna peaks to damask, accompanied by a dawn chorus filtched from a library CD, or the Korean equivalent of Vaughan Williams. Farts and plops would only destroy the illusion of The Intrepid Cameraman risking his life, although a 600 mm lens would make him appear to be Up There, his very being threatened by ice falls or frostbite.

It's so easy nowadays. Again and again we see wildlife programmes about leopards and lion prides, except that things have changed. Now there's always a cub called Tiny Tim or Orphan. Will he survive? Science anthropomorphised for the average viewer. Even the once-great BBC Wildlife Unit in Bristol has succumbed to dumbing down. Now we have camerapeople filming themselves as presenters, sitting safely in their Range Rovers with mounts fixed to their electric windows, their roofs caged by creature-proof mesh. They even have camera robots, covered in fur, infiltrating the big cats' most intimate moments. Want to see precisely how a lion defecates? We have the technology. Want to see exactly how they fuck? We can arrange that too. Animals as soap opera. *Everything* as soap opera. Everything cheapened.

We walked over a suspension bridge and through a Buddhist lichgate walled by prayer wheels, one of which was a drum, painted yellow, on which I read the name of a dairy product manufacturer. Still, I turned them just to know what it felt like; like a Nepali tourist in a High Church English cathedral lighting a candle. A corpulent monk in Beaujolais robes wobbled towards us like a witch doctor, holding a smoking thurible of juniper which, presumably, he believed would be useful.

An easy stroll through pines. Small birds; red, yellow and green, flitted amongst the branches, always too fidgety to wait for identification, although they were doubtless printed in my book and therefore truly existed.

Iman's way was his own, and we met no one as we trod silently through the forest, the river far below; the only sounds the wind in the pines and birdsong like a choir hidden behind a rood-screen. And occasionally the dull thwack of axes in the forest above us where trees were being illegally felled for timber and fuel.

No doubt denudation is a serious problem, leading to soil erosion and avalanche risk, but you can see it from the people's point of view: there seemed to be so many trees. Just one or two more lost can't make *that* much difference. And there were no police anti-chopping squads combing the woods. But with less soil to absorb the rain there is more run-off, and this can affect flooding a thousand miles away on the sub-continent. And the local people don't plant where they have reaped.

Even where the government has sold timber franchises, corruption has led to wholesale plunder; sycophantic and greedy officials making a quick buck. No different here than other Third World countries where those providing international aid seem incapable of constructing watertight, enforceable contracts.

We rested beside an automated prayer wheel, worked by water, sending its supplications around and around for as long as the stream flowed.

It began to snow, quietly, and we crossed a bridge which, for some reason, was forbidden to mule trains. They had their own, upstream, and it must have been ropy, for later I met a man who had seen a mule fall from it to its death in the river.

Looking back I saw a textbook example of avalanche risk. During our forest stroll we had not been aware of what was hidden above. Rock slabs, rising for thousands of feet, overlapped by linear cliffs, held fresh snowfields that had nothing to bind them. A rise in temperature and it would slip as inexorably as snow from a roof in a thaw.

Philippe and Marie, who had gone missing in Chame, suddenly reappeared at an altitude of 9,500 feet at Dhukure Pokhari, where Iman and I stopped for lunch.

I supped soup while the lugubrious French stuffed themselves, unenthusiastically, with yogurt.

I could tell that they couldn't wait to get home and tell their friends just how dreadful things had been. 'And the food! Could we find any cayenne pepper? And olive oil – they'd never even heard of it!'

I excused myself and examined the *mani* wall bisecting the street. These walls vary in length but most are clad with flat stone panels like grey gravestones propped against a country church, on which a prayer is chiselled, often half erased by the wind, or semi-illegible under a fur of lichen. *Om mani padme hum* is the prayer. Translated it means, 'Hail to the jewel in the lotus', although what it *means* is less easy to interpret. I have looked it up in the no-nonsense *Brewer's Dictionary of Phrase and Fable*, that states: 'The Lotus symbolises universal being, and the jewel the individuality of the utterer.' Are you any the wiser? Me neither. But we have to respect it. After all, it's been respected for millennia.

There are Christian litanies too. Petitions to God and his family. At benediction, in St Charles Borromeo, Weybridge, I used to participate in them between pumping the bellows for my father, the organist. The one to Our Lord Jesus Christ went on forever.

'Jesus, Sun of Justice' (audience response: 'Have mercy on us.')

'Jesus, splendour of the Father': response.

'Jesus, purity of virgins': response.

And so on.

It's all true. I've just checked it in *The Treasury of the Sacred Heart*. And in the same horrid book I have found the following: 'An indulgence of 300 days was granted by rescript, dated April 28, 1861, to the faithful in England for the devout recitation, by our Most Holy Father Pope Pius IX'. However, this decree was proclaimed some years before the same pope declared at the First Vatican Council that he was infallible. So does it count? And what does 300 days actually *mean* in terms of relief from purgatorial scalding? When you die are you sentenced, by angelic magistrates, to a thousand years or more of torture before gaining heaven? Such were the preoccupations of a small boy who should have been worried, instead, about finding enough wood to build a tree-camp. At least the litany to the Virgin Mary had poetic credence, with descriptions ranging from 'star of the sea' to 'mystic rose' and 'tower of ivory' – after which the congregation intoned, 'Pray for us'.

When I began my adolescent foray into writing poetry, one of my first efforts was a blasphemous parody of a litany. It was long, and long lost, but I remember odd lines:

God of Cancer
We pray for you.
God of Stillbirth
We pray for you.
God of Schizophrenia
We pray for you.

Even then I did not blame an unlikely and unlikeable God for human failings, for those depended on free will. No 'God of the Holocaust' or 'God of War'. Only those things which, as creator, he could have avoided, at his pleasure.

Those inscriptions on the *mani* wall were exquisite, but only, to me, in terms of the artistry. You don't have to be a Christian to appreciate the Sistine Chapel roof.

* * * * *

Snow swirled through the forest like gentle tornadoes until we emerged into a barren landscape at Lower Pisang, where we were destined to sleep. The dining room was already fuggy with international youth high-tailing it back to Kathmandu. After the quietude of the trail I still needed silence and so I sat at a table in the snow, drinking beer.

A man who looked even older than me approached, sat down and introduced himself. Fred, from Preston, declined the offer of a beer and sat, lost for words, staring up into the black confetti of snow squalling down from the surrounding peaks. He explained that he was a primary school headmaster who had suffered a breakdown and had come here, 'because I always wanted to'. He was on a paid sabbatical but had serious doubts about returning to his executive role.

'I became a teacher because I loved teaching but then I got pushed further up the ladder until I wasn't allowed to teach any more. All I do now is sit at my computer. I hardly ever see the children, except at assembly.'

His face betrayed betrayal, his jaw slack with resignation, his eyes habitually close to weeping. I flicked through adjectives to describe him, and *dour* sat on top.

'Fancy strolling up to Upper Pisang?' he asked. 'Apparently there's a monastery up there well worth seeing.'

'If you like.'

Upper Pisang, several hundred feet above, glimpsed through the snow, looked desolate. We were already nearly 10,000 feet above sea level and I thought the climb might help acclimatisation. We set off together until we reached a *mani* wall I wanted to photograph.

'You go on. I'll catch you up.'

But I never did. Fred was far fitter than me and sped up into the murk, leaving me to trudge after him like a toddler.

It seemed that tourists had not altered Upper Pisang. I suspect that it is as all villages in the Marsyangdi Valley must have been like thirty years ago. Muddy black alleys, splodged with cow pats, rose steeply between rectangular stone houses roofed by wooden tiles that were weighed down by boulders. Coughing goats with twisted horns were tethered to chimneys, and the windows of the houses were bleak orifices. I wondered what life must be like here in winter. Awful, by any standard.

I saw only three people: an old woman talking to herself as she turned prayer wheels obsessively, and two wives sitting sulkily at an entrance to a house resembling a dungeon. Prayer flags hung like dirty dishcloths above the squalid houses. I found the temple but it was locked, and so I made my way down through sodden fields.

I had witnessed such poverty only once before but then it was much jollier because of a combination of climate and a lack of formalised religion – despite evangelists lurking downstream.

I was staying in a village on the banks of the Javari River, a tributary of the Amazon separating Brazil from Peru, a week's paddle from sophisticated tin roofs.

The Mayuruna people lived in rudimentary grass huts but were surrounded by opulence: dense jungle howling and grunting with monkeys and wild boar to hunt, fruit and nuts to pick at will, and a rich river full of fat fish to catch. And always hot; an outdoor ambience where families intermingled, the sultry air tinkling with children's laughter.

In Upper Pisang it was harsh. No hint of Eden; the inhabitants having to live like troglodytes for half the year. No monkey stew on the menu, but an occasional scrawny hen. No fresh fruit, but lentils. The difference between a stark Methodist chapel and a baroque Italian church.

Two filthy children rushed out to greet me, and I took their photographs. They were dressed in rags and their faces were begrimed from a day's labour, planting potatoes. Suddenly their father appeared, demanding baksheesh.

'How much?'

He displayed all his fingers and thumbs and so I paid him ten rupees. Nine pence.

'Take my picture too.'

'How much?'

'Nothing.'

And so I did, reluctantly, but not before he had whisked a brown woollen hat from his pocket and placed it carefully on his head. A red sticky label adhered to it, and as I focused I read F.C. Bayern München. The Huns had been here before me.

I popped my head through the door of my lodge but the atmosphere was too youth-hostelly for my taste and so I headed up the deserted street in search of sophistication.

A smiling Buddhist lodge keeper leapt out of his emporium and said, 'Hey, man! You look like you could do with a stiff drink.'

'Too right,' I replied, reverting, involuntarily, to hippy-speak.

It was a lovely lodge but under-patronised and I shared

the communal table with three Dutchmen who were poring over maps. *Raksi* warmed my belly but I found myself disliking the dominant male; no reason except that he had short blond hair, high cheekbones, and rimless glasses. And he spoke with a foreign accent. Such is the power of stereotypes. He looked like every SS interrogator you have ever seen in all those POW and secret agent films they show on TV, usually played by Anton Diffring. Of course he was Dutch, not Deutsch, and his father probably risked his life for the resistance, but his perfect teeth, framed between fleshy lips, disconcerted me; probably for no reason other than I am ashamed of my gap-toothed Irish smile.

I glanced out of the window and immediately wanted to share the revelation. There, vertically above us, was a dream mountain of the kind drawn by children; a conical peak, suddenly framed between a break in the clouds.

'Oh that,' said the stereotype, who was called Piet. 'It's only Pisang peak.'

Only? It was an object of unadulterated beauty, dominating the horizon.

'It's just a trekking peak,' he explained. 'Nothing serious.'

It looked serious to me, its upper ridge glistening with lethal ice. Apparently anyone could climb it, for a few hundred dollars, but it's not a trek. You need to know your crampons from your ice-screws, and it's still 5,000 feet higher than Mont Blanc.

It was the scene of a tragedy a decade ago when a party of several Germans, inexplicably all roped together, fell to their deaths.

'Time for bed,' said Piet, yawning and folding his maps. I glanced at my watch. It was 7 p.m. 'At last we should be able to get some sleep. Last time *someone* went out and got drunk and came back after nine. He woke us all up.'

I felt like asking if they wanted me to read them a story, but I refrained.

Back at my lodge, I had to ask the international brigade to make room for me, which they did, grudgingly. After all, I was old enough to be their father and therefore almost invisible.

Iman was in attendance and offered me a menu, which I perused while an American woman opposite regaled us with a list of the really great beaches she had visited, ranging from Bali to Thailand and back again. They were all really neat, but she was having difficulty deciding which was the neatest. Although well past her teens, she wore a pink Alice-band that added a dozen years. Iman handed me a glass of *raksi* which I drained in a gulp.

'What's that?' demanded the American, frowning. Vertical creases, like inverted commas, appeared between her eyebrows.

'Moonshine.'

'You need that?' she challenged.

'I enjoy it. Can I have another glass, Iman? One for myself and one for the lady.'

It worked. She blushed with indignation, and the devil's advocate within me was fired.

'Not for me, thank you very much,' she said.

Suddenly I realised the advantage of these hot *kotatsu* tables where everyone sits blanketed like inmates in an old people's home. No escape. I turned my attention to a jolly Belgian who had retreated from Thorung La.

'It's bloody shits up there,' he told me. 'No chance. But what the hell? It's still better than Brussels.'

Iman handed me another *raksi*.

'No chance?' My irrational optimism was fuelled by alcohol. 'There must be a chance?'

'You could always say a prayer,' said the American.

'Why would I do that? I'm an atheist.'

She gawped at me as if I had just admitted to screwing a goat.

'That means I don't believe in God.'

'I *know* what it *means*.'

'Congratulations.'

'Don't you go getting all condescending just because you're English.'

'And what if I said I was a Communist as well?'

'I wouldn't believe you.'

'Why not?'

'Because they don't exist any more, except in Cuba and North Korea.'

'Don't forget China.'

'China's had its day.'

'But you're in a country run by Communists.'

'Pull the other one.'

'But you are. You're surrounded by them. You've got a porter?'

'So?'

'So how do you know he isn't one? Haven't you seen rocks painted with hammers and sickles?'

'So?'

'So what does that tell you?'

She paused, uncharacteristically, to gather her thoughts, and I decided to lighten the mood that had cast a guttering flame of gloom around the entire table. Something bland.

'How long've you been travelling?'

'Two years.'

'And you'll go back to the States?'

'No way. At least not for a while.'

'Why not?'

'I hate it.'

'So how do you survive?'

'I've kinda retired.'

Retired? She couldn't have been more than 25. 'How come?'

'I worked in real estate as a consultant and made some shrewd investments. The interest more than pays for all this.'

Having eaten, I excused myself, but came face to face with one of the Israelis who I'd admonished a couple of nights ago.

'Oh it's you,' he said, as surprised as me. 'You were right to talk to us like that, but you were more aggressive than you needed to be. Here. Give me your hand.'

And having shaken his hand, ambivalently, I went to my room, through snow, to face a night plagued by doubts.

I have been afraid of the dark ever since I can remember. The idea of waking in the night, opening my eyes and seeing nothing, is too close to death. In Hollywood films of the forties and fifties, characters would sleep wearing masks. How could they do that? Even the rim of a wardrobe lit by a hall light is enough to alleviate the fear; a hint of the material world. It's called nyctophobia, a word I had not heard before reading Martin Amis' book, *Experience*. It is part autobiography and part a biography of his father, Kingsley, who hated being alone at night. That's one of the things that makes writing worthwhile: the inadvertent sharing.

Martin Amis writes of having panic attacks on the Underground when in his late twenties. I had the same, and thought I was unique. Slippery with sweat, and shaking, I would have to get out of the Tube at every fourth station before reboarding. It became the same on railways, aircraft and boats. Despite rationalising the cause, in my case relating to my father's death when I was 13, the symptoms persisted, and still do to an extent, although I can cope now; Nepal and its aftermath a joint catharsis.

In Nepal, as never before, I learned to accept physical

danger, and when I returned to England I learned to accept death too.

My wife, Mimi, said that she was going to meet me at Heathrow. I thought it a little strange because she was working in a school in Devon, but I put it down to her desire to welcome me home.

Half an hour after landing I was on my way to a hospital where my sister Angela was being treated for pancreatic cancer. Angela, my best friend, still able to talk then, her husband and three extraordinary sons still optimistic about the prognosis. Ten weeks later I took a train from Devon to see her, at the hospice, for the last time. The train was late, and there were no buses or taxis at the station, so I walked the two miles to the hospice.

I was ten minutes too late. She had died. I kissed her, but her forehead was cold, her vibrancy and humour having fled. Although her family believed, deeply, that they would meet her again in heaven, I knew in my heart that she would only survive as a precious memory in all who had been privileged to share her sheer love of living and giving.

And there, seeing my dead sister, I no longer feared death, desperately hoping that my rationality had a flaw. We all want heaven. Father, mother, sister, children, reunited again. And despite my atheism, I prayed I was wrong; that I was merely a victim of an upbringing that had predetermined my rationale. Adolescent memories of Stanley Spencer's *The Resurrection, Cookham* come to mind.

Wouldn't it be luvverly if it were true; that we all rise from our graves? But painters and poets do that to you when you are young. You imbue them with wisdom beyond your own. But even the greatest poets have only asked questions, not answered them.

I'm reminded of a joke. A cab driver said to his mate: 'You know who I picked up today?'

'No, mate.'

'Bertrand bleeding Russell.'

'You mean *the* Bertrand Russell? The famous philosopher?'

'The very same. So I said to him, "Excuse me, Bert, but can I ask you a question?" and he said, "Indisputably." So I said, "Just one thing. What's it all about then?" And do you know? He couldn't tell me.'

12

I said goodbye to Marie and Philippe at breakfast. They were going back to Paris, convinced that Thorung La was closed for the foreseeable future, their desks waiting for them, needing them. I kissed Marie's cold cheeks and we exchanged addresses, each knowing they would never be written on envelopes.

Fred, dressed for the Himalaya, asked Iman and I if we wanted to accompany him on a high level route to Manang, but it meant a steep 2,000-foot ascent, and I declined. The promenade to Upper Pisang had already drained me.

The sun surprised us as Iman and I set out for Manang. Prayer flags fluttered from bamboo poles bending above a *chorten* outside the village, and I saw Annapurna IV and II, the latter over 26,000 feet, its fluted ridges cutting the sky like serrated white blades. I tried to gauge their immensity and only the fact that their summits, plumed with spindrift, were parting the jetstream made me appreciate their height.

Fred's porter, Bean, caught up with us and Iman and he immediately struck up a friendship. Bean, under five feet tall and as bony as a perch, carried Fred's well-stocked rucksack as easily as if it were full of feathers. A rumble in the bowels, and I told Iman I would catch up with him later.

I strolled up into the pines, chose a spot and dug a hole in the warm soil with my hands. But it was a false alarm and so I sat on a tree trunk in perfect silence. A partridge, its breast tattooed with black feathers like X-rayed ribs, scurried past, and rust-breasted finches skittered amongst the pines, oblivious of me. I sat there, not wanting to move, suddenly enveloped by a rare hot cocoon of contentment.

I caught up with Iman an hour later at a tea-shed on a

cusp separating forest from desert. Beyond us the valley, in a micro-climatic rainshadow, was all parched earth, trees greening it sporadically, as individuals rather than members of a tribe.

A haystack approached us, shimmering in a heat haze, stratified above the hot coals of stones baking in the midday heat. The haystack was carried on the back of a stooping woman who stumbled through the shale, her back parallel with the ground, her feet sliding rather than stepping, as she carried her incompatible load. She hesitated on a plank spanning a stream, but carried on, in obvious pain because it was compulsory. Her cows or goats had to be fed. She had no choice.

The view was perfect CinemaScope into which an aeroplane flew, centre frame, its silhouette heading for the airstrip at Humde. Wild horses roamed the desert, their backdrop gulches and yellow pillars of sand rising, kiln-shaped, from a plain, reminding me of the Badlands in North America. Wranglers, in yakboy hats, galloped and trotted up and down the village for no obvious purpose other than demonstrating their horsemanship; hooves sending mini dust storms across the street. There should have been tumbleweed.

We stopped for lunch at a first-floor terrace from which steps, chopped with an axe into a log, led up to a flat roof where prayer flags cast shadows on a solar-powered heating system whose clever cells faced south.

A man shouldering a Royal Nepal Airlines bag sat opposite, his back to the Annapurnas, wearing designer sunglasses and a posh baseball cap, the male equivalent of make-up. The restaurateur took his order deferentially.

'Where are you going?' the man asked me, like a man used to asking questions, a hint of the Bronx about him.

'Thorung La.'

'I doubt it. Where're you from?'

'England.'

'I've been there too.'

I took my cue. 'Where else?'

'The States mainly.'

'What do you do?'

'I'm Chief of Police for the Manang District.'

'Ah, a powerful member of the community.'

He shrugged. 'I have my responsibilities.'

'Is there much crime?'

'See those houses?' He pointed to the whole town as if he owned it. 'In the winter the people leave and go down the valley. And do they need to lock their doors? No way. No how.'

'You travel a lot?'

'Just flown in from Pokhara. One of those conferences. You know?'

I didn't, but I said I did. Not a Mister Big you'd want to cross.

'Why were you in the States?'

He lit a cigar, the first I had seen in Nepal. 'Learning things.'

'Like how to counteract terrorism?'

'There's no terrorism here.'

'I thought Maoists were a problem?'

'Not in my neck of the woods, mister.'

Iman and I reached a long display of prayer wheels, all brassy like cogwheels in an industrial museum. We passed on the left, as is the custom, and I ran my hand along them – hundreds of them – feeling the supplications as a blind man Braille.

We passed a temple, and I asked Iman if I might go in without offending the faithful.

'No problem, Peter, but you should leave a gift.'

A blood-red cylinder, several feet high and studded with gold prayers, turned to my fingers, its engineering impeccable, while the walls beyond were saturated by frescos, blue and brown predominantly, depicting the pantheon of Buddhist gods.

Aesthetically, as art, it was prodigious, but half my heart sank because the subject matter echoed the hierarchy of every religion; its poetic symbolism denigrated by middlemen into theological tenets. I left two gifts: coins and scepticism.

We checked into a police post guarded by a constable armed with a relic of a rifle, Lee Enfield by the look of it, its wooden butt buffed by generations until its original shape had been thinned into a wooden scapula. No wonder the Maoists, with their state-of-the-art arms, are winning. Antiques versus modern killing machinery. Bows and arrows versus flintlocks.

A red rescue helicopter flew over us, heading towards Manang. Someone was in trouble, and I was reminded that we were about to spend two nights there, acclimatising. Push on regardless and you can end up dead.

Braga is the last village before Manang, and it is extraordinary. We stopped by a stream oozing from a flowery water meadow above which the houses were almost camouflaged by a cliffy amphitheatre. Only prayer flags, protruding from the rooftops, and a white *gompa* squatting above, made sense of the architecture which was built into the crags like steps; the roof of the house below the terrace of the one above.

I should have climbed up to the *gompa*. I should have said, 'Come on, Iman, last one up's a sissy,' but the altitude, 12,000 feet, was causing lassitude. The heat was stupefying, and we still had to plod up a stony track into Manang.

The west was arranged with great peaks: Lamjung, Annapurna II, Annapurna IV, bits of Annapurna III, and Gangapurna. All those purnas, listed like that, sound prosaic, but that's what cartographers do.

A cornice, hinged to a ridge on Gangapurna and weakened by the sun, fell off. I couldn't gauge how wide it was; perhaps a few hundred metres, but it was no more impressive, in scale, than a trickle of sand caused by a lizard on a dune. The big one, Annapurna I, was out of sight.

In 1950 the great French climber Maurice Herzog couldn't see it either. Having arrived with a supremely talented team to climb either Annapurna I or Dhaulagiri, he had trekked to Manang with Gaston Rébuffat in search of the mountain and food, but was given short shrift by the locals who had enough problems feeding themselves. Herzog returned via the Khansi Khola and Tilicho Lake alone, heading for his expedition campsite above Jomosom. Having fallen into an icy stream, he almost died from hypothermia. He crawled into camp more dead than alive, but went on to find Annapurna I, which he climbed with Louis Lachenal. It was the first 8,000-metre peak to be pierced by crampons, but the descent was horrendous, resulting in frostbite that led to amputations. On the retreat, the expedition doctor, Jacques Oudot, had to operate.

> *'Ouch!'* [Herzog speaking.]
> *I felt a shock all over me and Oudot announced: 'The first amputation! The little finger!'*
> *This gave me rather a twinge. A little finger may not be much use, but all the same I was attached to it!'*

Oudot asked if Herzog wanted to keep it as a souvenir, but Herzog declined.

> *Every day one or two joints, either on my feet or my hands, were removed. All this was done without anaesthetic, in the open, how and when it was possible.*

If you haven't read *Annapurna* then do. It is a classic. And while I am about it, taste a book by another expedition member, Lionel Terray: *Conquistadors of the Useless*, an egocentric but fascinating account of a climber's progress from the Alps to the Himalaya and Andes. Aspirational books that inspired the climber I would never become.

Manang was not welcoming to Tilman either, who was also here in 1950.

> *On the whole they were not pleased to see us and I was not delighted with them. The traveller to remote parts wishes, indeed expects, to find the natives unsophisticated enough to regard him with the respect which he seldom gets at home. At Manangbhot he will be disappointed.*

This from a man who, great explorer though he was, displayed a callous attitude to those who did not have the advantages of a prep-school education.

And women! They were definitely beyond the pale.

> *It may be true that no home is complete without a woman, but it is possible to dispense with them in camp. No doubt our she-coolies were a comfort to the men, but for us they performed no womanly offices.*

It sounds like something a nineteenth-century explorer in darkest Africa might have sent home via a forked stick, but was written only 50 years ago. Thank God for Mick Jagger, Ken Loach, Jack Kerouac, The Sex Pistols, Neil Kinnock, Kenneth Tynan et al. Even the Beatles and Gore Vidal.

Tilman would have been scandalised by modern Manang and its decadence, its people now only subservient in a professional way. With him in mind, I relished the way I was shown to my double room at the Tilicho Lodge;

painted white and beamed with timber, complete with en suite personal pit with running water overlooking a view that no Going Places catalogue could hope to emulate. And across the field a building with a satellite link.

I was allowed two minutes, and heard my phone ringing in Devon, its sound bouncing off something unlikely in space.

I heard Mimi, my wife. 'Hello?'

'It's me.'

'Who's me?'

'Me.'

'Christ! Where are you?'

'Manang.'

'Where's that?'

'Nepal.'

'Are you all right?'

I could have been funny and said, 'OK apart from a broken neck', but we might have been cut off and an international rescue plan set into operation. 'Fine.'

I imagined her standing by the glass door tinged grey by March clouds blowing off Dartmoor.

'The boys?'

'Fine.'

'I've only got a few seconds left.'

'Keep talking. Don't stop talking.'

So I spoke incoherently until the meter clunked shut and left me feeling isolated – but not for long.

* * * * *

For three pounds a night I gazed out at the Himalaya, ate fine food, drank cold beer, and thought, 'Why the fuck have I waited so long to do this?'

Fred, still a bit puffed from his high-level route from

Lower Pisang, joined me and we drank, divorced from our previous troubled lives, putting the world to rights while the Annapurnas avalanched above us.

* * * * *

'No more cigarettes or alcohol until after Thorung La,' Iman admonished, winking at me mischievously. 'After tonight. You want to taste *chhang*?'

'Why not?'

'Come.' He was grinning.

I followed him down a street where leonine dogs, like photos from an RSPCA appeal, sprawled in the evening heat, their ribs like whale bones on a beach. No doubt some English loon will eventually set up a puppy sanctuary here.

Iman led me to a hut choked with woodsmoke. A stove was surrounded by an oblong of benches on which locals and porters sat, being plied with alcohol by a barmaid, Queenie, whose facial orifices were riveted with gold.

I was in a pub. Everyone seemed to be crying, but it was the fug. A dwarfish man thrust a glass at me. Not wishing to offend, I put the clear spirit to my lips, but it smelled of lighter fuel, making me retch, and I gave it back knowing I had failed a manliness test. Queenie poured the glasses of *chhang* from a jug and Iman and I said 'Cheers' before downing them.

Chhang is a home-brewed white beer, its consistency somewhere between milk and semen, and hypochondriacs should avoid it because it is concocted with unboiled water. Instead of a hangover you could get typhoid. Iman was reluctant to tell me all that went into it.

'Secret ingredients?' I asked.

'Yes,' replied Iman. 'Secret ingredients.'

He translated this for the clientele who fell about

laughing. We sat, tearful, knocking back glass after glass, and then the door burst open and a huge Tibetan man filled the frame. He was dressed all in red, with a Saturn hat rimmed with fur. He was Queenie's brother-in-law and pushed in beside me, his breath already fuelled like a fire-eater's. He asked Iman about me.

'He wants to know how old you are.'

'It's no secret. Fifty-four.'

Iman told him, and the man looked me up and down before speaking to Iman.

'He says you are strong.'

'Tell him my body is not strong, but I am strong in here.' I tapped my head.

Iman translated, and the tough guy's face crumpled into a smile, the crows' feet around his eyes opening like crevasses. He grasped my hand and shook it in a grip that could have crushed apples. Some chord had been struck, and he bought a round. Then I bought a round. Everyone bought rounds.

Dozy, I ate with Fred back at the lodge.

'You know,' said Fred. 'I am so *glad* that I am here.'

'Me too.'

I squashed my last cigarette into an ashtray. After all, we had a pass to cross.

13

A bang on the door at six and Iman was there, champing at the bit. Befuddled, chilled, and clad only in underpants, I saw the pyramid of Tilicho Peak lit by a spotlight of sun, while all around us the valley was blue with cold.

'You want breakfast?'

'I couldn't eat a thing.'

'Then I'll meet you downstairs in ten minutes.'

I puked pasta and chutney into the pit and joined Iman in the street where I followed him dumbly as he led me on our compulsory acclimatisation trek. I stumbled down a path, obediently.

'I thought we were supposed to go up.'

'We will, but first we have to go down.'

A family was already at work in the fields bordering the river, following black oxen dragging a plough.

A suspension bridge took us over a melt-water river and I shivered as I followed Iman to a powder-blue glacial lake under Gangapurna. Objectively it was beautiful, but sterile, and only a white wagtail hopping along the shore turned this still-life from stone to blood.

A colossal cliff of detritus, 500 feet high, plunged vertically into the icy tarn. It was a lateral moraine, sliced like a cake, its ingredients boulders, like gigantic halved almonds, that fell every so often, rippling the mirror and distorting a perfect reflection.

'Where're we going?' I asked without having to. Deep down I knew.

'Up there.' He pointed to the tumbling cliff.

Oh fuck! I thought. *I'm going to have to be brave.*

The first bit was easy, plodding up dust, but then the path hit the crest, the water directly below the friable edge. My knees turned to jelly, but I leaned to the left. If I slipped, I would only fall down steep scree. I was close to opting out. Bottling it.

And then it all changed. An animal, startled by us, leapt out from behind a huge boulder. It was mottled and I took it for a deer, but then it flew, without flapping, into the valley below. It was a Himalayan griffon, its wingspan longer than the tallest man. It fell like a stalled aircraft about to crash before finding an updraught that sailed it to a crag where it landed with the delicacy of a dancer. I watched it through binoculars which I handed to Iman while I checked its identity in my bird book, like a policeman.

The sheer excitement pushed all fear aside, and I followed Iman up through packed snow and smelly pines until we reached a belvedere beyond which Gangapurna and Annapurna III towered 9 kilometres above the sea.

We heard ice cracking colossally. Somewhere above us, seracs were falling, but so grand was the scale that we could see nothing. To the south was the cockscomb of Manaslu, like a distant Pennine peak.

I headed up, like a groupie needing to be close to his heroes, but Iman called me back. I ignored him and almost jogged up between the pines, inhaling air that tasted so fresh that no simile will suffice.

Iman caught up with me. 'We must go down.'

'Why? Can't we just sit here and watch?'

'You mustn't overdo it.'

'I feel wonderful. Do you think I'll have a problem on Thorung La?'

'No problem, Peter. No problem at all.'

Although I would have been happy to remain at altitude for hours, I took Iman's advice and followed him down, glad that he was convinced of my ability to cope with rarified air.

Iman celebrated by glissading down the steep snowfields between the zigzag path, and I followed.

We went back a new way, sliding on scree and picking

our way between boulders, whooping and screeching like children, enjoying our echoes, until we regained the valley.

* * * * *

Ravenous, I ate porridge and eggs. Already a day spent like no other – and it was not yet 11 o'clock.

Fred joined me, having completed his own acclimatisation day, walking up to a cave where the Lama in Residence guarantees a successful crossing of the Thorung La for the price of a bowl of rice; far less than the going rate for a Catholic mass.

It was festival day in Manang; the fifteenth anniversary of the Annapurna Conservation Area Project to which I had contributed 1,000 rupees at Tal. A village fête, mothers and children flecked with every colour, sitting behind men in their Sunday best. The women knew their place, like Jewish women in a synagogue or Muslim women in a mosque.

The mayor and his lady-wife were there, overhung by portraits of the king and queen, but the archery contest I had hoped to see was replaced by interminable speeches, and the bowmen slunk away, rescheduled for the following day.

I left too, and found myself wandering around the old town where yakburgers couldn't be found for love nor money. There were no slick entrepreneurs living here, but poor people, their goats tethered in muddy yards outside stone houses bordering alleyways reeking of dung.

A man in a cheap suit struck up a conversation, his English excellent. Suresh was a teacher in the school, which I asked to visit.

The building was functional; dark, earth-floored classrooms arranged around a courtyard, but Suresh was not a happy man.

'I've been here for three years.'

'Do you have a family?'

'Oh yes. Back in Besisahar, but I don't see them for ten months at a time.'

'Are you well paid?'

He laughed bitterly. 'Barely enough to survive.'

'But you're well educated.'

'Oh yes. I went to university and I have a degree. But teachers aren't paid properly. All the money goes to the administrators – the people sitting on their backsides in Kathmandu.'

'So why not try something else?'

He shrugged. 'I am a qualified teacher and I want to teach but it's so hard. Not the teaching, but the people here aren't educated. When the day's over I have no one I can talk to in an equal way, intellectually, and it's rotting my brain.'

He touched my down jacket. 'It's cold,' he said. 'Have you got another one?'

I assumed that he was concerned about my survival on Thorung La. 'No, but one should be enough.'

'But it's so cold here, especially in winter.'

Then I understood. He wanted my jacket. 'I'm sorry, I need it.'

He asked me to take his photo and send it to him; to remind him, no doubt, of his self-imposed exile.

'What happens,' I asked, 'when a clever child knows more than her parents?'

'It's a big problem here. Family is everything and when a child contradicts her parents all hell breaks loose. Parents come to me and say, "I tell my daughter so-and-so but she says you say I'm wrong."'

'So what do you tell the parents?'

'I end up compromising. Telling the truth is impossible here.'

'My mother told me that if I swallowed chewing gum it would wrap around my heart and kill me, but when I did basic biology at school I realised it simply couldn't happen. So I told her.'

Suresh frowned. 'Your mother really believed that?'

'Oh yes. It'd been passed down. But by saying it I was confronting her ignorance. It had to be done.'

'Not so easy here.'

Imagine it: Suresh telling little Tara, named after a goddess, that her namesake doesn't really have seven eyes, including ones on her forehead, palms and feet, and little Tara going home and telling Mama: 'Teacher says it's not true.' Oh the price we have to pay for honesty.

Back in the new town I attended a medical lecture. I didn't want to but I owed it to my family to survive, and if I came across a casualty I might be able to help him or her make it back. The Himalayan Rescue Association, run by volunteer foreign doctors, *does* save lives.

The middle-aged Canadian who addressed our alfresco class put the point succinctly. 'Those of you arriving yesterday might have seen a helicopter. It was evacuating a porter with acute mountain sickness. More than that, he'd suffered a stroke. He was the first non-Westerner to be airlifted out. We radioed the trekking company and said, "If you don't pay for his evacuation, we'll make sure your company never operates again." They acquiesced.'

Why the first? Naturally I thought of Iman whose insurance was paramount when I signed my contract with the trekking agency. Had Nepalis, hitherto, simply been left to die?

The doctor was a no-nonsense medico – telling it like it is – and, after her blackboard exposition of all the physiological symptoms waiting to ambush me on the pass, I was experiencing most of them. Apparently even experienced mountaineers can fall foul of bleeding brains and congested lungs.

A logbook listing our details – for next of kin presumably – finally passed to me, and when I filled in my age I realised that I was by far the oldest. Even Fred was only forty-eight. It didn't bode well, and reinforced something we all know is true. All mirrors are magic. Whenever we look in them, we are always seventeen.

The lecture ended with a voluntary oxygen count. Some improbable device measured the amount of oxygen your blood had absorbed on the way up.

A low percentage count could mean putting off the final ascent, perhaps indefinitely. If you registered somewhere in the 80 per cent bracket you had a good chance of avoiding a body-bag.

I waited until the end, listening to the squeals of the twenty-something, non-smoking, non-drinking Presbyterians who seemed to comprise the bulk of the trekkers. The high eighties seemed to be an average score. Like a confessor in a church, I slid back along the pew, until no one else was left.

The doctor, being a doctor, had my number. 'You a smoker?'

'Yes.'

'Too bad. You want to do it or not?'

'I might, but I'm still going over even if the reading's low.'

'It's your life. Give me your finger.'

Who can disobey a doctor? And so I put a forefinger into a device like a jump-lead whose curling wires led to a gizmo as compact as a pocket calculator.

'Congratulations. You're ninety-three.'

I almost said 'I'm only fifty-four' as a joke, but I didn't. I was too much over the moon. Ninety-three!

'You want pills?'

'Why not?'

There is a drug called Diamox whose function still

perplexes me. It does not mask the effects of acute mountain sickness, but allows you to continue if you're showing minor symptoms – although minor symptoms aren't to be sneezed at because they can lead to major symptoms. But everyone else seemed to be buying them so I joined the queue, concerned, in my Catholic way, that I might be cheating.

Back at the lodge Iman had joined a gambling syndicate of porters betting on the outcome of a game called *bagchal*, which translates as 'tiger move', the equivalent of our A Shepherd and His Dog. Played on a round board, there are four tigers and twenty sheep. The sheep have to gang up on the tigers, preventing them from pouncing into an empty square and 'eating' them. The restaurant was electrified by the contest. Each fan club yelled or booed at every move, until the final sheep was slaughtered.

Iman picked up his winnings. He had backed the tigers.

14

I woke to a blue dawn, and although Thorung La was still two dubious days away, I brimmed with hope.

Our next walking days were designed to be short, altitude rather than distance our goal. Time to stop and stare.

Having gently climbed to Tengi we walked steeply up to Gunsang, where we stopped for tea at a proper tea house – by which I mean we could have been in Devon: a beamed ceiling over bright gingham tablecloths on which vases of plastic flowers were expertly arranged. Chintz curtains framed windows in walls a metre thick. Only scones and clotted cream were missing.

I told the owner – a Tibetan woman old enough to be my sister – how much I loved her decor, and she offered me the best table. But I spoiled it by sitting outside, drinking black tea while white mountains measured the sky like a graph.

Oh how I wanted a cigarette, but I had promised Iman, and dragged on the chilled air instead. I could inhale this all day.

We wandered through country devoid of even the smallest tree, and I was reminded of Scottish glens, a stream gurgling below and scrub alongside the path; berberis, the Himalayan equivalent of heather and blaeberries.

'Stop!'

I stopped.

'Look down there.'

I saw nothing.

'There!'

A hint of movement among waterfalls, and I magnified the landscape through my binoculars.

'Sheep, Peter! Sheep!'

So what? I could see sheep any day on Dartmoor. But these were *blue* sheep: *bharal*, a rare breed that roams above the tree-line throughout the year, the favourite feast of snow leopards. But they aren't blue. They're brown and seemed a hybrid between goats and deer, strutting like deer but with horns instead of antlers.

Black yaks straddled the path, their heads perpetually downcast, as if saying, 'We're so, so depressed. Got any uppers on you?'

Above us one of the Chulu peaks printed itself into a sky so blue that a blue sheep would have aspired to it had it only known its own name. Below us a squadron of lammergeiers – bearded vultures – patrolled in search of carrion, their cruciform silhouettes no more than a sparrow's-width less than the griffon we had spotted the previous day.

And so to Yak Kharka, an unappealing collection of lodges whose sole purpose is to let people like me attune themselves to oxygen deprivation. I was shown a tomb of a room, and rebelled. Like all lone travellers I was being discriminated against, but a new building opposite had doubles with views, and so I crossed the tracks, aware that the single-glazing of my colour-slide windows would make for a chilly night; for we had crossed the 13,000-foot threshold.

A Romanian, his nipples sagging from hairy breasts, sat in shorts getting drunk, unaware – perhaps – that his semi-nudity was causing deep offence to the Nepalis.

I left town and picked my way down through boulders and thorny scrub to the river, where I sat in a rocky armchair smoothed out by pebbles when the river was in spate.

I watched birds and a herd of blue sheep that pussyfooted down scree for a drink. I had barely focused on them when the silent valley was assaulted by an

American man shouting 'Jeez! Just look at those deer!'

Why he shouted I don't know, for his companion was only a footfall behind, but the blue sheep panicked and stampeded downstream, out of sight.

'Jeez! They've gone,' he shouted.

I didn't move and the Americans didn't see me, but I watched. The shouter wore a black bandanna and matching Lycra leggings. Wraparound shades completed the colour coordination. They step-stoned the stream, and Bandannaman climbed onto a boulder where he immediately adopted a sculptural pose.

'This'll do,' he shouted to his boyfriend. And Boyfriend spent 15 minutes – and at least two films – immortalising Bandannaman as he adopted Rodinesque positions.

I half expected him to strip off, but Lycra is unforgiving, and I could see that his willy was even smaller than Hemingway's was reputed to have been.

They left, Bandannaman still shouting platitudes, until I had the coombe to myself again. I fell asleep but was shivered awake by shadows. Night was falling fast, but slower than the temperature.

* * * * *

Claire, an Irish woman at the table beside me, was ill: her head cupped in her hands, her *daal bhaat* congealing on her plate. Heat from the charcoal under the table only made her shake.

'You must go down,' I said.

'But I so want to go over. I've tried it twice, but it's no good. I think it's gone, but then the pain comes back, in my head.'

'You know what it is?'

'Of course I fucking know.'

'Then maybe you should go down now? Not wait till morning.'

'It's too fucking cold.'
'Tomorrow might be too fucking late.'
'Fuck off!'

* * * * *

I kept jolting awake, gulping air as though it were rationed. Through frosted windows I could see the Himalaya and a tapestry of pulsating stars; and I was elated because snow can't fall from stars. I might just make it over.

Guidebooks tell you what to wear but let me advise you. It is never enough. I got up and put *everything* on. Under a blanket, inside a down sleeping bag, I wore two pairs of woollen socks, two thermal long-johns, and trousers. And above the navel: thermal vest, vest, shirt, two sweaters, a fleece, a down jacket, its hood tied under my chin, and *still* I shook. And why the surprise? Because you kid yourself that because you are on a trek this somehow diminishes the fact that you are an individual, high on the earth's surface, doing something you aren't designed to do. You're a tourist, yes, but it is serious.

I woke with tears streaming down my face. I had just seen my sons, aged 5 and 3, and had heard their croaky toddlers' voices for the first time in 17 years; for, like a fool, I had not recorded them during that seemingly permanent time of parenthood where all is the present. Welsh days, playing in snow I thought would never melt.

I sat with Fred as we slurped porridge and drank several pints of tea. We could have been two ageing patients in a doctor's waiting room, enquiring discreetly about the other's symptoms.

'Have you taken your pills yet?'

'No need.'

'Me neither.'

A sip of tea.

My turn. 'Any trouble breathing?'

'Not so as you'd notice. You?'

'Not so as you'd notice.'

Claire passed by, her cheeks chalky, heading down.

'How old do you think she is?' Fred asked.

'Twenty-two, twenty-three maybe.'

'Pity,' said Fred. 'At least we oldies still have some advantages.'

Fred, Bean, Iman and I set off together, although our different paces pulled us apart as we climbed high above the Jharsang Khola, having been diverted from the gentler trail leading to the west bank because someone had been crushed to death there by a rock avalanche three days before.

The altitude and switchback trail began to take its toll, and I plodded behind Iman like a slave, not enjoying myself at all. Then we reached snow, deep and squeaky under our boots, and on a snowfield 15,000 feet high, we rested. Gradually the surroundings, their colour intensified by Polaroids, filled my perceptions; my skull a camera obscura into which images of sheer grandeur invaded me through the pinpoints of my pupils which, in the glare, must have been diminished to at least f22.

To the west, the Muktinath Himal glittered with sunlight refracted through the crystal blocks of icefalls, while to the south the Annapurnas, beyond the Grande Barrière that had hidden them from Hertzog, demonstrated their hierarchy: cold popes chiselled into a frieze. No wonder mere mortals have imbued them with sanctity.

When Joe Brown and George Band climbed Kanchenjunga in 1955, the third highest peak in the world, they deliberately left the summit inviolate by prior arrangement with the ruler of Sikkim, because gods lived there; as they used to on Mount Olympus, Mount Parnassus and Popocatepetl. For all I know, they once lived on Box Hill in Surrey, but they are not there now.

Iman used a finger to inscribe our names and the date in the blue snow, and I photographed it, the glare so great that without a neutral density filter I had difficulty getting an exposure even at a shutter-speed of a thousandth of a second. But as I focused, I didn't like what I saw. It was reminiscent of Scrooge seeing his own headstone.

Iman threw a snowball at me that I caught and threw back, and seeing my reflection in his mirrored shades, I was immersed in unadulterated joy. That was *me* I saw, and *here* with snowfields rising up to a wilderness of white, like a blank page on which I could write anything I wished.

We were almost the first to use the path that day, although actually no path existed; only a few footprints hyphening the snow with shallow shadows.

We set off and soon saw Thorung Phedi a mile or so away on the far side of the valley; a couple of lodges littering a rocky shelf above a deep canyon which I assumed was the route to Thorung La.

'No,' Iman explained. 'That goes nowhere. Thorung La is up there.' He pointed to snowfields hemmed in by high peaks green with seracs.

'Will we be able to do that?'

Iman shrugged.

To reach Thorung Phedi we had to descend 1,000 feet and at first it was a pleasure, kicking snow and watching it sparkle in the backlight. Then it all changed as we stepped onto a glacis, sloping north, which the sun had been unable to soften. We were on ice that swept down, unbroken, for hundreds of feet, and I began to be afraid. A fall would probably be fatal, for we did not carry ice-axes and our boots weren't spiked with crampons.

I had learnt to arrest a fall when on a mountaineering course in Snowdonia. I knew how to roll and use my body weight to drive the pick into the surface. I could even do it falling backwards. But now I had no ice-axe; only a bamboo stick. Iman had nothing apart from a cool head. Had this been Wales or the Lake District we would have retreated, but we had a goal, so went on.

'I'm not happy, Iman.'

Iman didn't reply, but edged along, taking extreme care.

'It's dangerous, Iman.'

Iman continued until he had to step down, awkwardly, poised on a frozen footprint. He turned and said, 'You are right, Peter. This is dangerous.'

I had never felt so exposed. Anywhere else we would have moved one at a time, linked by a rope, one of us belayed; but this was a path. It is marked as such on the map. So we persevered, my body flooded by adrenalin.

The slope eased for a bit and I relaxed, but then we encountered an even more perilous passage, crossing an outward sloping ribbon of ice as sheeny as baking foil.

Iman hesitated, then sidled down. Ugly boulders, like tank-traps, waited at the base of the white roof falling below us.

I was acutely aware of wearing a waterproof jacket and overtrousers; garb which my instructor in Wales had explained was the second fastest way of falling because of the utter lack of friction generated.

'Go slowly,' said Iman, truly worried for the first time, his brow scarred by a vertical furrow.

I slipped and nearly went over the edge. I began to shake.

'Easy, Peter. Easy.'

'Just give me a moment.'

Iman unselfishly held out his hand but it was beyond my reach, and as I moved I slipped again, falling on my back, beginning to slide, although I instinctively dug my bamboo pole in hard, and managed to maintain a precarious balance, the pole forming a single thin baluster. I dared not move and lay like an upturned turtle, my slippery carapace somehow adhering to the ice.

'Don't move,' Iman advised.

'I can't.'

All the energy drained out of me as I lay there helpless, knowing that if I went over I would have perhaps ten seconds before striking the boulders below.

Suddenly I was overcome by calm. I saw a rock above me and decided that I should make a grab for it, hoping that it was glazed into the ice and not resting on the surface. Very slowly, I removed the mitten and glove from my left hand, and threw them to Iman.

Do it, or don't do it? That was the question. I did it. I rolled and simultaneously thrust my bare hand out towards the black rock which I gripped as if my life depended on it, which it did. My fingers clamped around it and it stayed put. Somehow I pulled myself into a crouching position, cowering, and considered what the hell to do next.

'Well done, Peter.'

I stood up, gingerly, but there was no way I was going to attempt the *mauvais pas* again. The slope above appeared crustier, so I crawled up onto it and began to kick steps while Iman continued on his precipitous way below, parallel to me.

It took us an hour to get down and when we reached safety I slumped against a boulder. I broke my vow and lit a cigarette, but my left hand, wet and gloveless at 15,000 feet, was pink and puffy with cold, and melted snow, dripping from my fingers, soaked the cigarette, putting it out. I didn't need it and didn't light another.

I lay against the boulder for a long time gazing up at the slopes we had survived.

It may not have been mountaineering in the manner described by the great climbers, but I knew that I had been close to oblivion, so it was enough for me. And if I hadn't found my bamboo crook under a mattress in Besisahar? You'd be reading something else instead.

How I revelled in the sweaty trudge up to Thorung Phedi where I burst out laughing when I saw a bilingual sign outside a hut which read: 'Do not keep your goats inside the shelter'. Yes, it's not that funny, but why was it written in English? And you must allow for altitude and my renewed enthusiasm for simply being able to breathe and laugh.

We were almost as high as the summit of Mont Blanc, but the sky was squawky with black birds in their hundreds; yellow-billed choughs which have been recorded at over 27,000 feet. What they eat up there is a mystery, unless it is each other. Perhaps they simply enjoy the view? They look humdrum at first, mere black dots like crows, but their Bird's Custard bills and red legs add gaiety, like posies on a coffin. Red-billed choughs live here too, and can also be found in Britain, going under the international passport of *Pyrrhocorax pyrrhocorax*, named, presumably, after the ornithological Doctor Pyrrhocorax.

Choughs are one of Britain's rarest birds and I have seen them in the wild only twice: on the Lleyn Peninsula and in Snowdonia. But there are moves afoot to re-establish them in Cornwall, whose flag is adorned with a chough. They are breeding them for release on Cornwall's cliffs, where they died out because sheep no longer grazed above the sea, cropping the turf. Choughs need sheep like pushers need a pager, and so sheep are being reintroduced too. Thus does Darwinism get a helping hand.

The lodge was like a station waiting-room following a wildcat strike. Some people had been here for a week, going stir-crazy, having refused to go down. Irritability surfaced amongst parties stuck together for days in a place where there is absolutely nothing to do but eat, watch choughs, and get ill.

Fred moseyed in, and we sipped tea without cucumber sandwiches.

'Any trouble on the ice?' he asked casually.

'Just a bit.'

'Me too.'

'Actually I found it pretty hairy.'

'I'm glad you said that. I thought I was going to die.'

'Had a pill yet?'

'I thought I might soon.'

'Me too.'

We both delved into our packs and swallowed prophylactics. Diamox helps you breathe at altitude, and the effect was dramatic. My wheezing was replaced by an intake of breath as pure and regular as a life-support system, but then my fingers began to prickle, and later, when I tried to pick up a spoon to eat my garlic soup (also reputedly good for the breathing), I found that my fingertips were numb. My toes too, had lost all feeling. Fearing a stroke, I told Fred of my concern.

'Perfectly natural,' said Fred. 'Just a side effect.'

'Ah. A perfectly natural side effect.'

'Precisely.'

One of the Korean slimmers entered, followed by her friends, none looking too good, but I wanted to applaud.

Their crash diet had obviously done wonders for them. Only their weight seemed unaltered.

Iman joined us after dark and told me we must leave at 4 a.m.

'What?'

'The wind can get very strong in the morning when the sun rises and it could stop us going over. It may not be a peak but it is still a mountain, and we must do what we can to let it help us. I will wake you at three.'

I lay on my bed in a shed lit by a candle, worrying. The thought of returning to Besisahar was unthinkable but, even if the weather was kind, I did not know whether or not I possessed the tenacity to succeed. No delegation possible. Me, whoever I was. No one else.

Diamox is a diuretic and I woke several times to pee under a black sea in which stars shone greenly, like phosphorescence in a sombre ocean.

I was already dressed when Iman tapped gently on my door. We drank tea, then started out into a bitter night.

The path from Thorung Phedi doesn't ease you into the climb. It starts abruptly, zigzagging through scree on which I stumbled, unused to relying on a headtorch which only picked out details in its dim halo. There was no horizon, and my ears had difficulty telling me what was up and what was down.

I looked for lights ahead but saw none. We were the first to leave although, after half an hour, we noticed more torches emerging onto the scree, bobbing about as they appeared and disappeared behind boulders.

Then it hit me. It had to be acute mountain sickness for my skull felt as if a band of thick elastic was crushing it. And still 3,000 feet to go. I sat on a rock, disconsolate, and pulled off my balaclava. I was suddenly cured. The balaclava, bought in an army surplus store, had remained in my rucksack, unworn, waiting for Thorung La, and it was simply too small, its circumference designed for a soldier with a child's head.

A slow, slow, fade-up revealed a penumbra of peaks around us, but the sun was still rising somewhere over China, and we could only make out the vaguest of shapes.

More than 1,000 feet above Thorung Phedi, on a rocky col, there is a rudimentary lodge where well-acclimatised people, particularly those who have been delayed by storms, sometimes choose to stay.

It was still lit by oil lamps when we entered, with porters sleeping under blankets on the floor, or waking up scratching and bleary-eyed. Three well-heeled Austrians, two women and their male friend, were drinking tea served by their porter, a cadaverous man dressed all in yellow, although his clothing seemed inadequate for a height close to 16,000 feet. Was he really going to attempt the pass wearing battered trainers whose black soles flopped like cows' tongues? The Austrians were well clad in Goretex, and exuded wealth.

You can sniff money. It's in the details: the men's grey hair, still exhibiting the cuts of expensive stylists; the long-term tans, advertising free time; the teeth, too white to be real, capped by extraordinary dentists; the confidence exuding from those who know they can do what they damn-well please. Stroll by any Riviera café (the half-empty ones with cushions on the seats and no prices chalked against the list of aperitifs) and you will see them sitting there, at a loss.

The Austrians left, lightweight, their porter carrying a pack so heavy that he leant into the wind even though the dawn was still.

One of the sumo-ettes was crying outside in the snow as she was being interviewed, or rather harangued, by the cameraman. His programme depended on prodding her over, and I could tell that nothing was going to stop him getting it in the can.

I'd seen it all before in the media circus; personal ambition destroying the very personality of those who had, initially, hoped to do some good – politically or socially.

Instead they had become mere things.

One of my favourite poems is 'Prayer Before Birth' by Louis MacNeice who once worked as a BBC producer. An extract will have to suffice:

I am not yet born; O fill me
With strength against those who would freeze my
* humanity, would dragoon me into a lethal automaton,*
*   would make me a cog in a machine, a thing with*
*   one face, a thing, and against all those*

> *who would dissipate my entirety, would*
>   *blow me like thistledown hither and*
>   *thither or hither and thither*
>   *like water held in the*
>   *hands would spill me.*
> *Let them not make me a stone and let them not spill me.*
> *Otherwise kill me.*

* * * * *

The path gyred through precarious towers of frost-shattered brown rock speckled with snow, and I was reminded of those crumbling crusaders' fortresses, almost indistinguishable from the geology, once haughty above obscure Mediterranean desert towns where nothing now – or ever was – worth fighting for.

I was complacent. This wasn't so difficult. Yes, the air was thinner, but the difficulties no more trying than a trudge up Carnedd Llewelyn in winter. Then we reached a corner and I felt sick. Bootmarks traversed a steep snow slope for a quarter of a mile, the exposure even greater than the previous day.

I thought of my family, and recited a mantra at each step: 'Mimi, Pedr, Paddy. Mimi, Pedr, Paddy,' but I was not resorting to prayer, whose efficacy I disavow; each step, instead, imbued with the name of those I love most, aiding my concentration, transforming each moment into a commitment.

People do die here, from avalanche, falls, hypothermia and mountain sickness. There are plaques and cairns erected by grieving relatives linking this extraordinary pass to the suburban world, but I had no intention of adding to the tally.

When we reached reasonable ground we stopped and listened to the Austrians shouting at their porter who was plainly unwell.

'So if you want to go down, go down! We'll carry the fucking pack!' said the man.

'But I will lose my bonus.'

'I'll make sure you get your bonus. I'll pay it into your bank account.'

A porter with a bank account? Paper dollars were all he knew.

'I will be OK.'

'It's your decision.'

The Austrians and the porter set off while Iman and I rested, Iman concerned for his compatriot.

'He should go down,' said Iman.

'Shouldn't we say something?'

'If it gets worse we will.'

We continued through the snow until we reached the worst of traverses, a half-mile of drop across which we had to balance like ants on a white tent.

Again I employed my mantra, and when we reached the far side I collapsed in the snow, exhausted. But I had made a decision. There was no way I was going to reverse it, come what may.

The Austrians' porter was crouching in the snow, shaking, white sputum frothing from blue lips onto his cheap yellow anorak.

Iman addressed the Austrians. 'This man must go down. Now!'

'But we are so close to the top,' said one of the women.

'Now!'

'OK,' said the man. 'I'm a doctor. I know the problem.'

A doctor? Pray you never get ill in Vienna and consult him.

I joined in. 'So what are you going to do?'

'He'll have to go down,' the doctor said.

I looked across to the traverse and knew that to send the porter back alone would be potentially lethal.

'Not by himself,' I said.

'Of course not. One of us will go back down with him.'

'Good.'

And having resolved the problem Iman and I set off.

When you watch film of mountaineers in the Himalaya you cannot believe how slowly they go. Plod, plod, plod. Then a rest. They'll never make it. But that is how it became for me as we kicked up through snow-covered moraines, shaped like gigantic dolmens, that never seemed to end. And then my autopilot took over. I was full of energy and headed up, faster than anyone, treading in virgin snow until I reached the top. I turned to Iman and said, 'We're there. We're the first.' But I was wrong. More mounds of snow had to be surmounted. Then I saw the top of a startlingly red prayer flag flapping gently amongst whiteness like a stamp on paper.

Up became flat, and then nearly down. We were *there*, the distant kingdom of Mustang spread out below us, the peaks of Khatung Kang and Yakawakang rising in green iceballs and crevassed glaciers above us.

I walked up into the snow, needing to be alone, and cried my eyes out. My thoughts were with my family who would never share this unique moment. I reached into my bumbag for the crumpled family photograph I carried, wanting to kiss it, but I could not bear to see their faces frozen in our Devon garden, and left it where it was.

Those of you who haven't known the pain and wonder of children will not understand this; so have them, if you can. And those who understand will, I hope, take your children to such places, if you can afford to. For to reach such a goal, alone, is almost nothing.

Fred tapped me on the shoulder. He was crying too, and we embraced.

'It may not be much,' he said, 'but it's something, isn't it?'

'Oh yes.'

'I know I shouldn't say this, Peter, but we're both getting on so I don't care. I think we should be proud of what we've done.'

I could not see his eyes behind his shades but knew that they, like mine, were brimming with the springs of lost youth.

Later I wrote in my diary: *I think I have achieved something. I don't know what it is. Perhaps just a dedication to doing one thing and not giving up, even though I felt like giving up. A little expedition into my soul, whatever that is. The simple fact of doing something at the age of fifty-four where I had to rely on myself and did it. I am* elated, *and that is* rare *and to be cherished. It is my little Everest.*

People, young and old, began arriving in dribs and drabs, and the pass was awash with enough tears to water a whisky at a wake.

We were 17,769 feet above Los Angeles, Melbourne and Torbay. Nearly three and a half miles high; something I would never achieve again, and so we took the requisite photographs, but not before I had hugged Iman in true Californian style and thanked him for guiding me here safely.

I thought he might be blasé, having been before, but his face glowed with happiness; a man who truly loved the mountains. We had 'done it' but we were only a third of the way there. Ahead of us was a descent of 5,500 feet to Muktinath, which is a bloody long drop by anyone's standards.

Clouds floated in the distant sky like a flotilla of dirigibles, and vague memories of A-level geography made me suspect that this was an ill omen. A Buddhist was selling slices of cake but on closer inspection they became wedges of ice to suck.

We descended through scree and snowfields for hours, stopping frequently so I could sit and absorb the landscape;

the valley of the Kali Gandaki, hazy in the heat, with Mustang's peaks behind, some seeming no higher than us, which they weren't.

I had read that this descent can be hard on the knees, and halfway down one of mine took industrial action, complaining of excessive hours and insufficient tea-breaks. I explained that there was nowhere to stop, but it continued to whinge, holding me to ransom with stabbing pains aimed at my *vastus lateratis*, the muscle just above the joint.

Iman had gone ahead and at one point, on an icy section of the trail – above the ubiquitous drop – my knee simply refused to go any further. Arbitration was out of the question, all meaningful dialogue having broken down between management and worker. But we were both English so a compromise was reached. I stopped.

I stood there, unable to move, until Iman returned and led me by the hand as I shuffled like a casualty; Iman my nurse, and my crook my Zimmer frame.

Steep gulleys led to steeper hairpins that I took in first gear; but there were people walking *up*, despite the late hour. I thought they must be mad, until I realised that they were proper mountaineers, equipped with all the right tools: ice-axes in hand, crampons strapped upside down to their packs like gigantic dead insects, karabiners jingling like jewellery from their waists. But they were having a hard time of it, and it began to snow. Unless they were planning to bivouac they hadn't a hope of crossing the pass before dark.

Far below I saw smoke rising from a stone shack.

'What's that?'

'Tea house.'

'You go ahead, Iman, and order me a drink.'

'It will be cold before you arrive.'

'Beer. Not tea.'

'Is that wise?'

'Of course not, but I don't care.'

Iman sped off, leaping like a chamois while I hobbled down, glad to be alone and going at my own pace, like a Long John Silver with a bamboo crutch, delighting in my island.

An hour later I limped into a courtyard where there was a party atmosphere. I recognised old faces: Piet, the Dutchman from Lower Pisang, the saggy-titted Romanian, Fred and Bean.

Fred told me he was so overcome with emotion at Thorung La that he had said to Bean, 'You can have anything you want – within reason.'

And Bean had replied, 'A plate of potatoes.' And there Bean sat, eating potatoes.

The first sip of beer was true nectar but a litre was a mistake. There was still a long way to go, and we were still 13,000 feet high, but I had fulfilled my bargain. No alcohol or cigarettes. A cigarette! I delved in my rucksack and extracted a pack drenched by snow, the paper cylinders stained and as useless as wet kindling. So I begged, addressing the assembly like a true addict. Someone handed me a Marlboro, and I lit up.

Some say that tobacco isn't a real drug. Not true. It went to my head as fast as a rat into a sewer, and, coupled with beer, I became pleasantly disoriented. But then the atmosphere changed. The three Austrians arrived minus their porter. I asked them where he was.

'He went down,' the doctor said.

'Alone?'

'It was his decision.'

'No, it wasn't,' I replied, emboldened by beer. 'It was yours. You employed him.'

'He'll be all right.'

I hoped for the porter's sake, as well as the Austrians,

that he was, for to do something so heinous breaks all the rules, written and unwritten. Trekkers are responsible for their guides, some of whom live in the lowlands and don't come with altitude guarantees. It is up to the client to make sure that they are properly equipped, insured and treated responsibly.

The threesome sat alone in a corner, like the pariahs they were.

* * * * *

Two hours later Iman and I arrived in Muktinath. There is a temple here which is a Mecca for Buddhists and Hindus, but I didn't care a hoot. We had been on the go for almost fourteen hours and my only desire was to stop. Spindly poplars were planted in little coppices, the saplings supplied, I suspect, by some NGO, but they didn't look as if they were for practical reasons like replenishing felled oven-wood. They were there simply because they looked pretty, like a corner of an urban park where a mini-forest exists together with a plaque in remembrance of Councillor Smith who loved to walk her dog there. An icy wind swished through their silvery leaves and I thought how wonderful it was to see foliage again after the wilderness.

Wet flakes of snow fluttered into my eyes and I realised just how lucky we had been to have been blessed with the only possible day for our crossing.

We had descended a vertical mile, and the mountains above us were curfewed by a storm. The pass would be closed again, and I worried about the men I had seen three hours previously, heading up.

Ranipauwa is the village below the temple, and shawled women were sitting at dusk in the middle of Main Street weaving on portable looms, their quick fingers inured to the chill.

Those with a tight schedule can dash here in three days. Take a plane from Pokhara to Jomosom, then walk with spirit for three days, and there you are. And why not? Those who do this find themselves in a spectacular landscape, although Thorung La is out of the question; no time for acclimatisation, and the ascent from this side can be tortuous, even for the most athletic.

But access brings civilisation, including a Bob Marley restaurant with posters of the gaunt singer staring out into the street, his ganja cheeks framed by dreadlocks.

I had seen his photo several times in Kathmandu bars, and I asked Iman if this was because he epitomised rebellion that struck a chord with Nepali youth.

'Oh no, people just like his music. It's a bit Nepali.'

I wonder.

But the posters were depressing. Here, a mile from a shrine, was a reminder of another untenable religion: Rastafarianism.

Who can truly believe that the despot Haile Selassie was a Messiah? Just another case of the bigger the lie, the more the gullible will believe it.

I produced a programme involving the extraordinary painter Patrick Heron who lived in a house called 'Eagle's Nest', near Zennor in Cornwall. He showed me around the house. Upstairs one eyrie bedroom overlooked cliffs where Atlantic rollers were galing in relentlessly. 'This was Haile Selassie's room during the war,' he told me. And I wondered how the emperor in exile had coped with this sodden peninsula, so contrapuntal to his hot Abyssinia. But alienation is always good for the world's plotters. It brings the fatherland into focus. I could visualise him there, his bearded face reflected in the rain-streaked window, dreaming of the time he would return to a life of corruption in his own poverty-stricken acres.

In films, tired people fall asleep when their head hits

the pillow, and that's what I did, although a screeching animal in my dreams woke me. It was perfectly black, and I could still hear the creature which turned into wind whistling through the shutters. I assumed it was morning but the green digits on my wristwatch told me it was only 8.30 p.m.

The path from my stable to the lodge was blanketed by snow that blew horizontally. Lightning flickered far away, followed by a stomach rumble of thunder, just audible.

Iman was sitting at a table with a bald, corpulent Indian and his thin, young Nepali friend. The fat man was a professor of physics from a Delhi university, and his protégé, Molar, was an undergraduate in dentistry from the same institution.

'You look cold,' said the prof. 'This will warm you up.' He uncapped a bottle of peach brandy, brought up from Marpha.

'Cheers!' We clinked glasses.

'Bloody awful place,' said the prof in an almost-Oxford accent. 'Bloody awful weather.'

He turned to his friend and said, 'Be a chum and get me my woolly hat. And ask for some more blankets.' Molar disappeared dutifully, and images of Oscar Wilde and Bosie came to mind – or rather Peter Finch and John Fraser. I asked the prof what he was doing here.

'I am on a pilgrimage.'

'Why?'

'Why not? I am Hindu. Catholics go to Lourdes. I come here.'

'But why?'

'It is part of my heritage. My culture.'

'And you believe it?'

'Let's just say that there are more things in heaven and earth et cetera, et cetera.'

'But you're a physicist.'

'So what? Physicists no longer teach what they know for a fact. They teach theories – the ideas of unreligious men who are looking for an answer – and please don't start asking me questions like, "So what existed before the Big Bang" because I can't tell you. No one can. Now that certainty has fled we're all reduced to alchemists, floundering in the dark. But that's the fun! Physics is now the antithesis of certainty. Science has become philosophy again. We all have to begin anew. Play a game whose rules we no longer share.'

Molar returned with a silly white hat that the prof put on his head, like an egg-cosy.

'Are you hungry, Peter?' Iman asked, glancing up from the menu.

'Haven't you eaten yet?'

'I was waiting for you.'

'But you mustn't. You really mustn't. You must eat when you're hungry.'

'It is the custom.'

We ordered and, while we waited for our *daal bhaat*, I asked Molar how he could afford to study in Delhi.

'I am lucky. I was born into a wealthy family.'

'Reborn?'

'If you like.'

'And what will you do when you qualify?'

'Go to England or America.'

'Don't they need dentists here?'

'Oh I will return when I have further qualifications.'

'Are you sure?'

'Pretty sure.'

'My dentist comes from India,' I explained, 'but he's doing very well and intends to stay.'

'That is his decision, not mine.'

Will he come back? I doubt it. The First World offers so much despite its drift towards the Third.

The prof asked where we were going.

'Down the valley,' I explained, 'and then into the Annapurna Sanctuary.'

'Haven't you heard?'

'What?'

'A whole family has just been killed in an avalanche there. Too much snow. It just swooshed down.'

'Where were they from?'

'I can't remember. Australia. New Zealand. Somewhere like that.'

The peach brandy, coupled with altitude, made me benevolent but when Iman said, 'I'll wake you at six,' I protested.

Fred was sitting in a corner with the Western contingent, and I called out, 'Hey, Fred, want to go to the temple in the morning?'

Fred had been boozing too. 'Meet you here at nine.'

'So what time will we leave, Peter?' Iman asked.

'When I'm ready.'

As I left I heard an American saying, 'Good luck on Everest,' to a man I thought I had recognised passing me as I hobbled down from Thorung La; one of those with all the gear. Presumably he had been on an acclimatisation trek but had been forced down by deteriorating conditions.

I should have talked to him, but exhaustion sent me staggering through the snow to a bed which I embraced as though it were a lover.

– 17 –

The vertical height to the temples of Muktinath wasn't much, perhaps 300 feet, but Fred and I were now programmed to going down and so we shambled up the rocky trail, suffering from hangovers, passing a painted white cross of stones where rich pilgrims could land their helicopters. There must be one in Fatima too.

We passed a huge prayer wheel and trees planted beside memorials in a cemetery, then up, beside crumbling *chortens*, to a temple. Thousands of pastel prayer flags fluttered, their primary colours bleached by sun and rain, strung between bleak trees still waiting for their spring buds; like washing hung out to dry between apartments in an Italian slum. We were the first there.

There is a Hindu Holy of Holies, forbidden to infidels, where a monkish man sits, reciting scripture; but half surrounding it is a gallery of superb brass sculptures, 108 in all, comprising spring-fed animals' heads spouting supposedly holy water from their mouths. Some are recognisable as cows or buffaloes. Some are fantastic, like dragons, reminiscent of gargoyles rimming an English cathedral.

A man shuffled out of the shadows and said, 'If you bathe in this water it will wash away all your sins.'

Of course I did not believe him but I was intrigued by this universal belief in water cleansing the soul. We do it in England. We baptise babies in fonts, trickling magic water over their fontanelles to rid them of original sin. Otherwise they might go to Limbo, the semi-heaven God reserves for unlucky infants who die before the sacrament is administered.

Oh you Catholic priests! How can you peddle such nonsense? How can you believe this claptrap that causes so much pain to parents already distraught by grief?

Because you are afraid.

There is peace in water; a spiritual – whatever that is – aid to remaining sane.

There is a well on Anglesey that used to draw myself and my family like horses to water. It is close to a ruined priory founded in the sixth century by Saint Seiriol whose hermitage foundations are beside a crystal pool under a beehive hut made of white limestone covered by scabs of yellow lichen. Why we kept going back is a mystery I cannot explain, but there was a simplicity, a purity, about it.

So I washed myself under the icy spouts in Muktinath, not because I believed in their efficacy but because I could appreciate the symbolism; their poetry divorced from their literalism.

Fred and I clinked along a stony path to the Jwala Mai temple in which gas jets burned, the *raison d'être* of this shrine. Below crudely painted statues of fearsome gods the blue flames flickered behind metal cages beside a spring. This juxtaposition of earth, fire and water is the reason for its sacrosanctity. Once it must have seemed like a miracle, these flames glowing from stone, but we know now that it is a natural phenomenon. But still people come, in their tens of thousands, to worship here. Methane gas. It is guarded by vestal virgins, or nuns as they are now called, but we were too early for them. They were not yet on duty.

Outside the temple all was peace and reason. Yellow-billed blue magpies cackled in the trees, their extravagant tails silhouetted against Tibetan peaks, and a warm morning wind was melting the snow.

We passed the puffing prof and Molar on their way up, the prof dabbing his glistening bald head with a handkerchief, but still the sweat ran in rivulets, dripping into the holy earth.

Down we went, high above the Jhong Khola, a tributary of the great Kali Gandaki which, technically, has cut the deepest gorge in the world, although it is no Grand Canyon, its depth measured in relation to the gigantic peaks rising above it – Annapurna I and Dhaulagiri, still three days' walk to the south.

* * * * *

We left Ranipauwa late. Rounding a bend we saw the backdrop to a renaissance painting: the village of Jharkot which, seen from a distance, resembles a fortified Tuscan village built on a bluff overhanging a ravine. I counted a dozen griffon vultures riding the thermals above the houses like grim reapers sniffing for death. But Jharkot was the antithesis of decay. It was an oasis. Springs bubbled into meadows where fruit trees grow from proper green grass. Grey geese swam in a pond, and a bright yellow finch sang in a bush.

Alleys were bordered by tall houses with small windows, their stucco peeling as it does in Italy. A mangy white dog licked a red gash in a hind leg. A black yak ate a spillage of yellow hay. And always the tinkle of trickling water. Then, outside the town, a cat, the first I had seen in Nepal, but not just any old moggie. It had pointed ears fringed with tufts, resembling a lynx's, and black stripes across its face like warpaint.

Iman, Fred, Bean and I stopped for tea. A couple sat opposite. Barry introduced himself and his girlfriend, Crisp. I liked them immediately. Barry exhibited that rare combination of intelligence and guilelessness, and Crisp was beautiful, her sun-bleached hair wisping around a lambent face that didn't need make-up. They were both in their late twenties, and had met in Thailand. Barry was a plumber from Battersea, and Crisp had worked in an office before setting out to see the world. Now they were going home, to England, because they were running out of cash.

'How long've you been travelling?' I asked.

'Three years,' said Barry.

'Two,' said Crisp.

'Homesick?'

'Not on your life,' Barry replied. 'Oh I know it'll be nice being back in London for a few days, but I won't settle. I've been on the road too long.'

'So what'll you do?'

'Get a job, get some dosh, and set off again.'

'Why?'

'Look, man. Look where you are *now*. You'll remember this place, won't you? Always. This day. This hour. Drinking tea *here*. In England you only know what day it is because of what's on the telly. I was dying there, man. Fitting fucking pipes in high-rises in the docks built for fucking yuppies.'

Crisp had worked for a solicitor. 'Can you imagine what it's like sitting at a keyboard copying out conveyance reports all bloody day? If you can't I'll tell you. It saps the spirit – completely and utterly. I had to get out.'

'So what'll you both do?' I asked. 'Travel for the rest of your lives?'

'Why not?' said Barry. 'I used to take the tube to work and couldn't believe the unhappiness I saw around me. Pissed off. The lot of them. And for what? At least I'll have had some sort of life. Every day a memory. I mean – look at that, and that! You're looking at *Tibet*.'

'You're right,' said Fred. 'Most of us spend pissed-off lives. Good luck to you both.'

Iman was anxious to be off but I wanted to stay and chat, so Iman and Bean set off for Kagbeni to find rooms, leaving the English contingent to complain about their country. Tea turned to Tuborg and Tuborg to whisky. It was Friday night down the pub and none of us cared a jot about a schedule. That's why we were here in the first place.

Eventually we left, wandering tipsily across a desert of black stones, some piled into cairns by pilgrims in remembrance of their ancestors. Clouds became a mountain that dammed the horizon: Nilgiri North, 23,000 feet of ridge, stepped into fragile pyramids glistening like bone china. I imagined being a real mountaineer, looking for a way up, but it seemed impregnable.

We often had to step aside to allow horsemen, mule trains and yak herds to pass by. We saw a cowboy approaching. He was enormous, his belly sagging over the saddle of a puny pony that looked on the point of collapse. He wore a genuine Stetson, a chequered jacket and leather riding boots locked into stirrups that almost brushed the ground.

'Whoa there!' he said to the pony, who was only too grateful to whoa. 'You seen my guide? Man on a horse.'

I explained that we'd seen many men on horses.

'Shit! I knew I couldn't trust him. How far's this Muktinath place?'

'About two hours on a horse, I guess.'

'I don't know if my ass can take another two hours of this.' He sat up on his stirrups.

'Where've you come from?' I asked.

'The States.'

'No, I meant today.'

'Jomosom. Flew in yesterday.'

'Why're you going to Muktinath?'

'Someone said there was some kinda festival going down up there.'

I had to ask, just for fun: 'Are you a Hindu?'

'Do I *look* like a Hindu?'

Of course you can't become a Hindu. If, like Paul on his way to Damascus, the fat American had been struck to the ground and been blinded by Vishnu, he could not have swapped Seventh-Day Adventism for *dharma* and *karma*. Hinduism is exclusive. It's like the aristocracy. You are either born with a silver spoon in your mouth, or not. Nothing you can do about it. That's why Hindus don't proselytise. No one knocks on your door and there's no equivalent of *The Watchtower*.

For a start, it would be problematical allocating you to a caste. Would it be based on income, breeding, property? And what if you were a successful butcher? Would you automatically be relegated to the lowest of the low? Imagine owning the biggest chain of abbatoirs in the world and still being untouchable? It would murder your social life.

We turned off the main path and followed a gulch opposite an extraordinary yellow cliff of sandstone weathered into asymmetrical pillars. If Gaudi had been God he would have designed a landscape like this. There were holes in the rock but whether these were caves or pits left by fallen boulders was unclear, but I could imagine hermits here being enlightened after fifty years of asceticism. The answer to the universe and everything must have been blindingly obvious. It was 43.

Below us, we saw Kagbeni: its flat-roofed houses castellated by piles of firewood, its centre a red *gompa*; and all around it trees of the most delicate green like the translucent fronds of seaweed you find in rockpools at low tide. Beyond the village was the Kali Gandaki, a ribbon of blue meandering between shaly outcrops.

Iman sat outside a posh lodge on the outskirts, looking sulky.

'They won't give you a room, Peter.'

'Why? Do I smell?'

'They only have doubles.'

The differential price would have been peanuts but I didn't like it anyway: the wooden Nepali equivalent of a Hilton.

'So we'll find somewhere else instead.'

We walked under a hollow *stupa*, congested by goats, and found a lodge run by jolly girls pierced with gold like shrapnel. The front door led straight into an atrium that reminded me of Spain, and stairs climbed up to a roof with a hole in the middle. I peered down and saw flames crackling in the kitchen. Take care, I told myself. Too much brandy and I could tumble into a Hieronymus hell. A family of Indian Hindu pilgrims sat outside their room but my smile was met by sullenness. After all I was, by definition, unclean.

I absconded from the village and sat on a stone above the Kali Gandaki which threaded its way across a plain of pebbles a mile wide. In spate it must have been an awesome sight but that day the valley was an estuary waiting for the flood.

Women, bent double, worked in the fields below, and a stream of pilgrims passed by, some old enough to be great-grandparents, surgical socks and plastic flip-flops were all they had to insulate themselves from the snow above. Some had come hundreds of miles, some more, from as far away as southern India to pray before the blue flames and fountains. Holy men, half-naked, were the only ones to make eye-contact and say 'Namaste'.

I pre-set my camera. Nilgiri was as white as a seagull against a grey slate cliff of sky, and the pilgrims trod an unintentional catwalk of colour; mauve, pink, violet, orange, gold. My trigger finger itched. I zoomed to a wide angle and pretended to aim at the mountains but after a couple of disingenuous clicks I was inhibited by scowls, and sat instead, watching the shadows rise until the whole great valley began to shiver.

Back in my room I began to tremble with a fever all my clothes couldn't assuage.

I joined Iman in the cavernous kitchen, lit only by ovens and the odd candle, and ordered water into which I dropped iodine pills.

Iman saw me shuddering. 'You are ill?'

'Yes, I am ill.'

* * * * *

I woke in the night feeling something crawling inside my long johns towards my crotch. Lice sprang to mind because I had once caught crabs – and not from pots heaved into the sea. I had squashed one into a bar of soap where it lay imprinted like a fossil, and taken it to my GP who peered at it through a magnifying glass. He looked it up in a book and, delighted to identify it, showed me a photograph blown up into the most hideous monster you can imagine; all gristly and hairy like pork scratchings, with hideous arachnidan legs and a vampiric mouth. And these monsters were stalking the ferny jungle of my pubes, sinking their serrated straws into my skin and sucking my blood.

I was concerned because typhus is spread by lice, and so began a torchlit scrutiny of my genitals; each fold, each crease inspected pornographically.

Men lust after women, and vice versa, but it's all a question of scale. Look at your own wrinkles and folds microscopically and maybe you will wonder why people are ever attracted to each other sexually. *Vive le différence*: although the difference in BCU (big close-up) is merely two contrary cuts of meat.

I was awoken by a cock crowing, and when I crawled out of my sleeping bag I saw something leap onto the floor. It was a flea, the shape and colour of a cooked prawn, its body engorged with my blood, so I trod on it, leaving a red stain on the planks.

Jains would have disapproved.

I ate breakfast with a Swiss couple preparing to climb Thorung La from west to east and I worried about their frailty and naivety. And about the snow. They owned a health food shop in Zurich although their pallor and endemic neuroses, coupled with an almost skeletal physiognomy, propelled me into counsellor mode.

'Do you think you really ought to?'

'Body, mind, spirit,' she said.

'Sorry?'

'We can do all we want because of what is in here.' She touched her forehead and stomach symbolically.

'Maybe, but there's the altitude as well. I've got Diamox pills. Would you like some?'

The quiet man spoke. 'We don't believe in chemicals.'

'Not even at the dentist?'

He smiled that infuriating wiser-than-you lips-only smile that is designed to make you feel innately inferior.

The woman peeled a sock. 'Oh my God! A flea!'

It was identical to mine but whether it had hopped from me to her or had inhabited her own bed didn't bother me. Deep down I hoped it was one of mine.

Iman wanted to be away but I told him that I was ill and needed a rest day.

'What is wrong?'

'I have a fever. I have a cold. I have been bitten by a flea. I need to do nothing.'

I went in search of Fred to say goodbye, but he had already left his lodge, and I felt a little bereft. Travelling is a solitary pursuit but the acquaintanceships you strike up sometimes verge on friendship, and I was sorry that I hadn't said farewell.

But the sun shone and I explored Kagbeni, which is a bit like Bourton-on-the-Water in Gloucestershire, only different. A canalised stream, like a leat, bisects the village but the houses flanking it aren't holiday home investments. Real people live in Kagbeni.

A woman was shoving her young son into a woodpile, her hands grasping his heels. She tugged him out and in his hand he held a solitary egg, like a jewel; more precious than a Fabergé because it was edible.

I walked up through orchards pink and white with marshmallow blossoms, crossed the stream on precarious logs, and sat on the bank watching a wagtail pogoing between boulders. A dog like a jackal barked at me but, unused to silence, trotted over and I broke all the rules by scratching its chin. I was insouciant in the sun. Rabies? Fleas? I simply didn't give a damn. I was in Kagbeni; far, far from grey Protestant England.

Many of the mud-brick houses incorporated stables where livestock were garaged, with living quarters above. At the end of a warren I was prevented from going further by a policeman guarding a shed.

'You have permit, sir?'

'No.'

'So no go Mustang.'

From here Upper Mustang looked uninviting, its aridity no magnet for me now that I was amongst trees. It was an independent principality until 1951 when it was absorbed into Nepal, and in the following decade it became a base for Tibetan Khampa guerillas fighting the Chinese invaders. But you can go there on an organised march if you can afford it.

I couldn't, so, smiling at the guard, I walked five paces in and five paces back without being shot. Thus ended my sojourn in the almost-forbidden kingdom.

The red *gompa* is like a fort in the middle of town but you can't just walk in. It's like a National Trust property with an office manned by a monk who takes your hundred rupees and hands you a ticket. There were no other visitors, and having – compulsorily – removed my leather boots, made from dead cows, I had the place to myself.

Wooden stairs led to an ill-lit gallery of extraordinary paintings. Two gods with bulbous eyes, twirling beards and pierced ears glared at me in the half-light, their vestments vibrant blues, reds and yellows: wonderful works of art by any standards. Beside them was a circular painting, divided into segments, displaying Buddhist cosmology, depicted almost as a cartoon: the Buddha amongst mountains, overlooking men with strange long necks committing acts of violence; bowmen battling creatures – tigers, yaks, fish, birds – in an idealised landscape. Men despairing. Like Christian eschatology; a Dante's inferno. Sins of the flesh punished. The wheel of truth? Perhaps. At least a version of it. A divine comedy. Or a divine farce.

The inner sanctum was clouded with incense and cluttered with bright images that reminded me of baroque Catholic chapels in stately homes. An artist, crouching on the floor and lit only by a flame, was renovating a god, dipping his brush into an earthenware pot containing a colour that must have been ground from red rock or squeezed from a berry, for there are no Windsor & Newton outlets in Kagbeni. But the sense of timelessness was ruined by framed photographs of the Dalai Lama and his cardinals; the cult of personality invading this magical room which was, I thought, supposed to epitomise abstinence from ego. Popstars on a teenager's bedroom wall.

I escaped the odour of sanctity by climbing up to the roof where prayer flags fluttered between brass *lingams* – phallic symbols – or their Buddhist equivalent.

Spread out below me Kagbeni resembled a ruin, its people hidden in the narrow alleys, but down by the river I saw activity and a bridge leading to the far bank of the Kali Gandaki; access, perhaps, to forbidden trails.

Higgledy-piggledy stone walls led to the pilgrims' village; huts for the use of Hindus en route to Muktinath. Men and women crowded the lane and holy men sat cross-legged, some almost naked, their skin smeared with dye. One, with a yellow turban and long wispy white beard, was daubed from head to bare feet in grey ash and held a trident that signified that he was a follower of Shiva, creator and destroyer. He sat like a beached Poseidon but smiled at me with his eyes as I approached. He knew a few words of English and told me that he had been walking to Muktinath from Nagpur, in central India, for nearly a year. I asked him if he was glad to be so close to the shrine.

'No,' he replied, 'because my journey will not end there. It will continue.'

'Where will you go? Walk all the way home?'

He giggled. 'I have no home.'

There were no police at the suspension bridge and I was about to cross when I realised that I was overlooking the women's bathing place. Men began to stare at me. Embarrassed, I turned back and followed the river downstream, passing pollarded willows, until I chose a boulder where I sat staring at spindrift blowing off the corniced ridges of Nilgiri North.

This daunting peak was not climbed until 1962, by Lionel Terray. He had already reached the 25,292-foot-high Jannu in the Kanchenjunga massif in the spring, then popped down to Peru to plant his feet on Chacaraju East before arriving back in Nepal to lead the assault on Nilgiri from whose summit he could see the top of Annapurna I where he had played a crucial part in the epic adventure twelve years previously. Three years later he died in a climbing accident near Grenoble, the place of his birth. They all die. At least, most of them. Look at the group photograph of Chris Bonnington's successful Annapurna

South Face expedition. So many now just photos on widows' walls.

A dust-devil spiralled across the great alluvial plane of the river valley, and within minutes a wind sprang up, driving grit into my eyes. So I returned, feeling shaky, to join Iman who was sitting in the lodge kitchen keeping the gold-ringed sisters amused while they piled mountainous ranges of rice onto his plate. Throughout our journey I noticed how women were attracted to Iman, but he never took advantage because – I knew – he loved his wife deeply.

'Eat, Peter?'

'Peter not eat. Peter go to sleep.'

I lay on my bed feeling wretched, watching the afternoon passing me by, listening to my short-wave radio. Sons were killing sons in Macedonia and Israel and Africa. At least in Nepal, Hindus and Buddhists have learned to live and let live. Buddhists don't stone Hindu children on their way to school. Hindus don't murder Buddhist children sheltering in their fathers' arms.

How uncivilised the Western world must seem from their perspective.

18

A frantic rapping woke me.

'Yes?'

'Are you all right, Peter?'

'Come in, Iman.'

Iman peered around the door. 'I was worried. You didn't come down for supper but I didn't want to disturb you.'

'I was ill.'

'Are you still ill?'

'I feel wonderful and very hungry.'

'Shall I order breakfast?'

'Oh, yes please. Tibetan bread and lots of eggs.'

For Iman, appetite meant health and he smiled with relief. 'Three eggs?'

'No. Four. And pints and pints of tea.'

* * * * *

The path to Jomosom meanders through cliffs of conglomerate but in the dry season it is possible to follow the floodplain, hopping across rivulets on rocks and driftwood. This is the place to find fossils, but an icy wind blew up the valley and hailstones hurt our faces.

We stopped by a green tributary bridged by tree trunks to put on warm clothes, and watched pilgrims passing by, some barefoot, their heads protected only by blue plastic bags slit along a seam and worn like hoods.

An old woman was being cajoled by her son into crossing the bridge but she was afraid and so, still wearing her slippers, she waded through the glacial melt-water to emerge, crawling up the stony bank on her hands and knees.

Such is the power of faith.

* * * * *

Jomosom is a bit of a dump. We passed a locked park with a statue of King Birendra, dressed as John Wayne, staring out over the ramshackle town; then by a military camp where sentries in camouflage fatigues stood stoically in the cold guarding something or other, possibly each other.

A white palace, like a stale wedding cake, was stuck on a cliff, and Iman explained that it was a luxury hotel, just built, where you could stay for a hundred dollars a night. A tractor picks you up from the airstrip and drags you up to where *cordon bleu* cuisine awaits. And deep depression probably.

We crossed a bridge and trudged down the high street, which was made of mud with proper restaurants and shops touting for business – and lit by electricity. I was shocked by a familiar sound I had forgotten: an engine. A JCB trundled by, farting black fumes.

Iman shrugged his shoulders. 'Progress. They are extending the runway so it can take bigger planes.'

'Will there be more noise where we're going?'

'Not for a long time. There are no roads, only paths.'

The hail had turned to heavy snow and Iman led me into a lodge whose owner he knew well, and while they caught up on gossip I sat upstairs watching the construction of a new concrete control tower. I bought a quarter bottle of whisky and made myself an Irish tea.

Iman ate and ate, while I sat and sat, the whisky going straight to my head. Perhaps Jomosom wasn't as bad as I first thought? But it was, and we left in a blizzard along an airport road blasted out of the rock. Imagine a Welsh slate quarry in a storm. That's how it was.

The valley narrowed but I saw little of the country that was wreathed in murk from which snowflakes fell. I reached a rickety suspension bridge and set off along it before realising I had lost Iman. I heard him calling and retraced my steps.

'No, Peter, not that way. This.'

I followed obediently, wondering where spring was hiding.

Just above Marpha the snow stopped and the sun sidled out, briefly, lighting the village and surrounding forest in a way cinematographers can only imagine in their wildest dreams; whirlpools of dazzle spinning up the valley, turning the hillside pines blue and the orchard fields below into eddies of shadows.

I fell in love with Marpha at first sight. There is one narrow flagstoned street of white houses with exquisitely chiselled windowframes stained chocolate brown, with shutters carved into unnecessary shapes just for fun, and on every roof a vertical pole from which prayer flags flopped. Marpha is too close to Jomosom to be unspoilt but it won me over with its sheer prettiness, like a deb at a dance.

We were in the land of the Thakalis who originally settled here after leaving Tibet centuries ago, and despite populating a thin region less than twenty miles long they have their own language. And I had read that they were renowned for their hospitality.

Iman led me into The Sunrise whose stove fired the kitchen with blessed heat. The women of the house, recognising Iman, smiled perfect smiles.

Dental hygiene is a rigorous ritual in Nepal. Saunter through any village early in the morning and you will see people queuing up at the pump, toothbrushes in hand. On a purely practical level they have to polish their teeth like jewels; for in such far-flung places you can't just pop down the road for a bit of root canal work.

The interior was like a galleon; with nothing quite on a level and great timbers holding up the ceiling. Stairs leading down to the rooms were decorated with pots of red geraniums, and my room overlooked an orchard where a single apricot hung on from last year, still yellow after a Himalayan winter, its top capped by snow.

We were the first to arrive and I ate chow mein washed down with the last of the whisky before heading out into snow that now fell vertically, the flakes sticking to me as big as brooches.

I climbed the concrete steps leading to Solmi Gompa and stood in the courtyard beside a large prayer wheel, a gift from the Dalai Lama, although I saw no monks and the holy-of-holies was padlocked. Instead I stood in the silence, gazing down at the cubist town whose flat clay roofs were whitewashed with snow.

When I returned, the *kotatsu* was crowded with women, mainly Australians and Americans in their twenties, sprawling on the benches. I needed to warm my feet and so, in my English way, I said, 'Excuse me, but would you mind making room?' No one moved. 'Couldn't you squash up a bit? Please?'

A surly Amazon begrudgingly shifted a leg off a bench and I squeezed in, spreading the blanket over my wet trousers and feeling the heat from the brazier seeping through my leather boots.

'Wow! You oughta taste this apple pie,' one said to another without offering any, licking her spoon.

The *kotatsu* is a communal affair and so I made an effort to talk to them, but during the previous few weeks I had almost forgotten that I was a fogey. You may have read about them in Celtic folklore. They come from Fogeydom and are both invisible and inaudible to the under-thirties, so I gave up trying and listened instead.

'I mean this man was truly amazing. Real old and wrinkly and he read my palm and said I would live till I was ninety-six. He did tarot too.'

'You really believe that stuff?' a peer asked.

'Sure. They've been doing it for thousands of years so there must be something in it.'

'And what if it's really true?' I said. 'Just think of the nightmares you'll start having when you're ninety-five.'

'Very funny,' she scowled, displaying canines.

I felt a tap on my back, and there was Iman, beaming.

'I have brought you a present, Peter.' Like a naughty schoolboy he reached into his cagoule and extracted a bottle which he handed to me. I read the label: *Marpha Apple Brandy: 75 per cent proof.*

'Jesus! Seventy-five per cent proof!' My blasphemy was noted, creating a lull in the prattling. 'I can't drink all that.'

Iman delved into his pocket and pulled out two small glasses.

'Shove up,' I said to the antipodean next to me. 'Someone else needs to sit down.'

They must have respected rudeness because there was a shuffling of bums and Iman squashed in beside me. He filled the glasses to their brims.

'You really going to drink that?' Apple Pie asked.

'You want some?'

'No *thank you*.'

I fictionalised her childhood. Some hick town in the sticks with a Baptist chapel at the end of a dusty street. Tumbleweed. A black sheep of an uncle who'd turned to drink.

'Cheers!'

'Cheers!'

I took it down in one. Nothing happened for several seconds. Then someone lit sparklers in my stomach and I began to cough. Iman refilled the glasses, and I lit a cigarette.

'Do you have to?' Apple Pie asked, fanning her face with palms she believed mapped her destiny.

'This isn't California,' I said. 'Look, there's an ashtray. Anyway you're going to live till you're ninety-six.'

Iman was picking up the bad vibrations and said sweetly,

SHORT WALKS IN SHANGRI-LA

'We are celebrating.'

'Celebrating what?'

'Being alive. Being safe.'

'Where've you come from?'

'Thorung La.'

'Oh yeah? It's closed. Everyone knows that.'

'Now, maybe,' I said. 'And before. But not when Iman and I came over.'

Suddenly I was aware that they were looking at me differently, their collective antagonism melting into a slush of undeserved respect.

'Isn't that where you're headed?' I asked.

'No way,' said Apple Pie. 'Just up to Jomosom. Then we're taking the plane back to Pokhara.'

'Then where?'

'Go our separate ways. Some to Bali, some to Bangkok, some to Europe, some home.'

'And are you glad you came?'

'I guess so,' said Apple Pie.

'Guess?' I asked in amazement. How could she not be glad?

'Come, Peter,' said Iman. 'I must talk to you.'

Iman got up from the *kotatsu* and I followed him to another table.

'The snow is very bad this year,' he said. 'There still might be sun but ...'

'But?'

'I am not sure if we can enter the Annapurna Sanctuary as you want. It is your decision.'

'Why?'

'There has been another sadness. Another person killed in an avalanche. A member of the British Everest expedition.'

'Was he climbing?'

'No, just going for a trek to get acclimatised. Usually it

is quite safe but look outside. If it's snowing so much here it means that much more is falling on the mountains and they are very steep above the Sanctuary.'

'Let's see how it is in a few days and then we'll decide.'

'OK. You want to eat?'

I ate and wrote my diary, alone, trying to expunge the noise of Apple Pie espousing the merits of *Zen and the Art of Motorcycle Maintenance*.

I joined Iman sitting on the floor beside the stove, which was encircled by old women with rings in their noses and many gold earrings denoting their venerability. They were Indian pilgrims, shawled in cotton that would provide no protection against the weather. They held out their hands to the stove, then touched their foreheads for warmth. I imitated them, and it worked. They smiled, displaying gold teeth, reminding me, for some reason, of Egyptian mummies. Then I put my thumbs near the flames for a moment before sticking them in my ears. This made them cackle. Forefingers next, which I pushed up my nostrils, and they fell about laughing.

I asked Iman if I could talk to them, but even Iman didn't know their language and so I went to bed knowing nothing about them apart from their courage.

The snow had stopped, and the moon cast blue shadows in the orchard below my window. All was silence apart from the distant screams of an owl somewhere across the valley.

19

I woke to blinding sun and the sound of the *gompa* bell tolling, and left Marpha with regret, knowing in my heart that each step I took would never be retraced. Clouds blew in, bringing snow flurries. We walked through pine bluffs towards Tukuche which we approached along an avenue of poplars squelchy with the dung of yaks and goat herds being driven to pasture.

Children were playing volleyball outside the school in the town square, risking fractures as they flung themselves onto a court comprising knobbly bedrock. Superficially it is a dinky place, oddly reminiscent of Andalusia, but there is poverty beyond the façades of the tarted-up houses lining the main street. Toddlers in rags, globules of green goo bubbling from their nostrils, stood in doorways joining their hands and saying 'Namaste,' although, in reality, they were begging.

Tukuche was once a major trading centre where salt from Tibet was bartered for grain from the fertile fields to the south, but that trade had ended; sea salt from India having replaced the traditional rock salt which, without iodine, could not prevent goitre which now appears to have been eradicated.

Beyond Tukuche we joined a Via Dolorosa where men hobbled through lives leading to a perpetual Calvary. They are the timber carriers, their impossible loads crucified to their backs by headbands. One man carried eight four-by-fours, fifteen feet long; a staggering 23,000 cubic inches. Their only Simon of Cyrenes are stone walls every few hundred yards, where they can deposit their loads in temporary respite from the torture; for that is what it is. Your first thought is that they must be used to such loads but no one could ever become used to them. You see it in their faces as they pass, their eyes screwed up in agony, the veins in their legs bulbous from unnatural strain. I asked Iman what they were paid.

'It is according to weight. If it is a big load they might get five hundred rupees.'

'A day?'

'A week.'

'That's less than five pounds. And do they get free lodging?'

'Oh no. They have to pay for that, and their food.'

Paid slaves working for some greedy middleman living in a lakeside villa in Pokhara. So what if one drops dead? In a country of desperate people there will always be someone grateful to take his place; and always those willing to exploit them.

A man on a horse was fording the river, which still ran fast here, between sandy crags. He reached the far side but the slope was too steep for the horse, which stumbled back into the river. Instead of going a few yards downstream where an exit would have been simpler, he beat the horse and tried again, and once more the horse fell back into the water, almost toppling the rider.

'Why doesn't he get out where it's easy?'

'Because he wants the horse to know who is the master.'

He tried again, thwacking the horse on a flank as though it were a dirty carpet, and this time they made it. The man yelled out in triumph.

Blue sky waited around the corner, and there was Dhauligiri, its great glaciers tumbling from a knife-edged ridge that stopped at 26,794 feet, then went down again. Hertzog's 1950 French expedition attempted Dhauligiri but even the indomitable Lionel Terray declared that it would never be climbed. So they conquered Annapurna instead. But Dhauligiri was climbed in 1960 by the Swiss, whose expedition was supplied by an aircraft landing them supplies at over 19,000 feet. So by hook and crookery they made it, but many have not. For every six people who have reached the summit, one has died. In 1969 seven members of a United States expedition were killed by an avalanche, but the Americans succeeded, finally, in 1973.

In his excellent book, *Trekking in the Nepal Himalaya*, Stan Armington writes about Captain Wick airdropping supplies to the United States expedition from a Pilatus Porter aircraft:

> *Among the delicacies he dropped were two bottles of wine and a live chicken. The Sherpas would not allow the chicken to be killed on the mountain so it became the expedition pet. It was carried, snow-blind and crippled with frost-bitten feet, to Marpha, where it finally ended up in the cooking pot.*

The world's highest chicken, *ever*, reduced to drumsticks. A disgrace.

Iman and I planned to spend two nights in Larjung where we would dash up and down the 3,500 feet to the Dhauligiri icefall but Iman shook his head.

'Look at the snow, Peter. It is far too low. The trail is very steep and it would be very, very dangerous.'

So we headed for Lete instead, crossing the Kali Gandaki which widened here into a stony desert veined by streams crossed on logs or simply forded. The immensity of the landscape was highlighted not only by the great mountains but by the lines of pilgrims threading their way across the valley.

In photography there is the concept of *the circle of resolution*: the smallest image that can be discerned. These pilgrims could only *just* be seen. Imagine bookmites crawling across a ream of paper, and you will appreciate the scale.

We trudged for mile after mile but our discomfort was

trivial. Every so often we watched the oscillating figures of timber carriers staggering towards us through a heat haze shimmering above hot stones; blurred images that became people.

Apart from a temporary tea house halfway across this desert there was no place for them to set down their loads. If they were dropped they would be impossible to lift, and so they had no choice but to continue across a purgatorial plain despite having no sins to expiate.

An athletic blonde jogged past, just beating us to a log bridge. As Iman and I balanced across we were aware of heavy breathing behind us. A man almost elbowed us into the water, but apologised.

'Sorry,' he said, 'but I have to catch up with her.'

'Why?'

'I said something and she took offence.'

It was 1 April so I decided to play a trick on Iman.

We reached a deep tributary spanned by a particularly flimsy log bridge. I let Iman go ahead, then picked up the biggest boulder I could find. When he was halfway across I heaved the rock into the water, cried out and flung myself down on the ground to camouflage myself. The splash was stupendous and Iman turned, calling 'Peter! Peter!' I stood up, laughing, but he wasn't amused. I explained All Fools' Day; even the fact that because it was before midday it was a legitimate ploy, but the concept was lost on him.

I once wrote an article for *New Scientist* called 'The Llandudno Pentagon', parodying Erich von Daniken's risible books. It was about the Welsh equivalent of the so-called Bermuda Triangle. Sheep had mysteriously gone missing, eye-witnessed by farmers who had seen a strange green glow in the sky. The magazine did me proud with maps and moody photos of ancient stone circles. Of course it was their 1 April edition.

But there were letters; not complaining about the joke,

but about the fact that I had dared to misinterpret one of the leading thinkers of our time. Perhaps we are descended from aliens, but deep down I suspect that our ancestors were fish; hard to fathom, I know, particularly when you're tucking into cod and chips.

We left the river and climbed up into pine forest. Below us, timber carriers shuffled sideways across a suspension bridge, their loads as rigid as the wings of the Angel of the North.

I witnessed a duel at a bridge downstream between two muleteers who arrived at opposite ends simultaneously. Neither wanted to give way and the mules approached the centre with no room to pass. Both muleteers shouted abuse but gradually one train was forced to retreat; not easy, wearing hooves on planks swaying above a gorge. When the triumphant muleteer emerged, just below where I was standing, the loser picked up a rock of skull-cracking proportions, and threw it at his rival. It missed by inches.

Iman laughed, and I asked why.

'It is only a joke, Peter. Really they are friends.'

The joke was lost on me. It was almost murder. Cultural differences. Iman hadn't understood my April Fool jape either.

Kalopani and Lete are contiguous, both as ugly as each other. Lightning flashed as we walked along a mile-long highway, passing lodges that seemed to offer hospitality, but Iman had his own ideas. We stopped at a house next to the police station, which advertised a roof garden. A rickety ladder led up to a rain-lashed rooftop where two chairs, their broken plastic raffia backs streaming in the wind, would have entranced no one, even in halcyon weather.

The sullen lodge keeper seemed put out at being disturbed, but showed me to my hovel. It was only three o'clock in the afternoon but I didn't want to offend Iman so I sat in the dining room, freezing, and asked for a brazier. A guest asking for warmth? I could have been in Skegness. Much humming and hawing from Attila and eventually a can of dying embers was shoved unceremoniously under the table. The careers advisory officer in Lete had obviously made an error. At least, I thought, the place would fill up.

A German couple came in, saw the accommodation, and walked out. They were followed by a jolly Australian pair who, having seen the rooms, left too, with a 'Good luck, mate,' aimed at me.

There was a bookcase containing two tattered paperbacks left by trekkers: *The Way: An Interpretation of the Bible* and 700 pages chronicling the career of President Harry S. Truman. I would never finish it by morning.

'Food, Peter?'

There was so much hawking and spitting in the kitchen that I thought it sensible to ask for an omelette, but when it arrived there were unidentifiable flecks of green in it, and I pushed it aside.

Three policemen entered, propped their antediluvian guns against the wall and ordered booze. I watched them playing cards, slapping them down like rifle shots that preyed on my nerves. I ordered apple brandy and went into a sulk, but the journalist inside me prompted me to use Iman as an interpreter as I tried to interview the constables.

'Are you worried about being attacked by Maoists?'

'No.'

'Don't you get bored?'

'No.'

'Why have you chosen to join the police force?'

'It's a job.' So much for my interviewing technique.

It was only 4.30, and I rebelled. I picked a fight with Iman.

'Why've you chosen this awful place to stay in?'

'We can always leave and go down to Ghasa.'

'How far?'

'Two hours.'

'It'll be dark by then.'

The storm intensified, bringing a false dusk echoing with thunder. I began to read the turgid Pulitzer Prize-winning biography of Truman. He was only five years old when I gave up and slammed the book onto the table. I craved conversation.

'I'm going out!' I said petulantly.

'Where?'

'Anywhere's better than this morgue.'

I walked uphill through a blizzard looking for light which I saw, eventually, in a lodge full of people who gladly made room for me at the *kotatsu*.

I ordered food and drink, and spent a convivial evening conversing with bright people who had never had their palms read or their chakras attuned by crystals.

Outside there was a white-out and I slithered along the slippery flagstones searching for my lodge, relying on lightning to illuminate my way. I reached a forest before turning back, and eventually regained the lodge, identified from the sentry-box next door.

Having stumbled up to my room I burrowed into my sleeping bag and switched on my radio. That day a police post in eastern Nepal had been attacked by Maoists and there had been many deaths. Usually such battles were confined to the west and I hoped that Lete was not next on their list. Getting caught in crossfire would be a daft way to die.

20

When you loathe a place, you want to abscond, and so when I woke before dawn I strode out into the snowy countryside, making my way up through the abandoned terraces of a farm into a clearing where I watched Dhauligiri's summit emerging from the subfusc into a dim line just differentiated from the sky. Its tip turned pink, into a nipple, and I marvelled that men had trod there.

On the opposite side of the valley, in the Annapurnas to the east, the sky was a projection of sunbeams, pointed up at various angles into a subtle laser display.

'Hello, Peter.'

Iman was there, and I asked how he had found me.

He pointed down. 'Footprints.'

Iman! Always there, concerned, and I gave him a hug, embarrassing him.

'I apologise for my behaviour last night.'

'It's all right, Peter. I understand. We'll eat breakfast somewhere else.' He pointed. 'Look, Peter, there. Annapurna I.'

Its summit was just visible above its outliers, seeming no more than part of a contiguous ridge, but I had seen it.

We left the Unwelcome Lodge and headed down, steeply, through pines Christmas-carded with snow.

People ask, 'Are you fit?' and you invariably respond, 'As a fiddle.' But I really was. I felt extraordinarily strong as I leapt down the rocky trail, in complete physical control, my mind and muscles at one. Athletes talk of this, but it was a new sensation for me. I could accomplish anything. I was a demigod: a plain Narcissus.

We stopped at the village we should have stayed in the previous night, Ghasa, an alpine settlement where the climate was significantly lower. Fertile green fields of wheat, almost ready to reap, prickled into an azure sky, and lizards skimmed away at our approach. A porter passed with a wicker man stuffed with hens on his back, the birds clucking contentedly as they headed for sacrifice.

I sat in the sun dunking Tibetan bread soldiers into creamy saffron yokes, and watched a man opposite splitting bamboo with a carved knife he jerked towards himself with gay abandon, stopping each time with the blade only millimetres from his heart. His toddler son stood watching. No doubt in forty years he will be sitting there doing exactly the same.

Black buffaloes with mean-looking swept back horns roamed the streets but they were as gentle as pussycats. Birdsong filled the air with music I had missed; but the birds were elusive and I only identified yuhinas, like crested tits, and an eagle using updraughts to climb into invisibility.

An area of perpetual landslides needed a cool head in places but we threaded our way along the river over bridges, some suspended, some of timber, through trees like alders, until we reached a tea house under a spectacular waterfall at Rupse Chhahara.

I'm no foodie but the tomato soup contained real spiced tomatoes enhanced by an Englishwoman opposite who resembled Catherine Zeta Jones, but with fewer puffy folds around her eyes. I lusted in my heart.

She spoke to me. 'Excuse me,' she began, and never had these words seemed so sexy. 'My friend here's having trouble with his camera and we couldn't help noticing it's the same as yours.'

The friend turned. How could this callow, spotty youth have entrapped such a beauty? What did she see in him? Age is the answer. They were the same, less than half mine, and that is enough. So I spent thirty minutes instructing the boy about the computerised complexities of our Nikons, my concentration wafting away on Catherine's perfume.

In so-called British comedies there is a frequently used gag. An elderly man, ogling a young girl, turns to his mate and says, 'If only I was thirty years younger'. Cue sniggers. It was never funny but when you *are* thirty years older it takes on an air of tragic truth.

Catherine left, leaving me dispirited. In my twenties and thirties I had wondered what it would be like to become unfanciable. Now I knew.

Later, beside a bridge in a gully, there was a gathering of archers and I clambered down to sit amongst them. Young men with Tibetan bows, encouraged by their families, were aiming at a wooden target as thin as an Islamic headstone on the far side of the chasm.

They were very good, and had to be, for the scorers stood only a yard wide of the target as the arrows buried themselves in the wood or missed, the arrowheads sparking off boulders.

Have you ever watched Western archers in competition with their high-tech bows bristling with strange springs and counterweights, pulling back and aiming as if they were firing telescopic rifles? No fun, is it? Here they simply pulled back on their bows, shaped like Cupid's upper lip, and let fly without hesitation. Before guns such men must have been a formidable foe.

A crude cable car spanned the river north of Dana, its cabins enmeshed by wire. Iman explained. 'In the rainy season this river is impassable so it's the only way of getting people and supplies across. Otherwise all the villages above would be cut off for months.'

Dana is run-down but extraordinarily beautiful, its wooden buildings and balconies carved into a museum that keeps the lost skill of local artisans alive. It was, until recent times, the capital of the Mustang region, but the fleshpots of Tatopani, downstream, have attracted visitors away and, in retrospect, I regret not staying there.

An exposed path, complete with a tunnel, leads towards Tatopani, and I was so full of vim that I overtook everyone, not because I wanted to arrive first, but because I was taking sheer pleasure in my wellbeing; my ability to leap from rock to rock at high speed, the springs in my clockwork legs constantly coiled, the route finding as instinctive as it had been when I lived in the Welsh mountains.

But I hadn't reckoned on Methuselah who sprinted past, his walking sticks used like ski poles to push him forward in a flurry of dust. He must have been in his late seventies, and kept turning – without stopping – to tell his porter to keep up. Who he was I do not know because I never caught up with him, but he was English, his eyes bright as a boy's. Something about him was familiar and I wondered if he was a famous mountaineer who was drawn back year after year, like a ghost, to haunt the paths of his youth.

It's always in the eyes; people who have seen things, thought things, done things. Look at photographs of the late explorer Eric Shipton, whose appetite for new adventures knew no bounds. Even in his late sixties his eyes, beneath wiry white brows, reflected a wonder of a world whose obscure and different corners he had done much to reveal.

Flowers were suddenly everywhere; spiky red petals, yellow trailers like creeping Jenny, and delicate white blooms with flimsy leaves resembling wood sorrel. A stick insect on a blade of grass.

Tatopani is a resort, pure and simple, its claim to fame the hot springs spouting from the riverbank; a place for R & R. Just what I needed.

Iman led me into a lodge whose courtyard was overhung by oranges. The menu boasted pork and angerfish (*sic*) and it had solar-heated showers: bliss, because I stank. The sun had long slid behind the canyon in which Tatopani sits, and the shower was cold but I shampooed and scrubbed myself, and then washed my clothes which I hung up to dry in a warm evening breeze.

I sat on the terrace with Iman, drinking beer, effulgent with wellbeing, watching pilgrims picking their way through boulders towards their bivouacs by the river.

I wandered up the street and heard a coin clinking on glass. There was Fred, beckoning me into a lodge that would have passed muster in St Moritz.

He was seated at a table amongst familiar faces. There was the plumber, Barry, and his legal secretary friend, Crisp, Bean, and even Dutch Piet, who I had not seen for over a week. The Thorung La club.

They had all taken a day off to soak out the aches from their limbs in the hot springs, and had been on a binge, the table a gamelan of empty bottles.

Fred had been transformed from the rather dour old man I had met at Lower Pisang.

He had lost years, his taciturnity transformed into volubility, his confidence restored into the life and soul of the party, which was already in full swing.

A man holding a Spanish guitar introduced himself as Jim. He was twenty, and had spent two years as a steward on the Orient Express, not steaming romantically into central Europe and Istanbul, but to Newcastle and Bath on special trips; the kind people treat their spouses to on wedding anniversaries. Jim had ambitions to be a playwright and I asked, in non sequiturial manner, why he wasn't at university.

'Why do that and end up fifteen thousand quid in debt? I can read just as well here, and what do I need to prove? Write essays for tutors who're only interested in their own ambitions? I know what I think and I don't see why

I should get phony merit for putting it down on paper.'

I was sympathetic. I was almost thrown out of Durham University in my final year for refusing to dissect the love poems of W. B. Yeats for a virgin Ph.D academic whose knowledge of passion was shuttered between her hardcovers. Besides, what is a degree worth? My eldest son graduated with a good arts degree last year and now works for the British Council; not arranging lucrative tours for minor poets to Namibia, but changing light bulbs and checking the slide projectors in the boardroom. Handyman (BA Hons).

Miraculously, beer was transmuted into brandy, and I borrowed Jim's guitar. I played 'Greensleeves' perfectly, but when I attempted my *pièce de résistance*, Bert Jansch's 'Angie', my fingers had turned to wood and I gave up. I shook everyone's hands and said goodnight, promising Fred I would meet up with him in Ghorepani the following night, but I never saw him again.

21

Iman had scheduled a backbreaking climb for the following day in order to see a postcard of the Himalaya from Poon Hill, above Ghorepani. We could have carried on down instead, following the Kali Gandaki, but the panorama promised to be 'an unmissable experience' so I acquiesced, until dawn, when the thought of trudging from 3,900 feet above sea level up to 9,000 feet simply did not appeal. It would be the equivalent of returning to Kagbeni but at least we would have a better idea of whether the Annapurna Sanctuary was feasible.

So I said no. I was seduced by the thought of lazing in a hot spring and the luxury of writing my diary and letters in daylight for a change.

'Tomorrow,' I told Iman. 'Today nothing.'

He took it on the chin despite having been sentenced to a day of idleness amongst his friends.

I grabbed a towel and headed down towards the grotto. Warm springs would gush like fountains into a necklace of sylvan pools, coloured jade, overhung by blushing pomegranates where birds with rainbow plumage would flit, singing in avian harmony.

I bought my ticket at a bamboo booth and stood above a concrete pit 10 feet square.

The murky water steamed like unidentifiable soup and I hesitated, reminded of all those rumours about catching unmentionable diseases from hotel jacuzzis, tepidity bacteria's aphrodisiac. Still, I had paid my money, and climbed in.

It was pleasant enough but then I was joined by a New Yorker wearing William Morris-patterned trunks. His belly rose above the surface like a potato in a pot, and he wanted to talk.

'Isn't this something else?'

His toes rose like periscopes and I saw that his soles were covered with a coating of yellow skin that parboiling would shred.

I looked for a filter system but there wasn't one.

'You know,' he said, gazing up at the sun which was just splintering into light above a crag, 'this is really real in a truly profound sense.'

I guessed what was coming next. He would say, 'Have you read *The Snow Leopard*?' But I fled, found a flat rock upstream, and with my towel for a pillow, slept, lulled into unconsciousness by the unending rhythm of the water, my lean body drying in a hot wind blowing up from the Indian plains.

* * * * *

A woman sat alone at dinner, ordering her food in Nepali. Vanessa, twenty, was at a posh private university in Texas, majoring in anthropology, and had spent two months in Nepal studying women's issues. She told me things I already knew but with a vehemence and anger I hoped would remain with her when she returned home.

'The women are treated like shit here,' she said. 'It may seem all hunkydory on the surface but up in the villages girls are considered completely worthless. Imagine selling your own daughter to some pimp from Pokhara? They're told they're going to get jobs as domestics but the parents know they're going to brothels, some only twelve or thirteen. It's sickening.'

'So what's the solution?'

'It's so medieval up here I haven't a fucking clue.'

'Presumably mothers aren't any different here. They can't help loving their children. So how can they do it?'

'Because poverty's the daughter-fucking mother of invention. They pretend to themselves. It's either that or starve and then the whole family falls apart. And family's all they've got. It's devastating.'

'Any sympathy for the Maoists?'

'Of course. They've done a lot of good in some rural areas – only I'm against violence.'

'Isn't a corrupt government depriving their own people of medical care violence? You can kill a baby by stopping immunisation.'

'They're Communists.'

'But they have support.'

'You'd support them too if your village was ruled by people with guns.'

'The police?'

'No, the Maoists.'

'But they've set up banks and communal farms. And they deplore the caste system.'

'Because they're atheists.'

'Surely if the system stinks it doesn't matter what others believe or don't believe? You just want justice. Revenge even, but that can be the same thing. What do you do if your child dies of TB because some bloody civil servant on the take in Kathmandu steals the money? Write to your MP? Sign a petition? No. You want to change everything, and so you grab the only alternative offered to you.'

'Are you a Communist?'

'No, because I don't *do* anything – like a Christian who doesn't give all he has to the poor. But as I get older and see the wickedness in the world I'm beginning to believe that perhaps I am, deep down.'

'But it's never worked.'

'Not yet. It's failed but that's not the same thing. Marx died only a hundred and twenty years ago. Saint Augustine didn't go to England until five hundred years after Christ's death.'

'So in five hundred years we'll have a Marxist utopia?'

'I don't tell fortunes but almost anything has to be better than this.' I had the timber carriers in mind.

Vanessa, confused in her American way about the difference between conversation, debate and insult, yawned, and excused herself with the usual, 'It's been nice talking with you.'

No doubt she will now be putting the finishing touches to her thesis which will elevate her status from assistant to associate professor, with tenure. The American right will label her a liberal, which is tantamount to calling a Thatcherite middle-of-centre, and she will retire to a condominium, in Tampa, in 2040. Or maybe she will do some good. More than I have.

22

The suspension bridge beyond Tatopani gave me collywobbles. Not only was it very high above the river but juddered in a fierce wind. Rationalisation fled. I was pretending to be cool on a yard-wide pavement with holes in it, protected from a substantial drop by rusting chicken wire that whined eerily.

Be honest. If someone constructed something like this linking Big Ben with the top of the London Eye and said 'Walk!' you might refuse. Where had my new-found courage gone? Into my bowels, that's where, but it took 2,000 feet of steep ascent before I found one of the finest privies in the world, set on a rocky ridge at Ghara, its roof thatched and trimmed as neatly as a second home, with a tin can for a bidet. And the views! If I'd popped behind a bush on the way up I would have missed it.

Iman and I sat in the sun drinking lemon tea, gazing up into a fertile, spacious, terraced valley, the first we had seen in the west. We had left the influence of the Thalakis and entered Magar territory, Tibetan facial features having been replaced by almond eyes, *retroussé* rather than aquiline noses, and much darker skin.

With real soil in which to grow their crops, as opposed to stones and the odd alluvial floodplain in the Kali Gandaki gorge, these people were relatively well-off – by which I mean they were not quite as poor as most.

We sauntered up through fields of young green wheat and vegetables and passed stone corrals where buffaloes tugged at sweet-smelling hay. A trickle of a stream splashed alongside the path.

Iman stopped. 'Look, Peter! In the water.'

I saw nothing but rocks. 'What?'

'A crab.'

Six thousand feet above the sea? It was obviously a confusion in his vocabulary, or a joke, so I laughed.

'Really! There!'

Iman pointed to a little pool, and there was a crab, its diameter no more than three inches, complete with pincers and a shiny white carapace. I crept towards it with a photo in mind, but just as I focused it scuttled into a crevice. I knew about crayfish, but freshwater crabs? Another good reason for not drinking from streams. Big crabs must make little crabs, and imagine scooping up a nursery of them and putting them in your mouth? All those little creatures nipping your gums and getting wedged between your teeth.

This part of the trail was shadeless and by noon we were dripping with sweat. Time for a beer or two.

We sat under bamboo slats watching a farmer ploughing a field, urging his buffalo on with rocks aimed at the poor beast's rump. The buffalo was dressed entirely in black which was absorbing all the sun's rays. He must have been dying of heat and in need of a siesta.

We did not have the place to ourselves for long. A trekking party led by a harassed, ginger Englishman arrived. There were about a dozen in all, half in their twenties, half middle-aged or more, all just-off-the-plane pale. The older contingent were uniformly obese, the women in flowery cotton dresses, the men in shorts that revealed flabby white legs squiggly with varicose veins. I said a general hello but no one replied. They weren't even talking to each other. They slumped into two groups, a generation apart. *Something* had happened. A blazing row by the look of things.

The leader appeared to have no leadership qualities. No rallying the troops. Instead he sat on his own, sucking a Mars Bar like a solemn child who didn't want to share his lollipop with anyone.

Iman winked at me, and whispered, 'How sad to see them like this, but there's nothing they can do. They've paid their money and they're stuck with their companions. That's why it's never a good idea to sign up with people you haven't met. The young ones are fit and want to be off, and the older ones really shouldn't be here at all.'

'Why not? They'll get used it.'

'Look at them, Peter. You have to get in shape before coming here. Look at that one with the white hat.'

I glanced at a man whose ashen cheeks were awash with sweat, the hands holding his walking poles tremoring as if he were suffering from palsy.

'Someone like that will end up having a heart attack.'

'That'd certainly spoil it for the rest,' I said. 'They'd end up having to carry the body.'

Iman frowned, shocked by my callousness, but then I smiled and he grinned a little.

'English humour. Sometimes, Peter, it is so hard to understand.'

We passed a modern looking building. It looked deserted but there was a hand-painted plea on a planed log beside the trail: *Our school has trouble. We have no money from the government to pay our teachers. Please visit us and help us.*

'Why no money, Iman?'

He shrugged.

Like the Levite, I passed by.

We stopped for lunch at Phalate, a pretty village whose narrow street was blocked by roaring buffaloes I prodded away with my bamboo pole. Iman, true to habit, disappeared into the kitchen while I ordered onion soup spiced with chillis. A little dill, and possibly a pinch of cumin, was needed. In Ludlow this restaurant would not have merited even one Michelin star, but its rough ethnicity sufficed. Apple pie followed, its pastry a smidgen too soggy for my taste, and the chef's eschewal of cinnamon did the apple disservice. All in all an adequate meal which left me ultimately unsatisfied; but reasonable for seventy-five pence.

Iman told me that there was someone in the kitchen I should meet. There, sitting at a table, was a woman wearing mountain garb and climbing boots, eating rice.

'Meet one of the guides from the Three Sisters Agency in Pokhara.'

I had read of this band of female guides, and had seen them in a TV documentary. What they are doing in Nepal is revolutionary; women taking on what has been a traditionally male role, guiding travellers into the mountains. I wrote her name in my notebook, but so carelessly that I cannot decipher it. But it began with S and so, with apologies, I will call her S. I don't want to give her a false identity.

S had an aura of self-assertiveness I had not seen before in Nepali women. Until then I had met indifference, subservience and coyness, but S returned my smile with cool appraisal. She guided men and women, but I could tell that she would have a say in choosing her clientele. You would have to be able to hack it. Dollars wouldn't be enough.

She was new to the job, and her English rudimentary, although she had been an apprentice for two years. But I think her reticence was mainly due to the fact that Iman had, unwisely, said that I was a journalist. That's enough to put anyone on their guard, and when you are pushing forward the boundaries of social acceptance the last thing you need is misrepresentation. She was suspicious of me, and rightfully so.

I asked questions, via Iman, but quickly realised that I was getting nowhere.

'When you are in Pokhara, go to our office,' she said. 'They will tell you all you need to know.'

'I will.' And I did.

We were alone on the trail as we climbed into oak and rhododendron forests. Flat red blossoms, like rosettes, studded the dark green foliage but there was an air of melancholy, for no birds sang and the late afternoon sun had already fled the claustrophobic valley, and with terrible timing Iman chose this spot to tell me about a murder.

'Last year, near here, a Japanese man was walking on his own when he met a man who said, "There is something wrong with your shoes." The Japanese man bent down to see what was the matter, and the other man cut off his head with a kukri.'

'Why?'

'To rob him.'

'But why kill him?'

'The robber was an evil man.'

And then the strangest thing happened. A solitary Japanese youth walked down towards us. He carried nothing and did not acknowledge my hello. The hairs on my neck prickled for, although I do not think I believe in ghosts, I wondered if I had just seen one.

On my map the following day's stage of our trek had an arrow pointing to a specific place which read *Danger of Theft*. Further east, a trail was marked *Group Trekking Suggested*.

'Why's this place so bad?'

'Because of the forest,' Iman explained. 'Bandits can jump out at you and get away. They're impossible to find and anyway, who will look for them? There are no police.' It was true. I'd seen no coppers walking the beat.

'Is there much violence?'

'There have been quite a lot of crimes, but don't worry. I won't let anything happen to us. It's people alone mainly.'

Mainly? Did Iman and I constitute a group? Fear and

fatigue combined with mild paranoia, and when I saw a disreputable-looking man squatting under a tree in the middle of nowhere I became seriously afraid. He only had one eye, for God's sake. Had he been on the books of Central Casting he would have been filed under *pirate*. Was he a lookout? Would we hear him mimicking the call of a rare bird, signalling to his fellow buccaneers that here were rich pickings? After all, the cash I carried, not much by Western standards, could buy a lot in Nepal, including the sharpest kukris on the market.

But no one attacked us in this eerie forest as night gradually filled the gaps between the trees. Instead, in a clearing, a woman sitting on a rock jumped up in front of us. I guessed her age to be forty, but her face was so contorted that I might have been ten years adrift. She was dressed like a Romany; a white blouse, red skirt, and pendulous earrings that swung to and fro as she performed a strange staccato dance for us, the music inside her head.

What she was doing here, at dusk, far from habitation, was a mystery, although the glaze glistening in her corneas suggested serious mental illness. She spoke to Iman, and I asked for a translation.

'She wants money.'

We continued but after a hundred yards I refused to go on and returned. I tugged my money-belt over my navel, reached in and pulled out a 500-rupee note which I gave to her.

Suddenly she was still, and she stared at me with incomprehension. For me it was only a fiver; for her I don't know what, but a lot. She smiled a rare, toothless, Nepali smile, and I wanted to cry. And I did, quietly, wondering if Iman would notice. But if he did he said nothing.

Up we trudged, and I don't think I have ever been so exhausted. Thorung La was easy-peasy in comparison for there is a sting in the tail here. Just when you glimpse the outskirts of Ghorepani through the rhododendrons there is a vicious stone stairway that sapped my last reserves of energy.

It was dark when we entered the village and I sat on steps, refusing to budge while Iman looked for lodgings; but it was Bethlehem on the first Christmas Eve. No room in the inns.

I would have gladly pulled out my sleeping bag and crawled under a tree but Iman persevered and found us the last two rooms in the last lodge. Why so full? Because people had come here for THE SUNRISE, and Ghorepani is only a long day from Pokhara. We were in the Zermatt of Nepal where everything costs more.

Ever been to Zermatt? It's the pits. When we were students my wife-to-be and I ate a cheesy fondue that cost us a day's budget, and all because the proprietor had blown his overheads by substituting light bulbs for candles. When, a few days later, having been stormed off the Gornergrat, we dripped back into town, the snotty hotelier charged us an arm and a leg for a camp-bed in a cupboard and dry rusks for breakfast. Oh you mean, avaricious Swiss. May global warming melt all your glaciers.

Iman had checked us into a lodge where we draped our sweaty clothes above the stove, adding an air of onion. We were joined by an American and his recent acquisition, a Kiwi.

'Hi! I'm Bob from Boston.'

'Hi! I'm Mel from Auckland.'

'Hi! I'm Peter from Buckfastleigh.'

Iman arrived with a small bottle of rum, which he had paid for himself.

'I'm really pissed off with the Nepalese,' Mel said, with Iman sitting beside her. 'They keep ripping us off.'

'How much are you paying for him?' Bob asked, referring to Iman.

'You mean my friend Iman?'

'Yeah, him.'

'I'm not prepared to discuss it.'

'Don't get me wrong,' said Bob, 'but I just want to know if we're being ripped off.'

'What I'm paying is my business.'

Bob held up his palms, demonstrating that he wasn't carrying firearms. 'OK. All right. But last night we were charged ninety rupees *each* for a room and in the morning we learned that some Israelis had got a room for only *fifty-five*.'

'Ninety rupees. That must be at least one dollar twenty.'

'Too right.'

'Couldn't you afford it?'

'That's not the point.'

Rum and chronic weariness coalesced into rudeness. 'Listen, Bob, I simply don't want to talk to you any more. So me and Iman are going to sit at another table, OK?'

'It's true what they say about you Limeys. All so frigging superior.'

'The word's not frigging. It's fucking. And no, we're not superior but sometimes we simply speak our minds. I would've reacted the same way if you'd been a Dutch or a German arsehole.'

'Charming,' said Mel.

Iman and I moved, drank our rum and watched as Bob and Mel perused their supper bill, writing each item into their ledgers.

I went into town but, by 8.30, everything was closed. I could have been in mid-Wales on a Saturday night. People were taking the sunrise *very* seriously.

I saw a light in a lodge and banged on the locked door. Inside lay conviviality; a chance to meet interesting people.

I was let into a room where two yawning hairdressers from Swansea were pretending to enjoy a game of cards with the kitchen staff whose eyes constantly shifted from their hands to the coiffured bleached blonde anti-nymphets and their braless breasts shifting under matching angora V-necked sweaters. I ordered a beer, but when it arrived I paid and left.

Not so much Zermatt; more Staylittle or Llandrindod Wells.

Mel and Bob were in the cubbyhole next to mine and I overheard them talking about money. I put on earphones and switched on my radio. In Jerusalem a suicide bomber had blown himself up along with teenagers out for a bit of fun in a disco. And all for Allah.

23

Iman woke me at 4 a.m. and we set off into the night, along with many others, stumbling over rocks and each other. Looking down it seemed as if we were seeing miners coming off nightshift, head torches pivoting on a thousand foreheads.

Every so often I stopped to vomit into the roots of rhododendrons. Iman asked if I wanted to return.

'Yes,' I said, 'but I'm not going to. I have to see *the sunrise*!'

I had thought it would be a short stroll, but Poon Hill is 1,500 feet above Ghorepani and as soon as we reached the top my heart sank.

A viewing balcony, like a fire-watch tower of the kind you find in Idaho, had been constructed on the brow. Why, I couldn't understand, for being 10,495 feet high as opposed to 10,470 feet didn't make a blind bit of difference. Presumably the good burghers of Ghorepani thought it would add kudos.

A man sold hot chocolate, poured into plastic cups from a thermos flask, and I bought some to settle my stomach. Never, I vowed, would I drink 75 per cent proof liquor again.

People huddled on the hillside like extras in a biblical epic, only the costumes were wrong. Too much orange. And the Sermon on the Mount was to be given by the mute God of Nature.

I walked down through the throng so that I would have nothing but air between me and the impending revelation, but someone said, 'Hey, buddy, you mind moving? You're in my frame.'

His state-of-the-art camera was mounted on a sophisticated tripod. He was planning to swivel his powerful lens and produce a really wide composite postcard for the folks back home. I acquiesced, and moved back up.

The sky began to lose its stars, and a faint outline of mountains emerged, purple against a paling sky. The cheeks of Dhauligiri, the Annapurnas, and distant Manaslu, were effused by rouge under rumpled clouds like white wigs. But I no longer felt a part of the mountains. I felt apart. Objectively it was a stunning horizon but I wanted to be out of there.

People were oohing and aahing in a quiet, happy, one-hand-clapping kind of way but I have always hated being part of a congregation, and insisted on leaving. But we had the way down to ourselves and I stopped to watch a magical peak, Machhapuchhare – The Fish's Tail – which was first climbed by the author and poet Wilfred Noyce who was killed in the Pamirs in 1962. It stands alone, an outlier, its elegant summit more beautifully sculptured than the clutter of the Annapurna peaks; and all around us giant rhododendron trees stippled with blooms.

We ate porridge and decided what to do. Annapurna Sanctuary or not?

'I have spoken with other guides,' said Iman, 'and the snow is still very bad. More avalanches are possible.'

'So what do we do?'

'Go down, I think.'

'All right, but I'll come back in the autumn. Bring my son, maybe.'

'That would be best.'

'So we'll go to Langtang and hunt red pandas instead.'

'No, Peter. Not hunt. They are an endangered species.'

'One more or less can't make any difference and I can get it stuffed. Mount it on my wall.'

'Sometimes I think you are very silly.'

* * * * *

Frequently we had to step aside to let mule trains by, the sound of their bells muffled by oaks whose branches were tufted with moss, like straggly hair. Sometimes we passed groups of men sitting beside the path without loads, unsheathed kukris stuck in their belts like cutlasses, but we left the forest unscathed and entered a stony country which led to what must be one of the longest flights of steps in the world. Three and a half thousand, Iman said. For those just setting out, going in the opposite direction, it must be a brutal introduction, for there are no trees to provide shade, and no foliage to disguise the extent of the climb. No wonder the obese people we had met the previous day were already at the end of their tethers.

We reached the valley of the Bhurungdi Khola and waited while an entire school of children commandeered the suspension bridge, leaning out over the void to watch their spit falling into the frothy river.

I was sitting alone, supping soup, when I heard someone shout, 'Pete!'

It was Barry, with Crisp, along with a new companion. It was comforting to see them again.

'I thought you were long gone,' I said.

'Crisp got the squits so we had to stay over in some god-forsaken barn for a couple of days. Meet Al.'

Al shook my hand firmly, and said, 'How you doing, mate?'

He was 19 and from South London, with black curly hair, film star looks, and the concomitant confidence.

I ordered a round of beers and we sat in the sun while scraggy hens warbled around us.

'Where've you been, Al?'

'Here and there.'

'On your own?'

'Well you see I started out with this *really* nice-looking Norwegian girl I picked up in Pokhara. I mean she was *really* tasty, if you know what I mean. But what a teaser. I mean she'd share a room with me but wouldn't let me in if you know what I mean. So I dumped her.'

'You left her all alone?'

'No, mate. I wouldn't do that. I'm not a heartless bastard. I fixed her up with a bunch of Canadian virgins going up to Jomosom so she'll be all right.'

Al was off to university in October to study psychology.

'Why psychology?'

'Because it's a piece of piss.'

'Then what'll you do?'

'Dunno. Set up as a therapist or some such. Sex guru maybe. Something glamorous. Make a lot of pennies. Cheers, mate!'

I don't know what Barry thought about this Lothario but Al certainly had Crisp's attention. He had charisma and a libido as subtle as neon. But this is hugely attractive to many women whose lives are padlocked to the warders with whom they share an open prison.

We set off together but I kept stopping to watch birds while the others went ahead.

The river was a series of translucent pools that spilled into each other. A spindly man stood by the path with a telescope on a tripod. A serious ornithologist.

'Seen anything?' I asked casually.

English, he spoke in a Pooterish manner. 'Down there. A pair of crested kingfishers, not to be confused with the pied which are significantly more diminutive.'

I raised my binoculars and watched black-and-white plumage flapping between boulders until they perched, their bayonet beaks pointed at the water. One dived in and emerged with a silver fish.

Something else caught my eye. 'There's a common kingfisher just downstream,' I said.

'Indeed?'

'On that branch above the big flat rock.'

Pooter panned his telescope. 'How do you know what it's called?' he challenged, as though we were contestants.

'Why wouldn't I?'

In fact I had already seen one upstream and had looked it up in my book. The bird flashed orange, green and blue in the sun, plunging, tern-like into the river.

'Can you hear that?' I asked.

'What?'

'A cuckoo.'

'Indeed. But what cuckoo is it precisely? After all, several varieties are to be found in the vicinity and they're very hard to tell apart without visual corroboration.'

I imagined him talking to his wife when they were making love. 'Excuse me, dearest, but I have an interest in attempting congress in the manner of the sulphur-bellied warbler whose mating habits I observed whilst in the Himalayan foothills. If you wouldn't mind wearing this feather boa?'

We ambled through bamboo forest and left the Annapurna Conservation Area at the tidy village of Birethanti, but once across the bridge over the Modi Khola we left spick and span and immediately rejoined unsanitised Nepal. The Third World re-entered.

Mangy dogs and threadbare children roamed the favela-like streets of Nayapul. It's here that porters and muleteers – or rather entrepreneurs – strike up deals to buy and transport all manner of goods from kerosene to washing powder, trinkets to chickens.

Suddenly, after the mountains, I saw sadness in almost every face. That desperation. That knowing that unless a deal is struck the children will not eat. Men jumped in front of me like rugby forwards, offering this and that; things I didn't want or need. I declined, unable to hold up the Third World, like Atlas. And I smelt human shit again, for the first time since leaving Kathmandu.

Barry and Crisp were sitting disconsolately in a *bhatti* by the bus stop, having missed the bus.

'Where's Al?' I asked.

Crisp answered, enigmatically: 'We had a parting of the ways.'

I suggested a taxi, and we all crammed in, me in front, the seat belt as functional as a cummerbund.

Question: Why do cab drivers invariably drive dangerously?

Answer: Because they know you'll be so relieved to arrive alive you'll tip them over the odds.

Switchbacks led to a plain where the only verticals were the elongated necks of herons and cattle egrets reflected in drainage channels.

Pokhara's outskirts are ugly and chaotic, the traffic anarchic, the pedestrians on death wish missions; but all calms down in Lakeside where people like me stay. The difference between Hackney and Knightsbridge.

Promising to meet, we dropped Barry and Crisp off and went to a real hotel which seduced me, temporarily, with its hot shower and double bed with sheets. I sat on the terrace with a cold beer and a colder South African woman who was seeing the world as a penance.

We chatted as I watched a female Nepali hod-carrier balancing an impossible tower of bricks up a rickety wooden ladder onto the skeletal roof of a new concrete hotel.

I was back in a city, and loathed it: the sound of running water which had pervaded our entire journey replaced by a soundtrack of traffic, and the stink of carbon monoxide.

Iman appeared, beaming. 'Tonight, Peter, we go for a special meal to celebrate.'

He led me to a tourist joint. Nepali dancers performed

to live music on a stage around which tables were arranged, but it seemed as authentic as an item from a TV holiday programme. You know the kind I mean? Shots of the *faux* naive presenter pretending to be incapable of lying on a surfboard in Hawaii before cutting to the all-inclusive cabaret at the 'international' hotel where Gauginesque girls in grass skirts (with Methodist knickers underneath) shudder their hips, their breasts unethnically covered by bikini tops and garlands. But it was what Iman thought I wanted, so I said nothing.

It had been a long, long day. It was hard to believe that it had begun at 4 a.m. with Dhauligiri, five miles high, on the horizon. Fatigue and beer turned me maudlin.

'Thank you, Iman. For everything. For leading me safely and being such a companion.'

We clinked glasses and I choked, aware that a tear was running down one cheek.

'What is the matter, Peter?'

'The knowledge that what seemed a continual present has already become the past – now only a memory which will fade away like all memories.'

The roots of my sadness were deep-seated. Our journey was akin to the raising of my children: the awareness of irretrievable time that had precipitated my breakdown. My sons' bedrooms, upstairs as I write, redundant, still papered with their posters of basketball heroes and pop stars; their beds, carpentered by me, too short for them now, awaiting sporadic visits.

Objectively parenthood should be seen as a continuum but the cuddles have fled. No more reading them favourite poems or imparting enthusiasms, 'Look! Don't move. Just there, beside the stream. A roe deer.' And none of the insurance the religious have paid for. No hope, for an atheist, of reliving such love in heaven or its equivalent.

When I express my despair those with religious faith either pity me or adopt the posture of a military court, accusing me of cowardice in the face of what is obvious to them. Cowardice? To believe that when you die you don't 'fall asleep in the Lord' and are even denied dreams? Not cowardice. Not bravery either. Just what you believe.

Oh you cuckoo parents, so many of you, who can't wait to abandon your children in order to *get your own lives back*. A curse on you and your kind; you cold aliens for whom the human race offers no warmth, not even for your offspring.

24

I rose before dawn and was drawn towards the lake called Phewa Tal. Warm mist filled streets empty apart from sleeping black buffaloes huddled together like piles of peat. White egrets roosted in tall bamboo fringing the King's summer palace but I dared not take photographs because machine guns pointed from pillboxes, protecting the monarch from his people. After all, I might have been a Marxist mercenary planning a coup, my photos intelligence.

The great lake of Pokhara was a vast mirror, a templed island just offshore doubled in size by a perfect reflection. Looking back I saw Machhapuchhare, its silhouette new from this angle, turning pink. How I missed the mountains.

A flock of egrets flew down to the shore where they stood in the black mud, picking at tit-bit breakfasts. A fish-eagle skimmed across the lake, its talons spread, scooping a silver sliver from the quiet water.

An underfed man approached me. 'Tea, sir?'

'Yes, please.'

He returned a little later with a china cup and I sat on a rowboat, sipping, as the sun turned the wooded hills opposite to gold.

There was wealth here. Mansions, painted cream, made their statements in the forest, none impinging on its neighbours, and I was reminded of the Swiss lakes. Such enclaves of profligacy can be seen from the promenade in Como, although the have-nots there at least have social security. In Pokhara these palaces are an insult.

A barber owned a shed at the end of the alley leading to my hotel, and he shouted at me. 'Shave, sir?'

He reminded me that I now had a beard, flecked with grey, that was itching horribly in this subtropical climate.

'I'll do it myself,' I called back, but my disposable Bic failed. I managed an oblong on one cheek, resembling an aerial photo of a clearing in the Brazilian jungle, and realised that I needed professional help. I returned to the barber who welcomed me with open razors.

Aware that HIV is now a real hazard in Nepal, I said, 'New blades?'

'Of course, sir.'

I sat in a scuffed chair opposite an image of a sexagenarian or more who, I had to admit, looked almost distinguished. The cut-throat was not as lethal as I had envisaged. A blade like a scalpel's was peeled from a paper wrapping, like chewing gum.

'Look, sir, no tricks.' He doused the blade in Dettol before slotting it inside.

Shaving normally takes me two minutes but here it was different. It was a performance. No one had ever shaved me before. In fact I had never understood why anyone was too lazy to do it for themselves. All those Chicago gangsters pinioned to their barbers' chairs. Didn't they know it was a set-up? Hadn't they seen the movies?

He coated a brush with foam and rubbed froth into my skin for an eternity. Then the cutting began; cheeks first, the blade wiped on a cloth, then the chin, at which point the blade was substituted, like a sharp footballer. Doing the difficult bits – around my Adam's apple and top lip – he pinched the skin, and I relaxed. This is what he had done all his life. When it was all over, he began again: more foam, more shaving. Then a brick of crystalline stone was rubbed into my face.

'What's this?'

'Alum.'

'Why?'

'It's good for cuts.'

But there weren't any cuts, unless they were hairline.

My skin was as bald as a hard-boiled egg.

Oil was rubbed into my face and I thought it was all over; but then the massage – which I hadn't bargained for – began. Little pushes at first, above my eyebrows. Then my scalp, cheeks, chin, nose and lips. It was the nearest I've come to a homo-erotic experience in my life. My T-shirt was removed and he went to work on my arms, wrists and hands. A pink cushion was produced and placed on the sink in front of me.

'Head on that.'

I obeyed. For thirty minutes he massaged my back, his firm fingers ironing out all the tensions that had built up during the previous weeks, his hands only once going below the belt (but only just) to soothe my lower back muscles.

I sat slumped like a toddler having an afternoon nap, and like a toddler I didn't want it to end, the manipulations sending waves of comfort through my body.

'Sit up.' He clasped my head in a commando grip. 'You want a neck jerk?'

'Best not. No, thanks.'

It was over. I paid and left, feeling rubbery, my legs – which had been excluded – belonging to another, older, man.

I walked along the lakeside street, passing dusty pipal trees and steaming cow turds.

A grizzled hippy (headband *circa* 1967) sat cross-legged on the road, smoking a spliff.

'Hey, man, what's your hurry?'

He exhibited all the physiognomic traits of a long-term puffer: concave cheeks as wrinkled as deflated balloons, and eyes that were empty, the antithesis of a window of the soul: almost human but blank.

'Where're you going, man?'

'Just walking.'

'Just walking, eh?'

He nodded in the pseudo-sage way such people nod as if the jerking of cervical vertebrae was an empathetic Masonic gesture.

'That's what it's all about, man. Just walking. Learning about things.'

'What've you learned?'

'About things. You know? This and that.'

'No. I don't know. What?'

'If you don't know, man, I can't tell you.'

I never found out.

I passed Al, his tentacles wrapped around two blondes, but he didn't reply when I said hello. Perhaps he didn't recognise me without my beard? Or perhaps he was just the two-faced priapic phoney I'd taken him for.

I sat in a café, drinking coffee, thumbing through my *Rough Guide to Nepal*, looking for places to visit. I had won the book in a *Sunday Times* competition. Second prize. First prize was a family holiday in Florida, but I have a record of coming second. The first was in a *Woman's Own* competition when they supplied the first line of a limerick I had to complete, sponsored by Heinz. I was commuting to the BBC studios in Manchester from Wales at the time, and trains have always been a mainspring of creativity. Each Monday I composed a limerick as I trundled past Connah's Quay: six weeks of competitive poetry in the tradition of Edward Lear, and the promise of six weeks of fabulous prizes ranging from world cruises to jewellery. I came second four times and have four PVC Heinz aprons to prove it. But the best was a *TV Times* competition to win a piano. The package arrived. I had come second. I received a *How To Play The Piano* booklet along with a piece of narrow folded cardboard. It was a keyboard complete with all the notes, ebony and ivory, but when I touched them they were mute.

* * * * *

I knocked on the door of The Three Sisters but was asked to come back in half an hour. So I found a ramshackle bar, ordered a beer, and stared out onto the lake which had been whipped into an ocean by squalls that curtained the water with black and yellow organdie. Bucking boats caught in the storm, heading for the nearest landfall, were being blown back by the wind, but there was nothing I could do except hope for the rowers' survival.

Between me and the lake were the freshwater equivalent of salt marshes where women dunked washed clothes in pools, surrounded by their children and grazing buffaloes.

Lucky Chetri welcomed me with open arms; the first liberated female Nepali apart from the guide, S, I had met. She is one of the original three sisters (the others are Dicky and Nicky) – hence the name of the trekking agency, which had been inaugurated in 1993 to provide not only bespoke trekking services for female clients, but as a symbol of women's emancipation in a country where females are treated, by and large, like dogs.

'Professionalism is what gives us our credibility,' Lucky explained. 'Our guides have four years' apprenticeship during which they're paid, and we supply free accommodation and food.'

'Was it hard getting started?'

'Oh yes. Everyone laughed at us. Women going to the mountains! But why not? You've been to the hills. You've seen women carrying huge loads. So physically there's no problem. After all, you have female mountain guides in Europe. And women have climbed Everest.' She smiled. 'That only leaves intelligence, and although that's obviously not a problem for people like you and me there's a mindset in Nepal where women are considered chattels – not by everyone but by most.'

'How do you cope with the caste system?'

'By ignoring it. There are no restrictions. Even the

so-called untouchables are welcome here if they're capable of doing the job.'

'So you're a pioneer?'

Lucky laughed. 'I suppose we are, but attitudes have *got* to change. After all, what's the alternative? It's the twenty-first century and if Nepal's not to remain a backward country we must use all the talent we can.'

I hope she is right and that her philosophy blossoms, but courageous women like her have centuries of superstition weighing against them. Only yesterday I heard of two women being murdered in Nepal for being witches. Women can be sold for the price of a buffalo, and more than 50 per cent are the victims of domestic violence.

Of course the Brahmans, the priestly caste, don't help. Like clerics everywhere, they promulgate the status quo, hindering political and social progress. Five per cent of pregnancies result in the death of the mother, and female children are far more likely to die from malnutrition than their male siblings. Because they are not as useful, they are given less to eat. Simple as that. Evil as that. But what do the priests care? It is the way of the world. Fate. Sitting on their privileged arses as babies die around them. Brahmans: the warlocks in the machine.

Some say that tourism is ruining Nepal. You know the type: 'When I first came to Nepal in 1963 I would walk for days without seeing another Westerner. Now it's like Ibiza.' I'm glad, not only because tourists bring in much needed foreign currency, but because, by and large, visitors are serious and committed, and their example must rub off on the Nepalis. Many women trek into the mountains, and their independent spirit is noticed. It's not like Ibiza at all.

I took Lucky's picture and sauntered back to the town centre.

'You want marijuana, sir? Best quality. Give you a real buzz. Blow your mind.'

It might have been nice, sitting by the lake with a nostalgic joint, but I turned him down. Entrapment laws are lax in Nepal and I had no wish to see the inside of a Nepali prison, which are notorious for their squalor. As I write there are new inmates crowding the cells: journalists who have spoken out against government corruption. There has been a State of Emergency since the autumn of 2001, and the first casualty, as always, has been the truth. True, in 2002, there have been massacres of police on an unprecedented scale, and subsequent killing, on an unprecedented scale, of Maoists. The civil war – for that is what it is – has shifted from the far west to areas where tourists trek, and such publicity is bad for the economy.

The Maoists know that dollars help a proportion of the population, and so far no tourists have been caught in the violence, but they might be put off from visiting Nepal by accurate reporting. So what do you do? Simple. Put journalists behind bars. Report only the good news. It was always thus. Tourists have been robbed by people purporting to be Maoists but not by the genuine cadres of the elusive leader, Chairman Prachanda.

The storm hoovered up the valley and revealed the sun, and I sat on a lawn overlooking the lake, eating a rare sirloin buffalo steak in a setting which, in Europe, would have cost me an arm and a leg. The bill arrived: £1.50 plus tip.

Surrounded by exquisite palms I spent the afternoon writing and reading, noting new birds perching on spiky fronds: iridescent lesser racket-tailed drongos with ridiculous bladderwrack tail feathers trailing like wires, and crimson sunbirds with bills like thin arches, their plumage an exotic combination of reds, green and yellows.

I bumped into Barry in the street.

'Christ!' he said. 'You look so much younger without the beard. I hardly recognised you. Say, we're having a kinda party tonight for the Thorung La lot in the Maya. You'll come of course?'

'Of course. Seen Fred?'

'No, but the last I heard he was off to Everest Base Camp.'

Good old Fred; the boy within rediscovered.

* * * * *

I joined the party late. Much booze had already been drunk and I tried to catch up. I recognised most of the faces facing each other along the cobbled-together long table. There was Barry and Crisp, Al squeezed between two new women, the Dutchman, Piet, and many whose names were already half-forgotten. We ate and drank but I missed Fred. Most were young enough to be my children, and despite the jollity I gradually succumbed to melancholy during this last supper. I saw the exuberance in these young faces; the optimism, the potential. But I saw beyond. I knew the compromises they would be forced into making; the inevitable disillusion; the impossibility that this glowing moment would be able to warm their future lives except in dreams.

I imagined my own sons sitting there, growing older, with the battle of life ahead of them, their talents likely to be thwarted by the grey people who rule our country like malevolent bullies. In my mind I was seventeen, but to them I was fifty-four, and I was out of kilter. I was Banquo's ghost, and so I left the feast, quietly.

I walked down to the lake and sat watching the moon's reflection. All the sorrows welled up. Nothing religious, only the inevitable. My sons' future deaths. My wife's. Mine. This image of the moon over the lake extinguished forever and, in turn, the writing down of this image, read by my children, lost forever.

It is unfashionable to like Dylan Thomas. I don't like him either; I adore him. I love his passion for sounds, and having lived in a Welsh village for ten years I feel a strong affinity with *Under Milk Wood*. Polly Garter's song is the first of my Desert Island Discs and the dialogue between Captain Cat and Rosie Probert is poignancy personified. The old, blind, sea captain, with Rosie's name tattooed on his belly, talks to her in his imagination, and she replies:

> *Remember her.*
> *She is forgetting.*
> *The earth which filled her mouth*
> *Is vanishing from her.*
> *Remember me.*
> *I have forgotten you.*
> *I am going into the darkness of the darkness forever.*
> *I have forgotten that I was ever born.*

Clever modern poets despise him because he was original, unrepeatable; his heart written on his sleeve. And of course he was a sponger and a drunkard and an adulterer. So Bohemian! All that alliteration! All those compound words! So Gerard Manley Hopkins without even the excuse of a god!

Of course there are extraordinary modern poets. Seamus Heaney writes of his father with great affection, as in 'Digging', but no one can better Thomas' 'Prayer for My Father'. I think that it is the best poem ever written.

I too, raged, and tears dripped from my eyes, tingeing my lips with salt.

Holidays – call it travel if you will – are often the saddest of times. They thrust ordinary people into extraordinary settings where the humdrum of their lives is thrown into confusion: the loneliness of the thronged resort; the black nights without a routine to follow at dawn; the memory of aspirations shot down by vicissitude.

And funny foreign food.

25

We left Pokhara on a tourist bus, better than public, my fists full of bananas bought from depot traders. The interior smelled of deodorant, aftershave and gel, and there was room to stretch legs.

We were stopped by plain-clothed police in Dumre who demanded Iman's documents. After all, he was dark-skinned, a prune amongst apricots, and without his papers he would have been ejected like a Cape-coloured in South Africa before the rescission of the apartheid laws. But he was my servant, so legitimate.

With summer approaching, Kathmandu was hotter now, noxious grey fumes seeping like marsh gas through the streets, scouring my nostrils and throat with an abrasive stink.

Next day, Iman took me to the zoo in Patan to show me red pandas, crocodiles and rhinoceroses. However, it was Monday and the zoo was closed. Big cats howled beyond locked gates and I will never discover if they were imprisoned tigers or snow leopards.

Iman, apologetic, suggested a taxi back, but I wanted to walk. So we strolled through Patan, the St Paul to the Minneapolis of the Kathmandu Valley's twin cities.

Think of Athens as the Parthenon. Then think again. The rest is a hideous hotchpotch of concrete. Patan too: dusty streets littered with crap and flanked by foul-smelling butchers' shops, selling flies it seemed. Sacred cows pawed cones of discarded offal which we escaped, every so often, to visit temples whose carved wooden iconography was as incomprehensible to me as the bosses of a medieval Devon church would be to a Hindu tourist.

'What is that green man? What has he to do with Christ?'

'Nothing at all.'

'So why is it here?'

'A throwback to paganism.'

'But this is a church.'

'So why do you have men fucking donkeys carved into your temples?'

'It's emblematic.'

'Of what? Man's inhumanity to dumb animals?'

'Everything's open to interpretation.'

Interpretation. The usual excuse. Without it what would the world's clerics have left to do?

Iman made up for his gaffe the following day. He took me to Swayambhu, core of Buddhist belief in the Kathmandu valley. We arrived early but, because it was an auspicious time moon-wise, it was already heaving with people. Imagine being outside an Everton-Liverpool match half an hour before kick-off, and there you have it. Frenetic men in yellow robes danced to drums and horns, oblivious of their surroundings, as egocentric as Hare Krishna mantra-munchers in Oxford Street.

I was at a rave.

The flight of steps leading up the *stupa* was chock-a-block with countless thousands of pilgrims and I lost Iman in the throng as I bustled up through monks and laity whose eyes exhibited that frightening born-again quality: too much white, not enough iris. Are born-again Christians actually Buddhists manqué? Discuss.

As a work of art, the great gilded *stupa* is undoubtedly powerful; the unblinking eyes staring out over the city. There is symbolism everywhere that means everything to the faithful even though it is based on what I believe to be preposterous stories about a lotus blossom growing in a snake-infested lake, et cetera et cetera. You don't have to be a Christian to appreciate Renaissance painting. You don't have to be a Buddhist to appreciate Swayambhu. I don't believe in the goddess Athene either, but that doesn't make her temple on the Acropolis any the less sublime. I don't believe in a Christian god, but Chartres Cathedral is still well worth a visit if you happen to be in the area.

I liked the monkeys because they are considered sacred but are iconoclasts. Pilgrims threw offerings of rice onto little altars representing one or other gargoyle-like god or goddess (why do they *all* have crazy-looking eyes?), and the monkeys immediately leapt in to scoff the lot. I guess that's all right though, the monkeys being symbolic and all that. Designate the squirrels in Hyde Park sacred, and one could set up a Nutkin Cult.

Today, in Gujarat, India, Hindus herded twenty-seven Muslims – men, women and children – into a building that they sprinkled with petrol. A Hindu man struck a match and burnt them alive. And why? Because there was a dispute over the site of a religious building. Mosque or temple? Muslims have not only been murdered, but raped. And in whose name? Vishnu's?

Iman led me down past aggressive sacred monkeys to the Natural History Museum, empty apart from us, where I saw a stillborn rhinoceros floating in formaldehyde and many stuffed birds, their ancient plumage turned to rust. But no red panda.

We walked back to Kathmandu through dirty, poverty-stricken streets, crossing a sewer of a river, but one picture remained. I suspect that she was a whore. She leaned out of a window, her black, *black* hair cascading over a blood-red dress. Gold earrings hung from her lobes, and she was, quite simply, the most beautiful woman I have ever seen: a Matisse model of a woman, her skin the colour of sand, and I will never forget her.

26

A man in a cheap suit stared at me at the bus station. A thin tie, like liquorice, bisected his almost-white shirt and there was something horrid about his eyes.

Iman and I boarded the bus bound for Syabru Besi, the start of our trek into Langtang. I sat by the window, Iman beside me.

Just before we left, a gang of youths boarded the bus and crowded the aisle, leaning over us, and I asked Iman to ask them to move away. There was room in the back.

'They say they're getting off soon.'

It was 6 a.m. I'd already been up for three hours, and dozed off as we left the outskirts of Kathmandu through avenues serried with poplars, heading for the hills on our seven-hour drive.

When I awoke, the gang had gone but the road had become a test of nerve. My immediate inclination was to get out. Horrendous drops fell into valleys devoid of trees; nothing to stop a bald-tyred bus from tumbling thousands of feet. At one point, where a landslide had blocked a gully, the driver pulled out into air to avoid a boulder the size of a bus, and I leaned out as half the tyres gripped space.

It got worse. I could see the excuse for a road winding for miles ahead, its unprotected edges overhanging even more frightening abysses. And when lorries hurtled towards us our driver refused to stop to allow them through. Instead we confronted each other, like stags in rut, edging past in machismo duels for no purpose other than stupidity. No wonder buses fall off and people die. And for what? *Karma*, that's what. If it is written … What a lousy way to lose a precious life. A footnote, perhaps, in the *Kathmandu Times*.

In the previous day's edition I had read a report of a

tragic incident which had made me laugh out loud, not because it was funny, but because it was almost unbelievable. A man, depressed by his wife's alleged unfaithfulness had attempted to hang himself from a beam. His brother-in-law had entered the barn and cut the man down, and the man was so incensed at being brought back to life that he attacked his saviour with a machete, injuring him seriously. The suicidal man then threw a fresh rope over a beam, knotted it into a noose and attempted to hang himself again. But the rope broke. He was next seen trying to break his skull with a rock in a field, but without success. So then he threw himself over a precipice, but landed alive and was subsequently arrested for assaulting his brother-in-law.

* * * * *

We stopped for lunch in Trisuli but when I opened my knapsack a host of documents fell onto the *bhatti* floor. I had been robbed, but selectively. Only the outer pocket of my bumbag had been violated, the pickpocket having been kind enough to rezip it. And things he hadn't wanted had been secreted into my knapsack. Such gentlemanliness. He had missed my passport and my cash which were secreted in a money-belt stuck to my pubes by sweat. Not even the Artful Dodger could have delved there without provoking a tweak.

The thief had stolen only my AMEX travellers' cheques and return half of my coach ticket from Heathrow to Exeter. Wild thoughts coursed through my brain. Inform the CID in London. Pick up any Nepalis heading for Exeter on the date stipulated and the whole gang might be brought to justice via Interpol. Anger was almost immediately replaced by admiration. The man with the liquorice tie at the bus station had obviously been Fagin.

Such skill. Such sheer professionalism. Was there a slum in Kathmandu where manikins bristling with bells and bumbags were fondled by destitute apprentices seeking a life in crime?

The road became considerably worse. At one point a landslide, masquerading as a highway, switchbacked through mud. Conversation in the bus ceased. Surely there was no way up? And the consequence of failure was certain death. The driver ordered the roof-dwellers off first, to reduce weight, and they ambled up a rocky staircase in the hope of regaining the bus at the top of the hairpins.

Our treadless tyres skidded in saturated gravel, and the indigenous seat-holders were the next to be ejected, leaving only a handful of Westerners and Iman. The driver scrunched into first gear but we slid back. Much shouting. Helpers from somewhere wedged boulders behind the wheels, and thus began a tortuous ascent, the driver's brow oiled with sweat and sebum.

It was like playing a bit part in a scene from Clouzot's *The Wages of Fear* – only the driver didn't have the *sang-froid* of Yves Montand and I couldn't be confident of seeing him in his next film.

I had read of fight-or-flight and my instinctive reaction to *get the hell out of there* was countered by an irrational desire *not to let Iman down*, not to funk it despite the waking nightmare. After all the bus would make it, or not, independent of my sitting in a seat from which escape was via a barred window through which only squid could squeeze.

There was no system. Lorries, burning out their clutches, passed us on their way down, their tyres skis, edging us towards oblivion.

We finally regained the horizontal, all born-again, whatever our beliefs or disbeliefs.

Our luggage was hand-searched by soldiers on the outskirts of Dhunche, on the edge of the Langtang National Park. Ostensibly they were there looking for prohibited items such as firewood and automatic weapons, but in reality the huge army base is a symbol of the Nepali government's commitment to conserve national sovereignty over an area bordering Chinese Tibet. Dhunche was the end of the line for a majority of the Westerners but Iman and I continued along a constricted intestine of a road that terminated at the sphincter of Syabru Besi whose piles are claustrophobically built between buttocks of flabby hills. It's a gold-rush town en route to the nugget of a new power plant up in the mountains, and it is not pretty, its dusty streets clangorous with great trucks full of rubble.

A little girl with captivating brown eyes approached the table next to mine at the lodge. Dick, a dentist from Colorado, was in conversation with Paula, a chiropodist from Calgary. Boy, was he smooth-tongued, in a rough way, like a lizard. I had tried to engage him in conversation before the chiropodist arrived but he had spurned me soon after I had spoken, my teeth, presumably, falling far below par.

'You want to buy?' asked the little girl, offering Dick an intricately woven wristband. 'Only fifty rupees.'

'No kid, not now. Maybe tomorrow?'

Dick was twiddling his glass of sugar-free water so assiduously that all thoughts other than fucking Paula were patently an intrusion.

The girl came across to me and I bought the wristband. When I had handed over the banknote the girl's mother thanked me.

'She makes them herself. It pays for her pens and her paper for school.'

'Believe that and you'll believe anything,' said the dentist, unnecessarily.

I addressed my words to the chiropodist. 'Don't let him screw you unless you're truly desperate. He's a horrid person and you'll only regret it in the morning.'

Dick opened his mouth, displaying teeth in need of dentistry, and said, 'Now, you listen here,' before running out of vocabulary.

27

I woke before dawn to find a coronet of fire surrounding Syabru Besi, the forest ablaze. I dressed and went out into the deserted street. Flames were descending towards the town, blown by katabatic gusts, and I wondered why the band of fire was so linear. Had it been started deliberately to clear the precious forest for cultivation? Or had lightning sparked a dry branch into this conflagration?

The air reeked of smoke and I imagined the entire population huddling together in the river as the town was razed.

Iman was unconcerned. 'It will go out. They always do.'

'What caused it?'

'Some accident but now there'll be more room for fields, and the ash is good for the crops.'

'But this is a national park.'

'Writing something with ink can't prevent misfortune.'

If I wanted my traveller's cheques refunded I had to report their theft. Iman led me to a shed where I joined a queue to use the only satellite phone.

For some reason I had to phone AMEX's Delhi office.

'How can I help you, sir?'

I explained the robbery.

'Have you reported this crime to the police?'

'I'm in the Himalaya. There aren't any police.'

'If you call back later today with the cheque numbers I will put you in touch with one of our advisers.'

'I won't be here later today.'

'In which case, sir, we have a problem.'

I could imagine him in a starched, short-sleeved, white shirt sitting under a ceiling fan, hidebound by bureaucracy not of his own making. The phone went dead.

'Bugger it, Iman. I'll have to deal with it back in Kathmandu.'

We left Syabru Besi down a slope littered with rusty tins and plastic bottles, crossed the Bhote Khola and Langtang Khola, and found ourselves alone in a lovely wilderness which followed the river, winding up stone staircases and down again.

There was scrub and stunted trees at first, then bamboo and, beside the bubbly river, rows of thin-boled broadleaved trees I could not identify.

A dog like a hound from hell jumped out in front of us and growled. His neck was encircled by a leather collar three inches wide bristling with steel nails; the sort of thing you might find in a Soho S&M retail outlet. A man in rags shouted gruffly at the dog which trotted haughtily over to his master, its legs rippling with muscles, its teeth as sharp as a mantrap.

Goats grazed amongst the trees, their backs and horny heads dappled with shadows.

'Why such a collar?' I asked Iman.

'Because it has only one job, to protect the flock. At night it is let loose and if a bear or leopard tries to kill a goat it will attack – no matter how fierce the enemy. That is what it is trained to do. And a bear or leopard's instinct is to rip out the dog's throat. That is why it has such a collar.'

'Surely it couldn't kill a bear?'

'It would die trying.'

Few trekkers take this route, most preferring the path from Dhunche, and the only tea house was a rudimentary hut, thatched with bamboo, run by a woman and her seven-year-old son who lived there in a Lake Isle of Innisfree simplicity, the husband employed as a labourer at some far-flung government project. They were only a proper family during the winter when these paths are impassable. Even Yeats, I suspect, would have decamped to Dublin during the winter, his cabin of clay and wattles no protection against frosty winds blowing in from the Atlantic. And in summer all those bees louding it in the hermetic glade would have turned him insane. A pretty fantasy, though, to which we all aspire when problems crush us.

And that little boy would, I surmised, be off to Kathmandu as soon as his older legs would carry him. No one with whom to play here, the same horizon every day and only his mother for a friend. Missing his father, he leapt onto Iman's lap and put his arms around him.

In our wretched island a man would not dare hug a strange child. The boy would have been pushed aside for fear of wagging tongues. But here there was innocence; not Eden before the Fall but an approximation.

'Doesn't he go to school?'

Iman asked him. 'He doesn't even recognise the word.'

Half a mountain had slid into the river at a place called Landslide on the map. Purple and yellow blooms flared above the bushes growing there resembling buddleias and laburnums, and the air was flappy with butterflies; orange, black-and-white and steely grey. Red-billed blue magpies hopped amongst boulders searching for insects, and the edges of the exposed path were rockeries of alpine flowers with minuscule lapis lazuli petals. Bunches of wild strawberries sprouted like tiny pink scrotums from crevices but I was in an eco-tourist state of mind, and refrained from eating them.

A steep path led down to the river where a hot spring erupted into gravel thrown up by a meander.

'You want a hot bath?' Iman asked, and although I was drenched with sweat I was put off by the blue plastic lining that the tea house owner had employed to attract passing trade.

We climbed through oak forests click-clacking with crickets. I wanted to see them but every time we approached they stopped scraping their wings together. So I asked Iman to wait. We sat quietly beside a waterfall, and within a few minutes the boughs above us were thrumming.

'There!' said Iman, pointing.

'Where?'

'There!'

It took me five minutes, using my binoculars, to find the insect, camouflaged as a flake of bark, twitching as it added its noise to the massed choir, crooning in search of a mate. It sounded like all the rest, but who was I to judge? To a female cricket it might have been a knee-trembling Pavarotti.

Two pink-cheeked, ginger-haired women approached at high speed, but stopped when they saw me peering.

'What're you looking at?' The *at* was pronounced *atch*.

'A cricket.'

'What for?'

'Because it's there.'

They introduced themselves. Bridie and Maureen, nurses from Ireland, were on a whistle-stop tour, already worn out.

'Why're you in such a hurry?' I asked.

'Because we're mad March hares,' said Bridie. 'We're due back in Dalkey in a fortnight and can't afford to waste time.'

Iman adopted his serious expression, and said, 'But you must take your time. Otherwise you will become ill.'

'Nurses are never ill,' said Bridie. 'We don't earn enough to be ill.'

'Have you got porters?' Iman asked.

'Sure, but they're bloody miles behind.'

'Where're you going to tonight?'

'Langtang village.'

'That's too far,' said Iman. 'Too high, too quickly.'

'Sure, we'll be all right,' said Maureen.

'Nice meeting you,' said Bridie, 'but it's time to go.'

They sped off into the forest as though late for a very important date.

We stopped for lunch at Langmoche, a bare boulder of a place where the Langtang Khola disappears beneath colossal rocks to emerge into a cascade hemmed in by cliffs, but at midday the sun's rays fell vertically and it was a jolly place.

'See that lodge?' said Iman, pointing to the highest of several. 'Six months ago that was the only one here. The rest were swept away in a flash-flood.'

'People were killed?'

'No. They all got out just in time.'

Since then the entire community had been reconstructed, an amazing feat considering the difficulties of carrying in raw materials. And unlike the Annapurna region, mule trains are not used in this cul-de-sac of a valley with no trading access to Tibet or passes linking Langtang with other regions of Nepal: everything carried up by men and women on their backs.

I needed to pee. A hut was perched over a rivulet leading into the main stream.

That is why you don't drink from or swim in the rivers.

I succumbed to lassitude. Full of rice I sat in the sun, my eyes closed, absorbing the heat, my cheeks and eyelids barbecuing.

'Shall we go, Peter?'

'No.'

'When?'

'Soon. Or a bit later.'

The pressure was off. There was no Thorung La to cross. We planned to climb a modest peak of 16,000 feet but I was in fine fettle; strong and lean and full of confidence. What did it matter if we did nothing whatsoever for an hour or two?

Then I suddenly went completely deaf in my left ear. It was like emerging after a high dive. Sound disappears but if you hop up and down there is usually a click and a feeling of tepid water flowing from the inner complexities of anvil, stirrup and hammer.

I jumped up and down but it didn't work.

'What's the matter, Peter?'

'What's that?'

'Why are you doing that?'

'One of my ears isn't working.'

'It's probably just the altitude.'

Instinctively I was already turning my good flap towards Iman.

Shadowy woods led to a rickety suspension bridge and a shaly path took us up, relentlessly, through pines with the river flowing fast below and beside us, its anarchic course blocked by fortresses of rock which dwarf firs gripped with roots like talons.

Clouds ahead of us cleared to reveal a terrific postcard. There, framed by spiky pines, was a mountain range, the Langtang Himal, rising to a mere 23,000 feet but as impressive as a new car in a showroom, each innovation a delight to the eye. Such style. The sheer shape of it. That curve of the bonnet. The subtle moulding of the boot. And the quality of the paintwork! Himalayan-white of course.

Iman was delighted that I was delighted. 'Photos, Peter?'

'But of course.'

We were back in the mountains and I was suffused by pleasure. Why, exactly, mountains have this effect I still do not understand, but they do. Every time. Like women.

Easy walking took us to Changdam, crammed under cliffs, where we checked into the Lama Guesthouse. I sat on the earthy terrace peering down on a well-heeled group of German tent-trekkers watching their servants setting up camp and preparing the evening meal.

Iman was in sparkling form. He was amongst his mates, playing *carrimboard*. You see it throughout Nepal: a simple square table with holes in the corners like snooker pockets, but wooden draughts instead of balls, each opponent with different coloured pieces and no cues. They are struck with a thumb, flicked against a forefinger. It looks easy but when I challenged Iman to a game he slaughtered me, his dexterity inexorably accurate. I tried to cheat, using a finger as a cue, but it was no use.

Guides and porters gambled for small stakes but I never saw Iman lose a single rupee. Miffed at my humiliation (I pride myself as a better-than-average snooker player), I wandered down to the river where I sat pensively watching the water flowing amongst Tintern Abbeys of boulders. Solitude.

A man approached, picking his way carefully amongst the rocks. We pretended to ignore each other but as he passed I said, 'It's hard, isn't it? Here we are, trying to be alone, but all we do is keep bumping into other people.'

He grinned but said nothing. Wiser than me.

An elderly man was sitting on top of a vast boulder, sketching. Below him, his son – I was later to learn – was bouldering, delicately traversing across a mini-face of rock, solo, his feet encased in magically adhesive climbing shoes obviously bought specially for this purpose. What a fool, I thought. Fall off here and you're in real trouble.

I changed my attention to the river and watched dippers diving into the foam. Then a cry. I turned and saw the artist throw down his sketchpad. The climber had disappeared. Quickly, I made my way over the boulder field and found the father, distraught, comforting his son, who had fallen. A huge block of rock had come away in the boy's hands and he had landed on his back. The sharp wedge of rock had sliced into a foot that was spouting blood, sliming the ground with goo. Both were in shock.

I had no medical training but had made a habit of carrying my first aid kit wherever I went.

Stopping the bleeding, I knew, was the first priority, so I covered his horrid gash with absorbent pads that were immediately saturated with blood. I found a roll of bandages and wrapped it around the pads, using it all. The boy, in great pain, kept shouting out, 'Sheiser! Sheiser! Sheiser!'

'Do you speak English?' I asked the father.

'Yes.' He was trembling all over.

'Go and get help.'

He didn't want to leave but I pushed him away. 'Get help, for Christ's sake!'

Blood was pouring through the bandages and so I tied another roll around, as tight as I could, and it stemmed the flow.

'Sheiser! Sheiser!'

The skin around his wound was blue and swollen and I didn't know if his leg was broken, but there was no compound fracture; no white twigs of bone protruding. Serious but not life-threatening, although I didn't know if his back or skull were damaged or if he had suffered internal injuries.

'You speak English?'

'Yes.' His gums were bloody.

'It must hurt like hell, but you'll be all right.'

'Sheiser! Sheiser!'

Within a few minutes a platoon of the trek's servants arrived, bounding over the horizon, leaping from boulder to boulder in flip-flops, followed by the father. They carried the boy away and I returned to the lodge, in shock myself, and ordered a large *raksi*.

A white-haired man from the German trekking group came over to me.

'I'm a doctor. Are you the man who did the first aid?'

'Yes.'

'I need a doctor.'

'But aren't you a doctor?'

'Yes, but I need a doctor.'

I felt like asking if he was ill. 'Why?'

'I need a needle to sew a deep cut.'

I rummaged in my bag but I had left the skin sewing-kit at home. My wife had urged me to take it, but I had said, 'What possible use can I have for this? I wouldn't know what to do. Besides, I have the weight to consider.' So I had left the curly bits of steel behind.

Someone else, overhearing our conversation, shot off and returned with the requisite gear.

A middle-aged Israeli couple sat down, shyly, beside me.

'Excuse me,' the man said, 'but I am not feeling well. I have been on the lavatory for three days shitting all the time even though I have eaten nothing. I don't know where it comes from. Can you, perhaps, help?'

Suddenly I had become a barefoot doctor.

'I think it's better to let it all out.'

'But we can't stand it any more,' said his wife. 'It's ruining our trip.'

'I've got some pills.'

'Oh, please,' she begged. I hadn't even said what they were. They might have been ecstasy. I delved into my bag and took out a pristine packet of Imodium. I squeezed one out of its foil like a spot, and handed it to the husband.

'Can I have some more?' he asked, like Oliver Twist.

I gave him another.

'More?'

Four was my limit without a prescription.

After dark I sat in the communal room drinking whisky while all around me trekkers imbibed water. I attempted to start up conversations but there was a youth hostel vibe; mumbling people poring over maps and getting excited about apple pies.

An English foursome played bridge beside me, their conversation restricted to trumps.

'Why are they so strange?' Iman whispered into my good ear.

'Because,' I said, 'they're already dead. They play cards because they have nothing whatsoever to say to each other and so they substitute hearts for love, and diamonds for ...' No metaphor came to mind so I said, 'Diamonds for diamonds.'

Iman tapped my shoulder. 'Let's leave this graveyard.'

He led me into the kitchen where we sat cross-legged by a glowing stove; pine logs, bubbling with resin, filling the air with their pungent scent. A porter was playing a three-stringed instrument, the hybrid child of guitar and sitar parents, but he was an adept, the plaintive sounds as delicate as subdued birdsong.

An abandoned guitar, minus its A and B strings, lay in a corner and I picked it up.

A jam session ensued, and although the music must have seemed cacophonous to the Protestant trekkers next door, we had fun failing to amalgamate Nepali folk tunes with the blues.

Raksi flowed from a bottomless plastic jerrycan; and the music got worse. The ceilidh continued for hours, long beyond the bedtimes of the trekkers who had all deserted the dining room by eight. Songs, redolent of Irish laments, began to flow from the porters. Tears, dyed red by the firelight, seeped like lava down sad cheeks. I could have been in Kerry.

We stumbled out into a starry night, me to my room up suddenly lethal stairs, the porters to their camp beneath a precipice lit by crackling wood fires sending explosions of sparks into the darkness.

28

By first light porters were designing a red cross of cloth, weighed down by stones, on a patch of gravel to guide the rescue helicopter into a precarious landing.

I was eating breakfast when the casualty's father sought me out.

'I want to thank you, before you go, for your help.'

'He'll be all right?'

'There is a suspected fracture but it needs an X-ray. I'll be flying back with him.'

'And your wife?'

'The boy's mother will continue with the trek.'

I could see her packing her rucksack while her son was carried by four porters in an improvised sedan chair towards the *ad hoc* heliport.

I shook hands with the father. Obviously his parental feelings were stronger than the mother's.

The Israeli couple joined me.

'I'm completely cured,' the man beamed, 'thanks to you. No shits at all in the night.'

'Glad it helped.'

The woman glowed with gratitude. 'Now we can be normal. Enjoy ourselves again.'

I had performed miracles. I felt like a saint, and all accomplished with a Sterikit Medical Emergency Travellers' Pack now devoid of bandages. I would have to be careful from now on.

* * * * *

We left before the helicopter arrived, and an hour into the forest a wild man leapt in front of me displaying his teeth; brandishing his arms above his head to exaggerate his height.

It was a male langur who bounded into a clump of bamboo and chattered at me aggressively. We had stumbled upon a group of monkeys, although 'monkeys' does them a disservice. Langurs are almost people, living in troops, their brown eyes windows into souls of a sort. They are coated with silvery fur, their faces masked with black, like bandits, their tails long and puffy like draught excluders, designed for balance.

The clan was all about us. Females clambered amongst branches, eating leaves, their skeletal upside-down babies clinging to their bellies. Some sat breast-feeding, staring at us as though we were obscure cousins at a wedding reception.

Iman and I crouched by the path, quietly, while the langurs got used to us. Then, bored it seemed, they languorously headed uphill, our presence irrelevant to their lives.

The steep path veered away from the green river and led up through dark oaks. Porters, male and female, some with children, were brewing tea, their blankets still lying damply under the overhangs where they had slept.

The river must have become waterfalls, out of sight, for after several hundred feet of ascent, we regained its banks at a delightful plateau. Cliffs fell into a forest of pines, bright with clearings in which rhododendrons grew, their flowers more varied here than further west: pink, white, cream and shades of red. Birdsong filled the air and we sipped strong tea outside a shack, served by a pretty girl with Tibetan features, dressed all in red with orange bangles around her ankles.

A flock of babblers, their copper feathers flicking in the sunlight, landed in a tree beside us, babbled a bit, and headed off towards the river.

'Have we far to go?'

'Two hours. Three.'

'So no hurry.'

Iman smiled and ordered more tea while I tried to identify a warbler hopping in and out of an evergreen bush. But warblers are almost impossible to distinguish the world over, apart from by their songs, and here all their tunes were new to me.

We strolled through rhododendron thickets, and a bird almost collided with my face before landing in a cluster of white flowers that drooped under its weight. Its blue back and red breast glinted as it sucked nectar, I presume, from the blooms. It was not bothered by us and I had time to look it up in my book. Its name is a delight: fire-breasted flowerpecker.

The valley sides are steep in places, and the path becomes logs levered into the cliffs, but the way is safe enough, and the drops didn't worry me. All around us we saw peaks hazy with clouds, and as we climbed up towards Ghora Tabela it became colder, pines giving way to larches, and then a dearth of trees except in gullies and beside the river, far below, where they were protected from the wind.

Pastures, where horses and yaks browsed, led us towards Langtang village, melt-water falls cascading from the glaciers and snowfields high above us. We were in the land of *gompas* and prayer flags again. Langtang is a proper village compared with Changdam which is merely a collection of purpose-built wooden lodges. There are lodges in Langtang too but the town, comprising stone houses and farms with shingle roofs, exists in its own right, independent of tourists.

Bridie and Maureen were sitting by a stove, Bridie staring out at a *chorten* in a field, Maureen with her head buried in her hands.

Bridie turned. 'Hey, you two. Good to see you both.'

'And you.'

I meant it. Bridie was utterly guileless. Not naive,

simply exuberant. Pleasant to other people and nice to be near. Maureen raised her head, and smiled a weak welcome.

'How long've you been here?' I asked.

'It's our second night,' Bridie explained. 'Your friend was dead right. We came up too fast and we've been in bed all day. I'm not too bad, but Maureen's a little under the weather.'

'Why haven't you gone down?'

'Jesus, Mary and Joseph! It was hard enough fucking getting up here.'

'But you've reached eleven and a half thousand feet in just three days. No wonder you're feeling lousy.'

'Ah, we'll survive,' said Bridie. 'Get a bit of booze in us and we'll be right as rain. I suppose you can *get* booze up here?'

'Oh yes,' said Iman. 'You can get it anywhere but it is not a good idea for someone like you.'

'Who *is* this man?' Bridie asked, winking. 'The sodding parish priest?'

I wanted to explore the village before dark, and set off up the stony street. Prayer flags, almost torn to shreds, flapped in an icy gale blowing down from Langtang Lirung, 10,000 feet above.

I saw no one apart from a couple stained to the knees with dung, as they mucked out a stable while their child threw rocks at a buffalo tied to a wall like a victim of a fundamentalist execution, unable to dodge. But perhaps she deserved it? An adulterous or a lesbian buffalo maybe?

Last night on TV I saw terrible pictures, filmed covertly, of an alleged homosexual being hacked to death in front of an invited audience in Saudi Arabia. A piece of real theatre. The swordsman was inefficient. It took three swipes to decapitate this poor victim of bigotry. The stadium sand was stained with his blood, and the Saudi oligarchy's hands are smeared forever, but they are our allies. They provided bases during the Gulf War and, more importantly, they give us oil.

Twenty years ago, a documentary-drama called *Death of a Princess* was made. An Arab princess was accused of adultery and executed. I missed the programme but wanted to see it. However, the Saudi regime complained to the British Conservative Government. The Foreign Secretary apologised profusely, French-kissing the arses of the Saudi establishment. Our unelected representative, on his knees, oiled international trade by promising that the British public would never again be subject to such a misrepresentation of Saudi justice again. And he, like all good diplomats, was true to his word. I never saw the repeat because it hasn't been repeated.

I headed uphill hoping to see Fluted Peak over the rise but the mountains were swaddled by strips of clouds the colour of dirty linen. So I headed back, across the pastures, teeth chattering, passing only a yak herder with a suppurating eye; but he smiled, revealing a toothless cave of a mouth.

A party was underway in the lodge. Half-empty glasses of *raksi* were displayed in front of Bridie and Maureen, and they were surrounded by porters and kitchen helpers playing charades under the hiss of kerosene lamps. Bridie was miming something, holding out her fingers and thumbs.

'Fourth word.'

'Ten,' said a porter.

'So?' said Bridie. 'So what is it?'

'The News at Ten.'

'Well done!'

Maureen's turn next. She drew a TV screen in the air with her fingers.

'TV,' said a cook.

'Good.'

Four fingers held up.

'Four words.'

'Excellent. First word.' Maureen struck an imaginary match.

'Match?'

'Great!'

And the cook got it in the end. 'Match of the Day.'

'You clever man!'

Iman and I joined in, a jug of *raksi* adding to the jollity. We gave each other impossible titles. Bridie handed me *Encyclopaedia Britannica* which meant breaking it down into syllables and having to mime cycling and peeing. Maureen got it.

Iman, sat, somewhat bemused. 'Do people in England do this a lot?'

'Usually only at Christmas,' I explained, 'or when they're too far gone to talk intelligently.'

'I see.' Did he?

'Tell me, Iman,' asked Bridie, sipping *raksi*. 'Why's Kathmandu so filthy?'

'Because there's not enough money to get rid of the litter.'

'The garden next to the place I was staying in was like a tip, full of rubbish.'

'It's very simple,' Iman explained. 'When your garden is full of rubbish you throw it over the wall into your neighbour's garden. Then he throws it over into *his* neighbour's garden. That way your own place is never dirty for long.'

Bridie pondered this for a few seconds. 'Ah! Now I see. It's a sort of revolutionary new recycling system.'

'Exactly.'

An elderly man sat in a corner, reading. I had said hello earlier but had misinterpreted shyness for churlishness.

Judging people too quickly is one of my vices, and I had categorised him as a miserable old sod. Bridie, her fair Irish cheeks glowing with *raksi* called out to him to join us.

'No, thank you. I am quite happy.'

'Stuff and nonsense. Join us or I'll get all these brutes of men to carry you over!'

The man closed his book reluctantly and crossed the room, walking strangely, as if injured.

'You OK?' asked Bridie.

'Very well,' said the man, sitting down in a practised way.

'Blisters?' asked Bridie.

'Not on this foot,' replied the man, rolling down a sock to reveal an artificial leg the colour of copper.

'God! I'm mortified,' said Bridie.

'Don't worry,' said the man, touching Bridie's shoulder. 'I don't mind. Not any more'.

'Well at least you can't catch frostbite,' said Maureen, and the man laughed.

Jurgen – for that was his name – was in love with the Himalaya. Nothing could prevent him from returning. I asked him why.

'Memories. I was a mountaineer once. My whole life was the mountains. They still are, but differently now. I was never a great climber, but a good one I think, in the traditional style. Like your Edward Whymper.'

'You climbed in the Himalaya?'

'Oh yes.'

He was too modest to mention what he had done, so I pressed him.

'The only thing of importance was climbing to the summit of Gasherbrum II in the Karakorum in 1986.'

Only? At 26,000 feet it wasn't climbed until 1958, five years after Everest succumbed.

'Is that where you lost your leg?'

'Oh no. A silly skiing accident in the Alps.'

'Do you look up at the mountains and still wish you could climb them?'

'Yes. And no. They are dangerous, and because of this,' he said, tapping his prosthetic limb, 'I know that I cannot. And so I am alive. So many of my friends are dead. But in here, inside, I can still climb them.'

The *raksi* flowed as if from a clear, sacred spring, and Iman sang a beautiful song; a melodious lament, its trills almost Celtic, and I watched as Bridie's eyes become glossy with repressed tears. I asked Iman what the words meant and he explained that it was about a young couple in love. The boy was going away to the city and the girl had given him a piece of cloth to remind him of her. Should he leave it, flying like a prayer flag in the mountains? Or take it with him to the city where he could touch it as if it were her? A dilemma. As simple as that.

No one felt like charades any more.

* * * * *

My lost boys came to me in the night as they had done weeks before in Yak Kharka; again, perhaps, my brain supplying me with visions based on oxygen deprivation. Reciting mantras or singing Gregorian chants has a similar effect.

They were five and three, dressed as knights, holding the shields I had jigsawed out of plywood for them, painted silver with red St George crosses. They were Sir Pedr and Sir Padrig, long blond hair curling down from their plastic knights' helmets.

We lived in Welsh Wales then, surrounded by castles: Caernarfon, Harlech, Beaumaris and Conwy, which we often visited. I had made them a castle too, staying up until 5 a.m. on Christmas morning, waiting for the glue to stick before I could paint it Welsh grey.

'Why did we have to grow up?' they asked me in my sleep. 'And why are you so old now? Will you die soon? Will we?'

I woke, my cheeks again slippery with tears.

You don't have to worship the pseudo-gods, Jung and Freud, to realise that dreams are significant, and there was no mystery about this one. I was returning to a time of bliss, gone forever, and was concerned because, like all parents, I foresaw my children attending my funeral. And although they would survive without me, as we all do, I could envisage their own deaths, which was horrible to me.

But we are physical beings and I needed a crap. This was not en suite-land so I put on boots and my down jacket and shuffled out into the two-mile-high night.

There was a black boulder at the bottom of the stairs which became a massive sleeping dog dreaming, perhaps, of its long lost puppies. But it was big. Should I wake it and say, 'Good boy,' or attempt to step over it, risking a sudden lunge?

I stepped over, found the latrine, then wandered out under a sky so twinkly that I simply stood there, gazing up, refusing to believe that the nearest was four light years away, and that what I was seeing happened in 1997. Travelling at 40,000 mph it would take a spaceship 70,000 years to reach the nearest star.

Not wanting to return to my dream-hut, I carried on across a soggy pasture towards the *chorten*. All that symbolic architecture rooted in the lives of the people sleeping here, but an enigma to me. How I wished for such certitude although I knew that, with time running out, I would never snuggle down cosily beside a guardian angel.

Shivering, I fled back to my sleeping bag.

29

When H. W. Tilman first visited Langtang in 1949, he described the people as, 'Engagingly cheery, tough and dirty; but they have sufficient regard for appearances to wash their faces occasionally, and were scrupulous to remove those lice which strayed to the outside of their garments.' It was different now: no scratching, but soapy washes and much abrasive brushing of teeth at the pump outside the lodge, the rim of the basin spiky with a jaw of ice.

My stomach baggy with porridge, I followed Iman up into a valley roofed by cloud. We tramped through fields, off-course, disturbing flocks of snow pigeons whose grey and black wings clapped into the sky, their white-banded tails flapping with a hundred chevrons.

A farmer shouted at us as we clambered over a drystone wall to regain our path but we dislodged no precious rocks, for there is a simple technique which I learned in Wales and on Dartmoor. You keep your weight vertical, gaining the top of the wall with a deft mantelshelf movement, then jump down. Simple as that.

Mani walls, far longer than any I had seen previously, bisected the trail, and we passed on the left, as is the custom. Prickly scrub, bent immutably by the wind and smelling of cinnamon, lined our path, but there were flowers too, pressing up from the hard earth, which I thought were gentians. But they turned into wild irises, their delicate purple petals somehow surviving the wind's onslaught.

A woman, alone, was slumped by the path. It was Maureen.

'Where's Bridie?' I asked.

'Not far ahead. With the porters.' Her words were slurred; not the result of a hangover.

I turned to Iman. 'We must take her down.'

Iman scanned the horizon, put his fingers into his mouth, and whistled with an intensity I had never heard before. It hurt my teeth, like chalk scraping on a blackboard, echoing back from the mountains.

A silhouette on a rocky horizon half a kilometre away stopped and whistled back.

Iman whistled again. They were talking like dolphins.

'It's all right,' said Iman. 'They are coming down.'

We waited with Maureen until Bridie and two porters arrived, running.

'Your friend has mountain sickness,' Iman explained to Bridie. 'She must go down as fast as possible.'

'Ah well, maybe we'll make it next year,' said Bridie, hiding her disappointment heroically.

The porters got Maureen to her feet and they set off immediately, the porters supporting her as though she were a drunk or under arrest.

Bridie shook my hand. 'Goodbye, Peter.'

'Goodbye. And thank you for your company. I'll miss you.'

'Me too. I had some real mean charades lined up for you for tonight.'

'What?'

'You'll never know.'

I kissed a cold cheek. 'Bye.'

'Bye.'

Bridie turned and walked out of this page.

'Shouldn't we help them?' I asked Iman who replied by raising his eyebrows. I had insulted him. He knew the porters; knew that they were perfectly capable of taking Maureen to safety. But I, interfering like a bumptious colonial, was questioning his judgment. We carried on and I, ashamed, let Iman pull ahead.

I reached a little plateau where, in the middle of

nowhere, there was the most beautiful *mani* wall placed like a great sculpture in a gallery whose walls were air and white mountains. I took photographs, taking particular care about exposure and composition as if I were on an assignment, which I was.

'Peter!'

It was Barry, grinning, an ice-axe protruding from the top of his rucksack. Crisp wasn't far behind.

'Hello!' I said. 'What're you doing here?'

'Going up, as always. Except when we're going down.'

'Ice-axe?'

'I hired it. We're planning to go over the Kanja La.'

'Is that wise?'

'Anything to avoid the bus trip back. Crisp absolutely refuses to go through that again.'

'Too fucking right,' said Crisp, panting.

The Kanja La is not as high as Thorung La but more difficult, requiring mountaineering experience. Glaciers have to be crossed, and there are no lodges in which to stay. On the far side there is bandit country. Several Westerners have been murdered there in recent years. A guide is recommended but Barry and Crisp were alone.

'Where're you going?' Barry asked.

'Kyangjin. Then up the valley to explore a bit. Climb Tsergo Ri with a bit of luck.'

'How high's that?'

'About sixteen thousand feet.'

Sleet began to fall, greying the ground.

'Where's the fucking spring?' Crisp asked.

'It was lousy when Tilman was here too,' I replied.

'Who's Tilman?'

'Just another trekker.'

Iman and I huddled out of the wind drinking tea, gazing out into desolation. Upper Langtang drifted into a rocky valley of stones; a cold desert comprising pebbles scraped from the surrounding invisible mountains over millennia.

Hummocks of moraine led us up to Kyangjin which was already awash with snow; brown ponies, their backs roofed with white, foraging for food.

The lodge owner led me to a bunker and offered me a cell on death-row which I refused. Instead I insisted on a room with two cold windows which, in an average year, would have offered two beautifully framed vistas.

They make cheese at Kyangjin so I went to get some. It's made from yaks' milk but export is all – to India – and so I was only allowed to buy two hundred grams which I took to a lodge that advertised garlic bread.

I sat by the stove next to two Swedish couples who were playing Scrabble.

'How long've you been here?' I asked.

'Four days.'

'Why?'

'Waiting for the weather to clear.'

'Why?'

'Why not?'

The man resembled Bengt Ekerot in Bergman's *The Seventh Seal*, playing Death.

'There is an Englishman staying here,' said Death, 'who set off to climb Tsergo Ri this morning. He has not returned. The snow is bad. The wind is bad. We are concerned.' A tragedy would brighten his day.

I ate the cheese, hard and yellow as tallow, together with garlic bread consisting of half-risen dough nutty with uncooked garlic cloves. But as I was destined to kiss no one that night it would be all right.

I sat by the stove, my spine as cold as a fish finger, with nowhere to go. *Travel*. It sounds so romantic. There I was in a place which, until comparatively recently, was out of bounds to adventurers. And what was I doing? Just trying to keep warm in the company of Swedes playing Scrabble.

The door burst open and the Englishman entered, his face coated like an iced cake.

The Swedes welcomed him with disappointment. Shivering, he stood by the stove, thawing out.

'Did you climb Tsergo Ri?' I asked.

'Did I, fuck. Complete white-out conditions and my guide got us fucking lost. We couldn't see a bloody thing and we heard avalanches coming down all around us.'

'I was hoping to go up tomorrow.'

'You want my advice? Don't even think of it. Not unless the weather changes radically. It's fucking dangerous.'

'Where's your guide?'

'Don't know. Don't care. Gone off to get pissed with his mates, I expect. We had a row.'

I left him in the cold hands of the lugubrious Swedes.

There is a satellite phone at Kyangjin and I thought I should make one final effort to contact AMEX. I sat with Iman and the lodge owner who dialled the number in India. I set the stopwatch on my wrist.

A woman in Delhi answered. 'Hold the line, sir. I will be with you directly.'

I watched time ticking by.

'How much is this costing me, Iman?'

Iman asked the lodge owner. 'Five dollars a minute.'

'*What?*'

I had already spent 2 minutes and 51 seconds saying nothing, so I slammed the phone down and handed the lodge owner $15 which he pocketed immediately like a child given sweets.

Outside, a trekking party watched their porters putting up tents in the snow, and I recognised the injured German boy's mother. She recognised me too, but pretended not to and turned away.

The tents' ridges were already sagging under the weight of snow and in my thoughts I wished her an icy night.

* * * * *

The lodge dining room had filled up with middle-aged Germans and Swiss, who sat in silence worrying about food.

'Christ!' I said to Iman. 'Can you get hold of some *raksi*?'

'I will try.' He left on his quest.

A beaky girl with glasses squashed in beside me, placing a book on the floor.

She was a graduate student writing her Ph.D thesis about Langtang granite.

Meet her on her own ground, I thought, so I talked a bit about Dartmoor granite and the tors about which I had made part of a programme.

'How does it differ here?' I asked intelligently, or so I thought.

'It would be hard for me to explain.'

'You could try.'

'I don't think you'd be able to *begin* to understand.'

Obviously she had my number. I was too stupid.

Iman returned, triumphant, with a jug of *raksi* which we poured down our throats.

'What's that?' asked Beaky.

'Nepali hooch,' I replied. 'Want some?'

'I don't drink alcohol.'

'This is good *raksi*,' said Iman. 'And I know good *raksi* when I taste it. I've drunk it since I was six months old.'

Beaky's eyebrows formed Romanesque arches that almost touched her hairline.

'My grandmother used to give it to me when I was a baby,' Iman explained. 'It helped me sleep.'

'That's awful,' said Beaky.

'Why?' asked Iman.

'Drugging you when you were still a baby.'

I interposed. 'What on earth do you know what it's like raising a family on a poor farm in Nepal?'

'It's the principle that bothers me.' Spoken like a true Oxbridge academic.

'Tomorrow,' said Iman, unfazed, 'we will drink much *raksi*.'

'Why?'

'Because it is New Year's Day.'

'Tomorrow's Good Friday,' I said.

'Here it's New Year's Day, two thousand and fifty-seven, when we celebrate the birth of Shiva.'

'So we can celebrate the crucifixion and the birth of Shiva all at once?'

'Celebrate the crucifixion?' said Beaky.

'Why not?' I replied. 'After all, without it there wouldn't be any Christianity.'

'It's not the crucifixion but the resurrection that celebrates Christianity.'

'You don't seriously believe all that?'

'I believe that Christ is the risen Lord.'

Why, oh why, do such people use others' words to express their deep-seated thoughts?

'So, Iman,' I said, 'you believe that Shiva was born? A god born? In the West he's always been there. How can a god be born?'

'Christ was born,' said Iman.

'Yes, but that's just a story. Son of God and all that stuff. I mean how can a god be a man as well? It's a paradox. You're either a man or a god. You can be a god pretending to be a man or a man pretending to be a god but obviously you can't be both. It's illogical.'

Beaky spoke. 'Logic is the enemy of religion. Religion is a matter of faith.'

'And will faith be a part of your thesis about Langtang granite?'

'Of course not.'

'So it'll be based on science.'

'Naturally.'

'So how can you split your brain down the centre? Rely

on evidence for part of your thinking and superstition for the rest?'

'Faith isn't superstition. It's belief.'

'All faiths? Or only yours?'

'Every faith has something positive to offer.'

'Oh yes? Hindus too, with their disgraceful caste system?'

'If it works for them.'

'Cop out. It doesn't work for them. It makes people's lives unbelievably miserable. Ask any Harijan.'

Silence.

I looked up and the entire Calvinistic company was staring at me. I was an apostate, worthy of a warlock's pyre. Thus have we progressed more than two centuries on from the Age of Reason.

Barry and Crisp wandered into the void.

'Fucking snow!' said Barry, and I could sense Abbess Beaky flushing beside me. 'No way can we go over the Kanja La.'

'So what'll you do instead?'

'Go back via Gosainkund if we can.'

'Anything to avoid the dreaded bus,' added Crisp.

'*Raksi?*' I offered.

'Why the fuck not?' said Crisp, whose life would be lived out in total ignorance of granite.

Abbess Beaky huffed off, leaving a space for my new old friends, but her book remained on the floor. I picked it up. It was a New Testament.

30

Nothing is as silent or as insidious as snow – especially when you are entirely deaf in one ear. By morning the whole community was knee-deep in talc. Iman and I, our expedition over, sat supping weak porridge, killing time as we waited for others to break the trail down.

By the time we left the path had become a Cresta Run of ice down which Crisp, ahead of us, slithered unhappily, stopping every so often to regain her confidence, helped by Barry's outstretched hands. A blessing in disguise: Crisp negotiating the glaciers of the Kanja La could have proved fatal. We overtook them and reached Langtang village by mid-morning, so we carried on.

I had been concerned about retreating down the same path but it all seemed new. Only eyes in the back of the head would have superimposed a memory. And the sheer momentum was a pleasure. I glanced back, looking for sun in case our decision might have proved premature but the Upper Langtang valley was still a swirl of blizzard.

We descended 3,000 feet in no time, and even when the great grey tarpaulin of sky split, drenching us with torrential rain, we carried on, water dripping down my back turned to warmth by corrugated ribs that had become bony radiators.

We reached Changdam by lunchtime and stuffed ourselves with *daal bhaat* while our clothes steamed above the stove.

'Remind me what today is, Iman.'

'New Year's Day, Peter.'

'Time to celebrate.'

'*Raksi?*'

'Naturally.'

It was scandalous, drinking in the afternoon, the cold and empty room reminding me of Welsh pubs where, after a morning's writing, I would go to drink warm bitter and play snooker with elderly locals who tolerated me but despised me for not having a proper job like splitting slate at the quarry.

Wet walkers straggled in in drips and drabs, some going up, some down, and how uncouth Iman and I must have appeared, singing and talking too loudly, getting soused while the sun had yet to descend over the yardarm.

Back in the lodge quiet people sat reading paperback editions of *The Purity of Snow: Meditations of a Gulf War Veteran Turned Monk* (University of Death Valley Press, $9.99).

Having left university, I had taught in a primary school in the East End where the headmaster was a radio buff. He talked to people all over the world.

'What do you chat about?' I asked.

'There's an international convention,' he explained. 'We can talk about anything apart from politics and religion.'

'So what's left to talk about?'

He was nonplussed and I wondered why at the time, although he would have been completely at home in the lodges of Nepal in the twenty-first century.

Iman and I retreated to the kitchen where New Year celebrations were fully throttled; porters' throats draining down *raksi* and releasing babble and songs.

It's not given to many to leap forward in time. In 2057 – Greenwich Mean Time – I will certainly be dead. My children, if they survive, will be dandling my great-grandchildren on their knees. And with such melancholy thoughts in mind I got rat-arsed while the undead next door imported the culture of an English tea room to this extraordinary place.

Had there been scones they would have been ecstatic.

* * * * *

I had no memory of going to bed. Had we sung the Nepali equivalent of 'Auld Lang Syne'? 'Langtang Syne', perhaps? I couldn't remember. At least I was alone. No crone, her skin softened by midnight candles, beside me.

Still a bit confused I left town before dawn, heading downstream, stopping to watch yellow wagtails and white-throated dippers in the river whose water was the colour of the inside of oyster shells, swirling and oily in the grey light.

I had had enough of paths and climbed up steeply into the forest, my feet sliding on moss and brown earth concocted from rotting leaves, reeking of decay. I sat on a fallen tree, lacy with lichen, my back supported by an antler of a branch, and waited to be surrounded by wildlife.

I saw nothing but a red bird that might have been a minivet, and a brief flash of something small and furry like a squirrel: a pika possibly. Mist rose from the river speckling me and the leaves around me with droplets, but the sun's slant, rising above the gorge, slowly added orange then pink to this chasm; the light refracted, I supposed, from snow on mountains hidden from me by towering cliffs.

I sat for a long time as the day unfolded, glad to be doing nothing, half asleep but fully aware that I would never re-experience this long moment. When the sun finally showed itself over the crags it was already a fireball. The moss around me steamed and I stripped down to my T-shirt, already keen to retrace our steps up to Kyanjin; but when I slithered down to the path and looked up the valley I saw that it was dammed by an asphalt sky cracked by lightning.

Iman was pacing the lodge terrace like a sentry when I arrived back.

'Where you have *been*?'

'Wandering.'

'I was worried. Your bed was empty. You might have had an accident.'

'But I didn't. How're you feeling?'

'So-so.'

'Me too. So today we go nowhere. Today you'll find me a red panda.'

Relief at not having to trek anywhere was tempered by concern with having to supply me with a panda. Imagine a dad being asked to supply a particular teddy at a moment's notice for a child's birthday, and you will envisage Iman's expression.

'No panda, no tip,' I said sternly.

He remembered the joke and laughed.

Unencumbered by luggage we strolled up into the forest with no particular place to go. Rustling in the canopy drew our attention and we left the path, finding ourselves in a clearing surrounded by langurs nibbling at nuts and leaves, almost unmindful of our presence. Two males had a scrap while the harem watched, disinterested, it seemed, munching their leaves like tarts chewing gum outside a barracks. Males! All the bloody same.

Iman followed the troop up a mud chute oozing from a buttress of rocks, and was lost from view. When he returned, covered in muck, he said that he had got very close when one of the langurs picked up stones and pelted him. I took this with a pinch of salt but I have since read that langurs do, indeed, behave in this way.

At school I was taught that one of the things that differentiates us from other primates is our ability to use tools. That, of course, has since been disproved. Television is our witness. The other was the fact that only people use weapons. Not so. The scene in Kubrik's *2001*, where the ape uses a bone as a cudgel doesn't herald the transition between ape and *homo sapiens*. We both still use them. Men murder men. Chimpanzees murder chimpanzees. They can even paint pictures, even if they are invariably homages to Jackson Pollock.

Down by the river we watched another troop basking in the sun, spreadeagled on boulders like hairy nudists on a Greek island, grooming each other with great delicacy, picking out ticks and fleas like gastronomes savouring *petits fours*. But it couldn't last. The lager louts turned up, as they always do, exuding testosterone, and the inevitable brawls broke out. It might have been Faliraki.

Back at the lodge a heron-nosed Englishwoman in her sixties sat on the terrace, taking tea. There was a purple bruise on her cheek and I asked her how she got it.

'By falling off the path.'

'How did you do that?'

'I come every spring to watch the birds but I get so enthusiastic I forget to take my binoculars from my eyes and fall off things. I really must remember to stay still. Otherwise over I'll go again. Have you tried the cakes? They're frightfully good.'

* * * * *

That evening the base of the cliff just beyond the lodge was lit by a dozen wood fires in front of which porters and their families stood, casting their shadows onto the rock like cave paintings.

In the middle of the night I was woken by a great crash which I took for thunder but turned out to have been a rock avalanche. The porters and their families had slept close enough to the cliff to remain uninjured but the primeval forces shaping this wild country were epitomised when I walked over to see the debris. A boulder, like the blade of a huge chisel, had split an oak tree in two, revealing shredded white bark. Rocks had scythed through the hut belonging to a farmer who was already sitting, cross-legged, weaving a bamboo replacement roof, a wound over an eye where, presumably, shrapnel had gouged a new furrow in his wrinkled forehead.

But he was *staying put*: not moving his shack. Why not? Because, I suppose, of *karma*. What will be, will be. If the bullet's got your name on it ...

No one had died in the avalanche, but the whole community might have been wiped out. It happens. Build a home and it feels safe; gives a place that patina of human control. Not here. Horizons are restricted to the nearest crag. Above, rising for many thousands of feet, are more cliffs, and beyond them peaks heavy with snow. A minor tremor and it can all come tumbling down, humpty-dumpty; solid rock as flimsy as a house of cards, the lives of those below as irrelevant as a bug beneath a boot. No wonder the idea of reincarnation is more popular than rationality.

A Texan wearing shorts lay on a bench gladly suffering self-induced complicated isometric exercises. I attempted eye contact but he was too much in touch with himself to respond. His partner, a boyish girl with no tits and a pageboy crop, watched her Narcissus with reverence as she spooned white yogurt between her lips while he puffed and pumped himself up.

Iman and I breakfasted on *daal bhaat* with a surfeit of red chillies which I gnawed, hand-held.

'Be careful not to touch your eyes,' Iman advised.

I rubbed them on cue and had to rush out to bathe them like a mugger sprayed by Mace.

A young Israeli couple joined us. They were both called Ronnie – colloquially – and were dispossessed, wandering these hills in search of belief. The two Ronnies had emigrated from America several years ago but had found themselves increasingly at odds with Israeli policy towards the Palestinians.

'We went to Israel,' male Ronnie said, 'because we genuinely thought it would be a melting-pot. Judaism coupled with internationalism, but it's not like that. It's full of hatred and we don't know what to do. Try and change things from within, or give up? Go back to the States, maybe. Start again.'

He was the spitting image of Trotsky.

'Everywhere we go,' said female Ronnie, 'we are embarrassed. People say you treat the Palestinians in their camps like the Germans treated the Jews in the thirties and forties, and I can't think of any counter-arguments. Friends say I'm unpatriotic but I can't help remembering the words of Samuel Johnson, that patriotism is the last refuge of the scoundrel – and I don't want to live the rest of my life as a scoundrel.'

What, with my attitude to organised religion, could I possibly say? The seeds of doubt were already growing within them. I could only hope that they would be true to themselves, eventually, and do good without a god holding a gun to their temples.

31

Iman and I planned to amble down to Langmoche and spend the night there but the prospect of silence disquieted me. I had listened to my short-wave radio during the night, and the world appeared to be falling apart under avalanches of terrorism: evil regimes performing despicable acts against their critics. Palestinian teenage sons and daughters wrapped in sexless underwear comprising explosives, designer-labelled for indiscriminate carnage. Children exploited and exploded by religious maniacs whose wicked acts are, inevitably, excused in the name of God: bigots whose enemies have not yet learned to walk or talk. But, after all, didn't God demand the slaughter of first-born Egyptians, like Herod, later?

Going for a stroll as I was, meant nothing at all, and my impotence when faced with the great whore of the world was weighing me down. Yes, we saw more monkeys, flowers, butterflies: pretty and interesting things, but when we reached Langmoche my decision to hasten on, to move, was reinforced by young love. A beautiful couple were sitting outside their room after a night of love-making. How could I tell? I could tell. And I was filled with envy, regret and fear.

I saw myself in him, thirty years before, when time was sluggish and there was everything to live for, even if it were only the moment: the entwining, ecstatic moment: the naive hope in humanity's intrinsic benevolence; a belief that the world would inevitably change for the better, advised by history. And I sorrowed for them.

It is almost a year since I watched their lovers' looks. Perhaps they are still together, perhaps not. But that year has fled faster for them than their previous years. And for me, no time at all; the accelerator pushed to the floor on the road to oblivion.

My ear clicked, like a cricket, and I could hear again.

At Landslide we crossed a rickety bridge and drank dark tea brought to us by a five-year-old carrying a tray across hot pebbles, barefoot, and I could not stop the quiet tears I felt I had to hide from Iman.

We travel to break our routines, but travel is dangerous; not because of disease or violence. It is a retreat. There is the paradox. We believe that we are doing what we always wanted to do: getting away from the humdrum and inertia that has paralysed our 'real' lives. New tastes, new smells, new landscapes, new people. New, new, new. But we end up with the past; our old selves, the ones we have forgotten or eschewed, causing blisters on the brain that no guidebook will warn you about and for which there is no cure.

A thin path took us across the landslip which fell in dusty earth and boulders down to the river, then headed up, under broiling heat, on the steepest possible path for an hour, until we reached a shaded hut where two garrulous old women replenished our sweat with pints of lemon tea.

An elderly, frail Englishwoman, in a dress – yes, a dress: Laura Ashley-style, minus shoulder pads – was sitting with her granddaughter, taking tiffin, her walking-stick crooked over her chair, her complexion protected by a straw hat fastened by a ribboned chin-strap, her teeth perfect yellow. I was reminded of Merchant Ivory films.

'Bit of a bugger, isn't it?'

'Indeed,' I replied. Indeed? How often did I say 'indeed'?

'But worth the view, don't you think? There we have Tibet, and closer a drongo.'

The bird was sailing out from a pine, its wings silhouetted against peaks annexed by China.

'Are you going up or down?' I asked.

'At present we are doing neither. Merely resting.'

The granddaughter blushed from ear to ear with embarrassment.

'Have you been here before?' I asked.

'*Been* here? I *lived* here. For *years*.'

'In what capacity?' How often did I use the word 'capacity'?

'As the wife of a diplomat. Currently I'm a widow.'

'I'm sorry.'

'For what? You weren't responsible for his death.'

Eggs could have fried on the granddaughter's freckled cheeks had she lain horizontal and had there been eggs to fry.

'You must've seen many changes.'

'All for the worse.'

'Oh? In what way?'

'There's no respect any more.'

'For what?'

'For the way things were.'

Our path led along cliffs hassocked with wild grasses like green fur, then over a bridge and up into fields folding down from Syabru, an extraordinary village perched on a peninsular of rock bisecting a sea of crops.

Exquisite black wooden houses, their windows, doors and balconies carved by craftsmen, flanked the steep, stone-paved street, and I walked in time to a man tapping a bell and chanting his reason for living.

Our lodge was run by a house-proud Tibetan woman whose dining room floor I sullied by tramping across it in my boots, not realising that it was carpeted in powder blue. She scolded me and I scurried outside, strolling up to the village's extremity where I found a school from which I heard a teacher screaming abuse at a pupil whose crying proliferated into a scream.

A limping man approached me. Jurgen, who I had not

seen since Langtang village, greeted me with a broad smile. How he had managed the path from Landslide with one leg impressed me, and I assumed that he, like me, was going down.

'No, Peter, I'm going there if I can.'

He pointed towards Gosainkund and its sacred lakes – sacred to Hindus – hidden beyond a horizon backdropped by grey clouds and the smudges of snow squalls.

'This spring is terrible,' he said. 'The worst I have ever known. Never so cold and so much snow but if I don't get there what does it matter? There is always next year.'

He made me feel ashamed of the self-pity that had overwhelmed me earlier in the day, and I felt like hugging him. Instead, I was correct, shaking his hand.

'Good luck, Jurgen, I hope you make it.'

'Good luck to you too, Peter. I am glad that we met.'

'Me too.'

He set off up the path, his artificial foot scraping against the stones, and for the second time that day I could not control my tears.

32

Like a wildfowler I was up pre-dawn to ambush Tibet, which I shot with my camera, pointing the lens between underpants drying on a line. Iman joined me on the balcony as icebergs of peaks turned peachy above calm inlets of white mist.

'What's that mountain called?' It was exquisite and particular. In the Alps it would have been labelled the Whymperspitz or some such.

'No name.'

'And the one next to it?'

'No name.'

'So the one next to that must be No Name III?'

'How did you know that?'

Our lodge lady knitted intricate woollen socks for pin money, and I bought a pair for my wife, Mimi, offering double the asking price: fifty pence.

Iman and I walked through pine forests where I saw doves and heard laughingthrushes, the hot morning sticky and scented with resin. We stopped on a knoll to get our breath. A Westerner sat smoking a spliff, accompanied by three Nepali porters, their heavy loads their pillows. He looked Irish but nodded in my direction with a Dutch accent.

'Where've you come from?' I asked.

'Up there, friend.'

'Where're you going?'

'Down there.'

'Why so many porters?'

'I can't tell you that.'

Down we strolled along shady paths until we reached a hamlet surrounded by apple trees whose white blossom put the Tibetan mountains to shame, turning their snow to sludge. We sipped tea to the sound of bees while women, gaudy in red clothes and gold jewellery, laid beans in serried rows on saffron-coloured sheets. The Mystery Man, followed by his porters, passed by, giving me an enigmatic Churchillian V-sign.

Later we stopped for soup in a clearing. Mystery Man was sitting outside a bamboo hut where his porters were preparing *daal bhaat* over a wood fire. They were upwind and I could smell marijuana. Perhaps that's what constituted the load?

An airy ridge exposed us above villages 2,000 feet below, their roofs seen as if from an aircraft, their alleys a street map. We passed a school. It was break-time; the girls damming a stream while boys pissed yellow arcs into the air.

Then the last step from trail to road, which I trod as if it were a ceremony. We were back in vehicle-world, and walked into Bharkhu where I ordered an apple pancake devoid of apples. Teenagers sat at an adjacent table, playing cards.

'How do they survive?' I asked Iman. 'Is there any work?'

'Their parents help, if they can. Otherwise they end up in Kathmandu.'

'Any social security?'

Iman didn't understand.

'Does the government give them money if they can't find work?'

'If they can't find work it is their fault.'

'Just like England.'

'Really?'

'Oh yes. The government pretends it's socialist but the unemployed are treated like beggars, expected to live on pocket money.'

We walked through the slummy back alleys of Dhunche and booked into a hotel where I accepted my cell-like room as par for the course.

I walked out of the town, which was plastered with red Marxist electoral posters, and found myself sauntering above screes of rubbish providing forage for wild boars that trotted across the track in front of me like images filmed for a nature programme, the litter edited out.

33

The bus to Kathmandu was cursed. Stuffed in the back, we reached the horrendous switchback where a truck, heading up, had dug its punctured tyres into the mud. Iman slid out of the window and came back ten minutes later.

'We could be stuck here for a day. More maybe.'

'So let's walk.'

'If you want.'

'How far to pick up another bus?'

'Fifteen kilometres. Perhaps more.'

'Let's go.'

I performed a limbo movement out of the bus, climbed on to the roof, and released my pack.

We walked for three hours in the rain until we found a shed thronged with farmers, drinking *raksi* for elevenses. They invited us to join them and soon we were filled with optimism that was justified by our bus somehow arriving. We rejoined it and spent the next eight hours returning to Kathmandu, a puking baby and a clucking hen beside me.

The road heading down was even more unnerving than it had been coming up, the chasms easier to see plummeting beside a track as thin as a stray hair on a green blanket.

In Trisuli we broke down, as all buses do in Trisuli.

I bought tomatoes and sucked them while local people, some mechanics shouting advice, squirmed under the rusty entrails of our charabanc. Apparently it was only the brakes and the springs, so no major problem.

We reached Kathmandu after dark, six hours overdue, my legs paralysed from the thighs down, my brain numbed by the sheer relief of having returned alive after countless encounters on blind bends.

How sweet the pollution tasted as I inhaled it into my lungs.

* * * * *

First thing in the morning, Iman accompanied me to police

269

headquarters where I had to report the robbery. The uniformed inspector was thirty-something with a stunning figure and long black hair. I had to fill in a form and then write an account of the theft which she read carefully, somehow deciphering my appalling handwriting.

'So you are a TV producer?'

'Yes. When I can get the work.'

'That must be interesting.'

'It's a privilege. It allows me into other people's lives.'

'You should make a programme about us.'

'Perhaps I should? For a start I'm surprised to find a woman reaching the rank of inspector in Nepal.'

'Why?'

'I've read that women aren't treated seriously in your country.'

'I'm here on merit.'

'But your job's dealing with foreign visitors. Public relations. Giving a good impression. I mean, how many female police inspectors are there outside Kathmandu?'

'I don't have access to that information.'

'But it's a dangerous job. Particularly now with the Maoist uprising.'

'It's not my job to discuss politics.'

'I'm sorry. Old habits, asking difficult questions.'

With the police report stamped, we went to the AMEX office where a jolly man promised a full refund in forty-eight hours.

'Tonight, Iman, I will take you and your wife out to dinner. Anywhere you like. You choose. Will she come?'

'Yes. Your hotel at six?'

'See you then.'

I went for a late breakfast at Mike's, about which I had heard paeans, getting lost in backstreets and passing cisterns where shrieking boys somersaulted into scummy green water, then through a wasteland where soccer teams fought for goals made of bamboo. A holy cow, all horn and ribs, rummaged in rubbish strewn by the dusty road, and wafts of shit blew into my nose from mucky alleyways.

Mike's Breakfast is pristine but aimed at the American market, those looking for a 'real' cup of coffee, but it was not for me. Smart uniformed waiters brought me scrambled eggs as I sat awed by a linen tablecloth and marmalade in cut glass bowls around which high-class wasps buzzed. There was even an art gallery upstairs festooned with mediocre paintings. It could have been Mykonos.

I ate quickly, paid, and headed, I thought, towards Durbar Square, following my nose.

Follow your nose was the infuriating advice that a painter I once knew used to give me whenever we had a pub argument about *things that matter*. I would construct exquisite arguments that he would immediately shoot down with a whistling arrow whose message read, 'Follow your nose, Peter. Another pint?'

Never one to take the Arts Council route to success (clever applications for grants, glossy CVs, flattery) he was most at home in his mountainside patch, growing vegetables.

Last week I got a phonecall saying that he had collapsed in his garden, and had died from a stroke, leaving a wife and a daughter bereft of their seed-sower. So, John Evans, my epitaph for you is that I followed your advice and got completely lost – which is, maybe, what you meant all along.

For hours I wandered through a maze of streets not mentioned in the guidebooks, the only foreigner observing the day-to-day struggle for survival: a butcher fanning flies from his meagre supply of meat with a flip-flop; fruiterers picking squashed berries from their shallow dishes; barbers with silent scissors hoping for a snip. Everywhere the destitute, cowled against the heat, selling matches and plastic bags as loss-leaders, their real offering hands cupped into begging bowls.

Eventually I found Freak Street which, in the sixties, was the hangout of egocentric post-war babies who, having been raised on free orange juice and cod liver oil, now sucked joints. And all legal, then. No doubt I could've acted being one of them in 1967, had I made it.

Now there is no trace left, and I was glad because it was an era of self-indulgence that hardly merits an iota in the footnotes of social history.

Durbar Square is the Vatican of Kathmandu. It is a museum of art, architecture and untenable beliefs. Religious and cultural tradition surrounds you like a winding sheet, stifling any hope of intellectual progress. Believers offer offerings to Technicolor gods glaring out at an imperfect world of their making. Sex manuals, carved in wood, assail you from the rafters of temples, including perversions which I doubt even the pornographers of Amsterdam could persuade junkies to perform. But the most depressing exhibit is a courtyard where a living goddess resides. Yes. Really. An incarnation of the Hindu goddess Durga.

Apparently abused girl children aged between 3 and 5 are shoved into a room amongst bleeding buffalo heads while holy men, dressed as devils, terrify them. The one who wins is the one who shows the least fear. Or the dumbest. She is called the Kumari, and is sacred until she menstruates when – naturally – she becomes impure. Then she is discarded and, apparently, becomes unmarriageable because there is the curse of early death bestowed on all suitors. Who, I wonder, thought up that fairytale?

Although Durga is a Hindu god, the poor toddler is chosen from a particular Buddhist clan. Oh, those Buddhists again. Don't the starry-eyed Western Buddhists who flock here for enlightenment *know* that such criminality exists? Don't they *care*?

You can bribe officials for a glimpse of this living goddess who will appear, for a price, at her balcony, her eyes made up to the nines like a paedophile's dream.

I heard a child laughing behind a wooden screen but the Kumari did not appear for me. What I did see was a Coca-Cola machine slotted into an alcove below the Kumari's apartment, thirsty for rupees. But is this the *real* Kumari? Across the river, in Patan Durbar Square there is *another* one. Which abused child is authentic? You pays your money and you takes your choice.

Holy men jostled to smear me with dye, demanding money like pre-Lutheran priests offering indulgences, and I took refuge up some temple steps.

You can't avoid taking postcards here, and my Nikon hung around my throat as tempting as a rare necklace. I headed down, and a well-dressed man confronted me. He looked concerned. 'There is something wrong with your shoes, sir.'

Instantly remembering the poor Japanese man whose head had been severed by a robber, I stared the suit in the eyes and said, 'There is nothing whatever wrong with my shoes.'

I was meant to bend down, and my camera would have been whipped from my neck, depriving me of slides of the Coca-Cola machine in the Kumari's courtyard.

The suit seemed surprised by my response and I pushed by him, roughly. He followed me, but I continued to take photographs including one I pretended to take of him. Then he disappeared into the crowd.

I sat on a roof overlooking the Taleju Mandir, the city's biggest temple, which is barred to non-Nepalis. A woman sat at the temple entrance cleaning gold plates with a rag, while close by a guard in battle fatigues protected her, a black gun slung from a shoulder, a cigarette held rigidly between his lips, smoke rising like an offering into the noisy air.

34

I awoke with herbivorous visions after green dreams. I was Peter Rabbit in a cage. After weeks of rice my body demanded that I eat green leaves. Green anything. So I went to the restaurant where all salads are soaked in iodine for forty minutes. I devoured lettuce, cucumbers and cress heaped into a soft mountain, but they must have been all out of iodine that day for I barely made it back to the hotel before the volcano inside erupted, top and bottom, simultaneously. Thank God I wasn't on honeymoon. It would've been doubly anti-aphrodisian.

So I never took photos of the *stupa* at Boudha. Instead I lay in a darkened room, shivering and sweating, leaping to the loo every few minutes. No wonder it's called the trots. But I had a dinner engagement, and stuffed myself full of Imodium. By dusk I was cured.

Had I roamed the city I might have witnessed a violent demonstration in Ratna Park by the coalition of left-wing parties demanding the resignation of the Prime Minister.

In the local newspaper I read that Nepal was going to participate in an international conference in Durban, South Africa, against caste discrimination. I read, 'Even after the restoration of democracy in 1990, caste discrimination in Nepal has increased.' The article went on to report 'the atrocities committed to the rest of the people of the country in the name of caste.' Brave journalism in a pseudo-democracy where writers are arrested for expressing their thoughts.

In the countryside a civil war was being waged; police killed simply for being in uniform. But why? Because since 'democracy' the police have murdered many.

I have an Amnesty International report naming names, too many to quote in full, but here is a small sample. Each is worth a few seconds of your time.

Bin Bahadur Pariyar, aged 30, reportedly dragged out of his house by a sub inspector and shot dead, allegedly because he had refused to sell police his goat.

Bhakta Bahandur Sunar, aged 31, was reportedly arrested and died in custody of police, due to torture.

The Maoists are no better, their moral highground eroded by beastly acts.

Mani Ram Khatri, aged 35, hacked to death by masked men with kukris while he was buying cigarettes in a shop.

Balaram Pokharel attacked in his house by ten masked men who dragged him outside and stabbed him to death.

If I believed in an afterlife I would pray that they might rest in peace, but I don't. There is only politics, and I hardly believe in that either. All I can do is hope that their children grow up in a less violent world. But I don't truly believe that this is possible.

I don't *believe*.

* * * * *

Iman arrived at my hotel with his beautiful wife, Suja, who spoke only a smattering of English – or spoke more but was too shy to practise it. He had chosen a restaurant that he thought would impress either me or his wife or both of us. It was lit by ultraviolet and boasted a stage on which dancers, dressed *circa* 1965, mimed to Nepali rock music which made conversation difficult. But I was filled with happiness at meeting Suja who was not the hard-faced travel agent I had imagined but just another poorly paid worker in just another business.

I had bought wrapping paper and string, and gave Iman my first gift: a guide to the birds of Nepal.

'But this is not yours. It is new.'

It was sheathed in cellophane. 'Yes, it's new. No one else has read it.'

'Thank you.'

He unwrapped the next present: my binoculars.

'These are mine? Truly?'

'Yes.'

Then an envelope enclosing his tip, in dollars. I hoped it was enough.

Suja whispered to Iman. 'Suja says you must come to dinner at our apartment tomorrow.'

'Tell her I accept, with pleasure.'

* * * * *

The following evening Iman led me through backstreets to his apartment which turned out to be a cell in a concrete apartment block; a room ten feet by eight. No toilet; no running water; a small window, barred; a bed; a stove fuelled by bottled gas; a chair. Nothing else. Cramped inside were Suja; Iman's father, Dhan; Iman's mother, Dhan Kumari; his sister, Maina; and his little brother Kalyan who had all come down from the farm for a visit. How they all managed to sleep there was beyond my understanding.

Iman handed Dhan and I bottled beer and I asked Iman to translate my conversation with his family who glowed with charm and inquisitiveness. We talked of the farm and how they missed Iman when he was away, but his mother and sister said little, as though not used to having their opinions sought.

Iman was overcome with genuine modesty when I asked him to translate my praise of him to his parents, but his mother smiled, as all mothers do when their children are complimented.

Suja had cooked a chicken which we ate with rice and

chillies, drinking *raksi* which appeared from under the bed in a huge plastic bottle.

'My father brought this down from the hills,' Iman explained. 'It is the best.'

Lit only by an oil lamp it was like being in a cave, the women's gold jewellery catching the light like veins of ore in a mine.

'I'm sorry my house is so small, Peter,' said Iman. 'But one day we will move to somewhere bigger.'

'When you have children of your own?'

He giggled. 'We hope so.'

They kept their secret well. Perhaps it would have been bad luck to mention Suja's pregnancy, but three months later Iman wrote to tell me of the birth of his first child, a son, whose presence had been cunningly kept under wraps.

I asked how his family could afford the things we in the West take for granted, like medical care.

'It is so difficult. My little brother Kalyan nearly died last year. He has a bad heart, and needed an operation.'

Iman talked gently to Kalyan who opened his shirt to reveal a great scar stitched across his tiny chest.

'Somehow we found the money. We are poorer now, but we manage to eat and have a place to sleep, and I still have a brother. So it is not so bad.'

Iman was content with so little, materially, and showed no obvious bitterness at having to live in such privation. The family unit was palpably inviolable; a closeness which most of us have lost in our clever West.

'My father says you are welcome to visit his farm next time you come.'

'Tell him I would like that very much.'

Kalyan fell asleep, his head on his father's lap, and I said goodbye with deep regret, wondering if I would ever see them again. Iman walked with me through unlit alleyways until I recognised a street, and we said goodnight, shaking hands.

'See you in two days?'

'See you in two days, Peter.'

Iman turned, and was soon lost from view in the shadows.

A flock of fruit bats, like little pterodactyls, flapped overhead, briefly, in search of orchards.

35

There were only three days left before I flew home, and
I decided to spend two nights in Nagarkot, 6,000 feet up
in the hills, a two-hour bus ride from Kathmandu.

A metalled road rises from Bhaktapur, leaving the smog
behind, to the village of Nagarkot above which lodges are
clotted along a ridge of pines. The road was constructed
to give the army ease of access, but the spin off is a resort
where those without the time, inclination or knees to visit
the Himalaya proper, can get a glimpse, at dawn, ranging
from the Annapurnas to Everest.

I appeared to be the only visitor at my lodge, which
was luxurious by previous standards: a large double room
with en suite bathroom opening onto a terrace dotted with
potted pink geraniums.

All around there were similar hotels, each resembling
the house in *Psycho*; tall, Gothic, built of red bricks, each
with a crow's-nest of a viewing tower from which the
dawn splendour could be savoured; but not in the
afternoon, which filled the gap between ground and
horizon with vapour.

I ate dinner alone in a rotunda of a dining room
wondering how such lodges could exist without guests.

* * * * *

Before dawn I climbed iron treads that shuddered and
creaked like the spiral staircase in *The Haunting*. I waited
to be entranced. The lodge had provided a semi-circular
brass guide with arrows pointing to essential peaks. The
sun rose over Sikkim and there were the peaks, as billed,
but I felt cheated. There was Manaslu. There was
Annapurna I. There, I think, Everest, but it was a dreadful
disappointment. Postcards lie. They show these peaks,

taken with telephoto lenses, squished together. With the naked eye they are shot with a wide angle lens and fill only the bottom ten per cent of the frame. You are away from them, and I felt like a day-tripper, divorced from *being up there* amongst them. Silhouettes of other gatherers were filigreed on other towers and I was overcome by anticlimax. Don't go there unless you are on a stopover and only have a day or two to kill.

In the village a band was playing traditional music, but I carried on, passing a grotesque luxury hotel with barber-pole barriers on hinges, like frontier posts, which they were. Then into woodland where bivouacking soldiers, bleary-eyed, were cooking breakfast.

Dozens of black kites were floating on early thermals, and I took off into a forest loud with silence where I lay on hot brown mulch, staring up at the green feathers of leaves crackling in the heat. Birds, carmine and sulphur, flitted above me picking at pine cones, but Iman had my binoculars and I could not discover their names. Still, the colours were enough.

I fell asleep and woke to see a lizard staring at me from a log. Above me the kites were still wheeling, but closer now to a dazzling sun, their wings acting as heliographs.

I walked back down to Nagarkot and chose a lane at random, that led me to an exclusive hotel where the waiter viewed my unshaven face and ragged trousers with alarm. Nevertheless I was a sahib, and he dared not turn me away. After all, I might have been a pukka eccentric millionaire. I plonked myself down in an exquisite garden, gaudy with unlikely flowers amongst which superior butterflies pranced. My Tuborg tasted no better than the last, despite costing four times the price.

A couple sat down at an adjacent table and perused the menu, ordering, at long last, exorbitant meaty meals. I said hello but the man suddenly seemed incapable of moving his mouth. I got a curt nod instead. He took a magazine from his briefcase. It was the *British Medical Journal*. His wife opened a book. Jilly Cooper.

I had nowhere to go so I sat for two hours, drinking beer, watching the butterflies, and in all that time the doctor said not a word to his wife, nor she to him. A perfect English marriage. After all, you cannot fight over words unsaid.

A narrow man approached me on a thin road.

'Excuse me, sir, but where are you from?'

'England.'

'Are you going back to England soon?'

'Too soon.'

'Then, sir, will you post this letter for me when you arrive? It will be quicker for me.'

I was wary of accepting it. I had heard too many stories of people carrying contraband and getting caught in customs. But it was an airmail letter which could only contain paper.

'OK,' I said.

He joined his hands in thanksgiving. The letter was addressed to Colonel X who lives in an opulent area of Hampshire. 'It's very important, sir. I am a guide and the gentleman promised to return to Nepal this spring and employ me. But he has not answered my letters. He said he would send me money but he has not, and I have many money troubles.'

'Posting it will be the first thing I do when I land in London.'

Perhaps I should have given him some cash there and then, but he was not begging and I did not want to demean him, so I carried on. A hundred metres down the track I was racked by guilt and returned, but he had disappeared into the dust.

Again I sat alone in my lodge restaurant, sucking

noodles, but then the door opened and *another guest* came in. She was in her forties, her ginger hair falling around her face like a seventeenth-century wig. Nell Gwynne without her oranges.

I introduced myself. Morag was from Perth – Scotland, not Australia.

'Why're you here?' I asked.

'I needed to get away.'

'From what?'

'From him. From everything.'

She had the look of a pledge-taker and I assumed that her slur was a symptom of antidepressants, for she had ordered water.

'Are you happier here?' I asked.

'What business is it of yours?'

'None.'

She delved into a handbag resembling a litter bin, and pulled out a book to talk with, like a paper partner, so I gave up. She supped her soup, noisily, and read – or pretended to.

My double bed was far too big for me so I put my sleeping bag on the terrace and slept under the stars.

An owl warbled, and meteors performed brief fireworks, sprinkling a black sky pulsating with red, blue and green jewels.

* * * * *

Dutifully I climbed my tower again at dawn but the Himalaya were invisible behind a bank of fog; even the sky devoid of circling birds deprived of updraughts.

Time to leave.

* * * * *

Back in Kathmandu I went in search of Iman but he had gone to the mountains with a sudden new client. The final celebration I had planned evaporated and I missed him dreadfully because he was a true friend, found by chance but invaluable; guileless, honest, and a man who I had trusted with my life. Gone.

I had promised to treat him to a farewell meal at the Everest Steak House but I went there alone. I ordered a sirloin steak but when the dish arrived it consisted of *three* steaks, imported from Bombay, all of which I ate in recompense.

A resident English gay asked to join me and made up a bit for Iman's departure with his wit, but I drank too much, and staggered back through dark streets to my hotel with memories of Iman and his family already consigned to a photograph album.

– 36 –

On my last morning I went to the holiest of Hindu shrines in Nepal: Pashupatinath. Woodsellers were already bargaining with people buying fuel to cremate their relatives on ghats beside the Bagmati River where devout believers bathed in turbid brown water. Widows once committed *sati* here, throwing themselves on their husband's pyres, but this is now illegal, thank God. A small step, but a step away from lethal superstition.

The most sacred temple, the Pashupati Mandir, is out of bounds for non-Hindus so I never got to see the *lingam*, the stone representing Shiva's phallus. At least I did not have to give the temple priests a donation for the privilege, as the pilgrims must.

I spent the morning wandering around the site amongst monkeys, and sadhus daubed like clowns, seeing symbols as esoteric to me as a Holy Ghost might be to a Hindu tourist in Canterbury Cathedral. But instead of celebrating it all as an affirmation of cultural heritage and belief, I left profoundly disturbed by its anachronism. It was a dagger pointing into the past; beliefs, devoutly held, holding a whole population to ransom.

If only all this energy could be channelled into social reform: the reduction of infant mortality, the fair treatment of women, the casting out of the iniquitous caste system. But it will continue despite what I, and others, think.

Nowhere in the world are there shrines to humanism. Just as well. If there were, it would, by definition, have failed.

* * * * *

I bumped into Barry and Crisp at the airport.

'Going home?' I asked.

'Not exactly.'

'Meaning?'

'We're going to Greece for the summer.'

'Why?'

'Because we're putting things off.'

'How'll you survive?'

'We'll find jobs. After all, anything's better than a dingy bedsit in Clapham.'

Almost anything is.

Message

It used to be fashionable in the unsophisticated post-war years to ask, 'What's the message?' when referring to books, plays, poetry, paintings or songs. And although such creative acts still intone a message, we dare not speak its name. It is out of vogue. We are too cool, too worldly-wise. But I don't care. I've got one. A message.

Go to Nepal. Or to the place you've always hankered for. You can do it. I did. It doesn't cost much. And unless you do you will regret it for the remainder of your short life. *Go* before arthritis gristles up your joints. *Go* before a stroke numbs your mind and your limbs. *Go* before you need a clever device to lower you into the bath. *Go* before you merit a gold watch for long service in a stultifying job. *Go* before you are saddled with grandchildren to babysit.

GO! GO! GO!

Message ends.

Hotel On The Roof Of The World

Five Years In Tibet

Alec Le Sueur

The Holiday Inn, Lhasa, would have proved any hotel inspector's worst nightmare. An hilarious behind the scenes look at the running of an unheated, rat infested and highly confused hotel set against the breathtaking beauty of the Himalayas.

• Highly entertaining but also illuminating and informative

• No other foreigner has spent so long in Tibet since the days of Heinrich Harrer

• Le Sueur provides a fascinating insight into an intriguing country which so few foreigners have been permitted to visit.

Paperback £7.99

Heartlands

Travels in the Tibetan World

Michael Buckley

A glimpse into the spiritual soul of hidden Tibet.

Reaching Lhasa is the dream of all Tibetan pilgrims, but China's brutal occupation has reduced this ancient civilisation to a shadow of its former self. If you want to discover real Tibetan culture, you have to go elsewhere on the plateau – to Ladakh, Bhutan or Outer Mongolia.

Exploring these remote regions in a series of trips, Michael Buckley embarks on a quest to come to grips with Tibetan ways, from the celebrated spirituality to the downright bizarre, and finds himself balanced somewhere in between magic and reality. A fascinating and personal journey of discovery, Buckley rubs shoulders with hardy nomads, encounters giant phalluses and stuffed kangaroos, cycles snowbound passes, chats to the Dalai Lama and survives interrogation by Chinese police.

Paperback £7.99